BY THE
COLOR
OF OUR
SKIN

BY THE
COLOR
OF OUR
SKIN

THE ILLUSION OF
INTEGRATION
AND THE REALITY
OF RACE

LEONARD STEINHORN
BARBARA DIGGS-BROWN

A DUTTON BOOK

DUTTON
Published by the Penguin Group
Penguin Putnam Inc., 375 Hudson Street, New York, New York 10014, U.S.A.
Penguin Books Ltd, 27 Wrights Lane, London W8 5TZ, England
Penguin Books Australia Ltd, Ringwood, Victoria, Australia
Penguin Books Canada Ltd, 10 Alcorn Avenue, Toronto, Ontario, Canada M4V 3B2
Penguin Books (N.Z.) Ltd, 182–190 Wairau Road, Auckland 10, New Zealand

Penguin Books Ltd, Registered Offices:
Harmondsworth, Middlesex, England

First published by Dutton, an imprint of Dutton NAL,
a member of Penguin Putnam Inc.

First Printing, January, 1999
10 9 8 7 6 5 4 3 2 1

 REGISTERED TRADEMARK—MARCA REGISTRADA

Library of Congress Cataloging-in-Publication Data
Steinhorn, Leonard.
   By the color of our skin : the illusion of integration and the reality of race /
Leonard Steinhorn and Barbara Diggs-Brown.
      p.   cm.
   Includes bibliographical references
   ISBN 0-525-94359-5
   1. United States —Race relations.   2. Race discrimination—United
States—History—20th century.   3. Afro-Americans—Civil rights—History—20th
century.   I. Diggs-Brown, Barbara.   II. Title.
E185.615.S7238   1999
305.8'00973—dc21   98-29906
                                                              CIP

Printed in the United States of America
Set in New Baskerville
Designed by Leonard Telesca

This book is printed on acid-free paper. ∞

To Sabine, who made this possible.
—LS

To Carrie, my hero, my mother, with love.
—BD-B

Contents

Acknowledgments

Many brooks and streams flowed into the making of this book, so many, in fact, that we fear not being able to thank all those who gave us their support, encouragement, insights, and ideas. We both have drawn great strength from our families, friends, and colleagues, and we stand eternally grateful for their patience and understanding during these past two years.

We owe special thanks to American University for providing a generous grant to support our research. Our colleagues in the School of Communication at American University have provided a superb support system, and our dean, Sanford Ungar, has been an enthusiastic backer of this project since day one.

At the foundation of this book is our research, and we could not have gathered and organized it all without the help of our graduate and undergraduate assistants who diligently tracked down leads, mined various libraries, searched databases, obtained reports, and checked some very stubborn facts. Our thanks go to students Sarah Ackerstein, Keri Bartok, Dawn Bergantino, Stephanie Bluma, Melanie Brown, Pamela Feifer, Jodi Glou, Rodney Hill, Monique LeNoir, Anne Maginnis, Kelly McCormick, Lisa Parsons, Anna Plaza, Tad Segal, Sally Shoquist, and Theresa Spinner. We also owe our gratitude to Renée C. Sprow for her precise and rapid work in transcribing tapes of interviews we conducted.

There is no greater gift than to give one's time, and so we are especially grateful for the hours and days that various friends have spent reading drafts of the book. To Brent Crane, Sam Fulwood III, Victoria Pope, Richard Shenkman, Douglas Stanglin, and Renée C. Sprow—each of you has improved this book through your thoughtful comments and recommendations.

Jennifer Moore, our editor at Dutton, believed in this project from the outset. Her guidance, comments, edits, and genuine interest in the book have made the painstaking work of authorship so much easier to bear. Our agent, Nina Graybill, helped us shape the initial book proposal and has been a consistent supporter of our efforts.

Author Leonard Steinhorn would like to offer special thanks to the people in his life who made writing this book possible. To Sabine, my wife, best friend, and soul mate, this book could not have been done without you. Without your confidence in me, I might never have even tried. Your unceasing patience, love, and support kept me going day after day and page after page, and your keen observations and insights made this a better book. To my children Ariella and Max (ages five and two), you may not realize at this young age how much strength you have given me, but you have. Ariella, I will never forget your gift to me, a page full of words to help me finish the writing sooner. To my parents, Paul and Adele Steinhorn, you taught me values and a love of ideas, and you believed in me. To my mentors, Bernard A. Weisberger and John Higham, let me take this opportunity to say what I have always wanted to say: thank you for inspiring and educating me. Finally, to Barbara, my co-author, a true partner in the pursuit of truth, thank you.

Author Barbara Diggs-Brown also offers special thanks. God, thank you for the blessing of writing this book. Thank you for sending me to search deeper within, where I found the people who have loved, inspired, and sustained me. Thank you, Roy—my life partner—for your abiding love and devotion, and for reading the manuscript, again and again. Cari-Shawn and Courtney, thank you for the research you provided and for your understanding of the amount of time this book took me away from you. To my parents, Carrie and William T. Diggs, Sr., and to my sisters and brother, thank you for your comfort and constant encouragement. To my dear friend Renée, you helped me focus. To my best critic, Toni, who left me along the way, I miss you. To my co-author, Lenny: Thank you for writing the manuscript.

Together, we offer one final and customary note: As co-authors, we assume sole and complete responsibility for the ideas and conclusions presented in this book.

We are all condemned to live together.
—ALBERT CAMUS

"But he has nothing on!" all the people
cried at last. The emperor felt a shudder go
through him, for he knew at once that it was
true, but he had to continue to lead the
procession. And so he walked on beneath
the canopy, and the chamberlains held up
the invisible train.
—HANS CHRISTIAN ANDERSEN,
"The Emperor's New Clothes"

What's past is prologue.
—WILLIAM SHAKESPEARE
The Tempest

Preface

One of us is white, one of us is black, and we are the two authors of this book on racial integration in America. Barely a day passes in which we haven't talked, chewed over an idea, reviewed a research problem, or worked intensively on this project. Our time is often spent discussing complex ideas about race, or sharing our dreams and fears about human nature and the ability of black and white Americans to live together as one. During the two years we have worked on the book, we have grown to trust each other and to know each other's personalities and idiosyncrasies. Surely the fact that we could collaborate so closely confirms the promise of integration in our country. From a distance, we appear to be perfect symbols of racial progress in America.

But often we wonder how much our paths would have crossed had we not chosen to work together on this project. True, the white author once was the only white staff member in the office of a black member of Congress. And true, the black author has been the first black throughout her career—most recently the first black woman to receive tenure in the School of Communication at American University, where we both teach. So we have both made an effort to integrate. But then we look at the rest of our lives.

The white author grew up in an all-white suburb of New York and currently lives in an all-white suburb of Washington, D.C. He rarely ventures beyond the predominantly white parts of town, and knows almost nothing about the black neighborhoods nearby. The black author grew up in an all-black neighborhood of Washington, D.C., and now navigates between her predominantly white world of work and her predominantly black personal life. Our friends and acquaintances tend to be of our own color, and so are our social environments and engagements. Race influences the magazines we read, the books we buy, the media we follow, the entertainers we recognize, the vacations we take, the lifestyles we lead, and the choices we make for our respective families. At work in the university, the white author is surrounded by people who share his features, and he never thinks twice about standing out. The black author thinks twice about it, every day. She has been mistaken for cafeteria help in the faculty dining room, and as one of the few black professors on campus feels personally obligated to reach out to and mentor the students and employees of her color. We then look at the fact that our families have never socialized together, and ask whether color is the reason why. Only once have we done something together outside of work, when the black author came over to the white author's home for a Sunday brunch. The white author has never been to the black author's home, and has never met her spouse.

Sadly we must acknowledge a reality we would prefer to leave unsaid, that a simple but complex phenomenon, the color of our skin, serves as a wall between our two lives and worlds—as well as the way we perceive them. Working on this book together has allowed us to look over the wall, but rarely are we anything more than guests on the other side. Our two lives have intersected on this project, but they have not really integrated. And so we ask: Does our own experience epitomize the state of racial integration in America?

This book attempts to answer that question by taking an in-depth look at American race relations. This is a book not about laws or policies but about institutions and people. It is about the way black and white Americans live, learn, love, play, interact, relax, and think. It is about the images we hold and the choices we make, about the shows we watch and the communities we build, about the myths we spin and the frustrations we feel. It is not uncommon for a novelist to say that he or she did not write the book, the characters did. We feel much the same, for in many ways the American people have written this book and we are merely the scribes. Our only goal is and has been to pursue the truth, to look beyond the images, to hold up a mirror to our great integration experiment and to evaluate the strength and resilience of our nation's color line. If there is anything that made achieving this goal difficult, it is the extent to which myths and illusions camouflage the underlying truths about race in America. This book is about what we saw once we cleared the brush away.

Unlike many books on race today, ours did not originate in a need to support or oppose affirmative action or any other political agenda. As you will see, we view the affirmative-action debate as a symptom rather than a cause of our racial disease, and it must be treated as such. Nor do we engage in the usual blame game on race. To be sure, it would be easy to point the finger, as so many authors have done before us. The targets seem so inviting: liberals and conservatives, white politicians and black leaders, and of course the media, all committing excesses and making the usual excuses. But just like affirmative action, they are mere bit players in the larger theater of our nation's racial history. The blame game is an endgame that serves no purpose. We also don't provide readers with the proverbial happy ending to this book. There is no parting vision of black and white Americans walking arm in arm to the promised land, no twelve-step formula to help us overcome our racial demons and usher in an integrated future. We realize that our ending runs against the American grain. In our Hollywood-saturated culture Americans have grown accustomed to books that match a hero for every villain, a possibility for every problem, a solution for every dilemma. Such a story line is attractive, and we wish we could write it, but our evidence simply does not support it. It is said that Americans fall into two camps on race relations, one of optimism and one of pessimism. But to us that is a false and misleading choice. We prefer realism. We would rather be the child who says the emperor wears no clothes than the courtier who waxes eloquent about his majesty's beautiful new threads.

The book is organized into three sections. In the first we examine both the image and the reality of integration in America. We ask whether our national devotion to the integration ideal hinders or helps race relations, and whether integration is a workable goal our nation can achieve or a fiction that merely salves our conscience and makes us feel good about ourselves. We also compare integration facts to the integration ideal, and probe the depth of racial separation in America. As part of our inquiry we take a new look at the 1960s, asking whether integration was truly possible during the heady years of the civil rights movement.

In the second section we ask why: Why do whites and blacks make certain choices and see the world differently? Why do so many whites believe our problem with discrimination is a thing of the past? Why do blacks seem so angry? Why do whites avoid intimacy with blacks? To find our answers we examine the role of history, culture, the media, perceptions, and politics.

In the third section we explore where we go from here. We look at three integration success stories and ask whether they can translate to the rest of society. And we offer recommendations designed to make Americans think beyond the racial box that so badly walls us in.

At one point in the book we paraphrase Winston Churchill's famous line about Russia and call race relations in America a riddle wrapped in a quandary hidden inside a history. We do not fool ourselves into thinking we have solved the riddle. But we do hope we can move our nation a little bit closer to understanding it.

PART ONE

INTEGRATION ILLUSION, INTEGRATION REALITY

CHAPTER ONE

The Integration Illusion

It was an emotional, inspiring moment meant for an audience of millions. The opening ceremony of the 1996 Atlanta Olympics was designed as a pageant not about athletics but about race. Carefully choreographed in ebony and ivory, blacks and whites performed together as brothers and sisters, climaxing when a mixed group of four blacks and four whites carried the Olympic flag around the track. Moments later the music stilled and the powerful, stirring voice of Martin Luther King, Jr., echoed throughout the stadium, evoking once again his dream that the children of former slaves and the children of former slaveholders could sit down at the table of brotherhood. The camera flashed on President Clinton as tears welled up in his eyes. Through symbolism and words, the Atlanta Olympics had reaffirmed with great fanfare our national commitment to racial integration. Our task may not yet be complete, but we shall overcome. We shall overcome.

Barely a few months later another symbol of the great American melting pot was in the news, but this time the story line was very different. In an article buried on page 49 of the Sunday *New York Times*, a black man described the "pride and dignity" that surged when the National Park Service made him a ranger at the Statue of Liberty—until it dawned on him that he and other black rangers were being isolated from visitors at the statue and nearby Ellis Island simply because of the color of their skin.

Other black employees described racial intimidation, a secret ban on the hiring of black maintenance workers, and rampant prejudice that was most profoundly manifested in keeping black personnel of the Statue of Liberty out of the public eye.[1]

The Statue of Liberty story never made the front page, and unlike the Atlanta Olympics it never will be publicized or broadcast to millions as an allegory about American race relations. But its portrayal of black Americans literally being quarantined from our most powerful symbol of inclusion—with the implication that black faces might taint our national image—tells us more about race relations in America than any pageant, political speech, or public event ever could. For it illustrates the stark and striking contrast between our very public ideal of a racially integrated America and the daily, grinding reality of a society deeply divided by race—a society in which almost 70 percent of its black children attend predominantly black schools, a society in which middle-class whites flee from their suburban communities when equally middle-class blacks begin moving in, a society characterized by racially distinct perceptions, images, choices, and experiences. And it begs us to ask whether this reality is ever likely to change, whether the integration ideal can ever amount to more than a futile illusion or tantalizing dream—and what we should do if the answer to these questions is a sad and poignant no. Herein lies the new American dilemma on race.

Certainly, it was not supposed to turn out this way. In the decades after World War II, no other national goal captured the spirit and imagination of American democracy more than racial integration. "Integration," said Martin Luther King, Jr., "is the ultimate goal of our national community." It is the "Promised Land," a destination worth all our sweat and sacrifice, where "all of God's children" would live together in a "beloved community" of harmony and peace. It is about believing "in the possibilities of one America, one community, one house, one family," wrote civil rights veteran John Lewis.[2] Like so many others of his generation both black and white, Bill Clinton has repeatedly called integration the most important moral idea he grew up with.

Born in the heady and hopeful days of the civil rights era, the integration dream was fueled by a national culture eager to validate its commitment to decency and pluralism. It was perhaps the ultimate expression of the melting pot ideal, that the most victimized and vilified part of American society could be integrated seamlessly into mainstream life, and that the white majority could overcome its prejudice and welcome black Americans as full brothers and sisters in our national community. Integration spoke to what Lincoln called the better angels of our nature, the idea that blacks and whites can live together in harmony, friendship and mutual respect. So powerful was the ideal that for many Americans it overwhelmed any doubts about the possibility of achieving it. Right after the Supreme Court struck down separate but equal schooling in the 1954 *Brown* v. *Board of Education* case, Thurgood Marshall and Kenneth Clark, two giants of the civil rights movement, expressed confidence that America would be integrated by the mid-1960s. Many others, black and white, simply assumed that blacks would begin to assimilate as millions of immigrants had done earlier in the century.[3] Let us be "knit together as one," wrote Massachusetts governor John Winthrop more than 300 years ago, and that vision of the American community still holds sway today. Realistic or not, racial integration remains a thoroughly American ideal.

What exactly is racial integration? It is about the realm of life governed by behavior and choice, not by statutes and institutions. It should not be confused with desegregation, which means the elimination of discriminatory laws and barriers to full participation in American life. Although desegregation is a necessary precondition for integration, it is entirely possible to desegregate without integrating—for blacks and whites to attend the same schools without ever learning much about each other or becoming friends, or for blacks and whites to work for the same employer without mixing much on or off the job. Desegregation may unlock doors, but integration is supposed to open minds, which is why some say that integration makes desegregation look easy. Indeed, what makes racial integration so compelling is that it is about people, not laws. It is about the way we perceive each other, about the way we act toward each other, about whether there will ever be room in our hearts, homes, classrooms, and communities to welcome each other comfortably as neighbors and friends. Steeped in the pluralist tradition, integration is both color-blind and color-conscious. It insists on a color-blind approach to character, ability, and personal relationships—that people be judged not by the color of their skin but by the content of their character. It is built on a universal acceptance of people as individuals. Yet it appreciates and welcomes the different black and white traditions, perspectives, and historical experiences that make our nation whole. Its model could be Protestant-Catholic or Jewish-Italian relations in America today, a mutual respect that acknowledges the differences and embraces the similarities.

In a racially integrated America, blacks and whites would choose to live side by side, socialize with ease, see each other as peers, recommend each other for jobs, harbor little mutual distrust, respect each other's outlook, and appreciate each other's contributions to American culture. Prejudice and stereotypes might not completely disappear in an integrated society, but they would not define relationships, images, and behavior as they do today. Skin color would become incidental rather than fundamental. In a color-blind society, a middle-class white person would feel equally at home living, learning, or working in an environment 80 percent black or 90 percent white; the black-majority neighborhood would perhaps feel different but by no means threatening or disagreeable. For blacks, as *Atlanta Journal-Constitution* writer Tom Teepen puts it, it means finally having the "opportunity to define themselves and to calculate their lives non-racially—as architect, say, or bass fisherman or Republican."[4] Or, as former civil rights strategist Bayard Rustin used to say, we will be truly integrated when a black person can make the same mistakes as a white without anyone drawing special attention to it.

To hear most white Americans talk about it, they are living up to their end of the integration bargain. As evidence that race is no longer a barrier in America, whites point to Colin Powell, Michael Jordan, Vernon Jordan, Oprah Winfrey, Denzel Washington, Bill Cosby, the late Ron Brown, and the scores of black lawyers and executives in fine wool suits and tasseled shoes who seem to inhabit the corridors of social and political power. Most whites believe the core of the problem was solved with the landmark civil rights legislation of the 1960s, when the nation outlawed discrimination, ended legal segregation, and created a level playing field in the eyes of the law. Almost every public opinion poll shows large white majorities saying that black Americans have at least as good a chance as whites to obtain a quality education, a decent job, and their choice of housing. Whites also point to affirmative action as proof of how they bent over backward—albeit grudgingly—to guarantee access to the system and right any lingering wrongs from a bygone era. If there's any problem at all, many whites believe, it's because too many blacks have brought it on themselves through crime and loose values, and then have tried to blame white people or racism for their mistakes. As white America sees it, every effort has been made to welcome blacks into the American mainstream, and now they're on their own. "No place that I'm aware of makes people ride on the back of the bus or use a different restroom in this day and age," wrote a white respondent to a survey in *Essence* magazine. "We got the message; we made corrections—get on with it."[5]

Whether you agree or disagree with this perspective, it's hard to blame people for having it when our public life is filled with repeated affirmations of the integration ideal and our ostensible progress toward reaching it. Integration as a goal may be hotly debated among a few intellectuals within the academy, but within our major institutions it is almost beyond criticism. Integrationist symbols pervade American politics, whether in campaign rhetoric, nominating conventions, or presidential inaugurals. Conservative Republican leader Newt Gingrich feels as comfortable as Democrat Bill Clinton in quoting Martin Luther King, praising the 1960s civil rights movement, and calling for racial unity. We have governors proclaiming ours a "color-blind society," and even a firebrand politician like Patrick Buchanan celebrating America as "a nation committed to racial justice." The Republican party may have few black members, but that didn't stop it from showcasing a disproportionate number of black speakers during the precious prime-time hours of its 1996 convention. Even the conservative Christian Coalition has acknowledged that its adherents were on "the wrong side" of civil rights a generation ago and has now established a "minority outreach" program to absolve itself of this sin, complete with photo opportunities of coalition leaders praying hand in hand with black ministers.

Integration has been enshrined in the Martin Luther King

national holiday, in the ritualistic replaying of King's "I Have a Dream" speech, and in Supreme Court decisions that sanctify color-blindness, warn against balkanization, and strike down policies that might "carry us further from the goal of a political system in which race no longer matters." The NAACP has expelled chapter presidents for questioning the ideal. It is the framework for corporate and university diversity programs—certainly it is hard to find an institutional brochure that does not feature blacks and whites comfortably working together. Nor should we forget the role of the almighty and ubiquitous media, which are filled with countless images of racial harmony, uplift, and interaction, from sports broadcasts to the happy talk on the news to the racially mixed operating rooms on medical dramas. Indeed, few images are as appealing to a photo editor or television news producer as one where blacks and whites are embracing or holding hands in common cause or in response to tragedy.[6] Go to any major theater production and the cast will likely be racially mixed; a show like the Tony Award–winning *Rent* or the Washington Ballet's *Nutcracker* will feature an unpretentiously color-blind cast. Given the ubiquity and power of the integration image, it is no surprise that Americans in public opinion polls estimate that blacks constitute up to 40 percent of the population—more than three times the actual percentage.

Few would dispute the notion that the public culture of America today is decidedly antiracist, with racism in this case defined as the overt, crass, hard-core expression of antiblack bigotry. "Racial prejudice has declined so significantly in the United States that the white politician who appears to be anti-black hurts himself with white voters," wrote columnist Mark Shields back in 1983.[7] So powerful is the antiracist norm that many whites imagine it more palatable to be a victim of racism than to be accused of racism. The portrait of a bigoted person is someone uneducated, narrow-minded, boorish and unsophisticated—a redneck perhaps. Even former Ku Klux Klan leader David Duke has tried to distance himself from his own history, claiming that he is not antiblack, that he only opposes welfare and affirmative action. In the aftermath of the O. J. Simpson murder trial, a Gallup Poll surprisingly found that Simpson's 62 percent unfavorable rating among whites (24 percent favorable) was dwarfed by the resounding 88 percent unfavorable rating (four percent favorable) given to Detective Mark Fuhrman, apparently because of his racism.[8] So when President Clinton vows an "all-out assault on hate crimes," everyone rightly applauds and feels good about our fight against intolerance. As *Washington Post* writer Richard Cohen put it after observing that most people don't use the word *nigger* anymore, "So I think—I know—that things are getting better here."[9]

To many white Americans, this broad consensus is compelling evidence of our national goodwill on race. It suggests we are moving inexorably—even if haltingly—toward the Promised Land of integration that Dr. King envisioned three decades ago. "Most whites desperately wish to see the fulfillment of King's vision," wrote columnist Charles Krauthammer soon after the first O. J. Simpson verdict. "They may argue over the best way to implement it, but it remains a powerfully unifying theme." To another columnist, James K. Glassman, "The lines between the races are fading." Journalist Jim Sleeper, writing with the deep conviction of a color-blind idealist, describes "a transracial belonging and civic faith for which Americans of all colors so obviously yearn." Novelist John Updike puts it this way: "An ideal colorblind society flickers at the forward edge of the sluggishly evolving one." More decisive is the language of Supreme Court Justice Antonin Scalia: "In the eyes of government, we are just one race here. It is American."[10] So pervasive is this integration consensus that people who pride themselves as students of American race relations are often unprepared when confronted with evidence of its breakdown. "I thought I knew a lot about how people of different races viewed things in America," President Clinton observed when the first O. J. Simpson verdict revealed the deep racial fault lines we rarely acknowledge, "but I have been surprised by the depth of the divergence in so many areas." Shock and surprise are sentiments expressed by one or another political leader almost every time overt racial conflict breaks out—these incidents must be the exception, not the rule.[11]

Apart from seeing legal segregation end in the South, white Americans feel the greatest pride in what appears to be the profound transformation of their own attitudes toward blacks. This pride is seen in the affluent white urban apartment dweller who puffs up at the mention of the five or six black families in his three-hundred-unit building. It is seen in the white workers who feel their tolerance affirmed after talking basketball outside the bathroom with black coworkers. It is seen in the casual acceptance of black athlete role models for white kids. It is seen in the elevation of Colin Powell and Bill Cosby to national father figures. "Can't you see how we've rejected racism," white people say. Indeed, countless polls show widespread acceptance of complete racial integration in America. A 1994 Harris Poll found that two-thirds of whites favored "full integration." A Gallup Poll the same year found that 87 percent approve of school integration. There are surveys showing that most whites would work with blacks to advance race relations, that a majority of whites would prefer living in racially "half-and-half" neighborhoods, that nearly half of all whites believe racially mixed schools have improved educational quality for white children, and that nearly three-fourths of all whites disapprove of laws against interracial marriage. One poll reported that only six percent of whites rated themselves as prejudiced. A survey of the Chicago metropolitan area, considered the most residentially divided area in the nation, found that a majority of whites supported programs to attract blacks to predominantly white suburbs. This list can go on and on, but the point is this: these polls are universally described as "good news"—strong evidence that whites have accepted full integration and support real racial equality.[12]

Given this apparent integration consensus and the professed devotion to it on the part of so many whites, it is fair to ask why there is so much racial angst in America. Isn't it enough that almost every public institution has made integration a formal priority? Shouldn't whites be praised for a tolerance almost unthinkable just a generation ago? Do we pay too much attention to the doom and gloom crowd in the civil rights movement, who may have an organizational stake in bad news? Hasn't remarkable progress been made? Lurking behind these questions is the one heard for almost forty years: What more do "they" want?

This is where American race relations turn deeply bittersweet, and this is where our story begins. For when you look behind the words and symbols, when you focus on what we do rather than what we say, when you explore who we are rather than who we think we are, a very different and racially divided America unfolds before us—so different that you would think it wasn't the same country as the one of goodwill gestures and expressions of tolerance described above. Indeed, the history of American race relations is in many ways about the sad reality hiding behind the professed ideal—about the contrast between the lives we actually lead and the way we want to see ourselves. This contrast was evident from the beginning of our nation, when our founders declared that "all men are created equal," but maintained slavery in their midst. It was evident when we fought two world wars to make the world safe for democracy, but with racially segregated army units. And it is evident today—albeit more subtly—as the private lives we create for ourselves belie our public protestations of integration. "The lady doth protest too much, methinks," wrote Shakespeare in *Hamlet*, and so do we about race. We have created a mass fiction of interracial comity, a grand illusion of imminent integration, perhaps because as a culture we have lost our ability to distinguish between symbolism and reality, or perhaps because we don't want to face the unpleasant truths about our beloved but divided America, or perhaps because we do indeed know the truth but for any number of reasons simply want to deny it.

Consider the many survey findings that herald the good news of white America's tolerance. A significant majority of whites say they would prefer to live in a mixed neighborhood, perhaps as mixed as half black, half white. But almost everywhere you look in every part of the country where more than a token number of blacks live, whites begin to flee from their communities the minute the first black family moves in. Often these are suburban communities where the new homeowners are middle-class or even affluent blacks. It is a classic case of the domino effect: each black family that moves in increases the likelihood that the remaining white families will leave. Integration exists only in the time span between the first black family moving in and the last white family moving out.[13]

The very era that we applaud for racial progress tells a different story in communities like Sherman Park near Milwaukee, which lost 61 percent of its whites between 1970 and 1990; or Palmer Park, near Washington, D.C., which went from being virtually all white in the 1960s to virtually all black today; or the middle-class Philadelphia suburb of Yeadon, which doubled its black population in the 1980s, going from one-third to two-thirds black, and saw a corresponding decline among whites. Real estate agents will tell you that prospective white buyers show no interest in moving to these neighborhoods. And even if whites and blacks share the same zip code, they usually live on different sides of town. Near Atlanta, which bills itself as the city too busy to hate, residents of the predominantly white Gwinnett County overwhelmingly rejected a proposal in 1990 to join the area's rapid transit system, despite clogged roads and traffic jams, apparently because they did not want to open the gates to black suburban migration. It seems that everyone is for integration except in their own neighborhoods. None other than radio personality Howard Stern, not known for his racial sensitivity, summed it up best when talking about the transformation of the Long Island neighborhood of his youth: all the adults "preached brotherhood," he said, "and overnight there was an exodus, as soon as there was black skin in the community. That community didn't have to become all black at once. It could have become a fully integrated community. But people were phonies and left."[14]

The story is no different when it comes to schools. A majority of whites support mixed public schools, but apparently not for their own children. A 1993 survey of whites from the Minneapolis suburbs found that two thirds favored sending white suburban children to the predominantly black Minneapolis public schools as a way to increase integration, but only seven percent said they would send their own child.[15] Indeed, few whites will say they object to sending their kids to school with blacks—it just depends on how many blacks. The public schools in Southfield, Michigan, have an active PTA and graduate about 90 percent of their students, which should appeal to any parent. Twenty years ago Southfield was nearly all white, and whites made up nearly 90 percent of the children in public schools. Today whites are still a majority in Southfield, making up about two-thirds of its population, but the schools are 70 percent black, as nearly half of the white school-age children opt out of the public schools. In community after community, the story is the same: blacks make up a significantly larger proportion of schoolchildren than their percentage of the school-age population, which means that large numbers of whites begin to flee the system for private schools when the black student population inches above the token. Wilkinsburg, Pennsylvania, is 53 percent black, but its schools are 97 percent black. Oklahoma City is 16 percent black, but its schools are about 40 percent black. As of 1998, there were fewer than 4,000 white children left in Atlanta's public schools. Nor should we be misled if the numbers for an entire school district make it appear integrated; the actual schools themselves are often segregated by race. In Illinois, Michigan, New York, and New Jersey, almost three in five black public school students attend schools that have fewer than 10 percent whites.

Even self-consciously progressive whites have their integration threshold, though they are often unwilling to admit it to themselves. A 90 percent black private elementary school tried to set down roots in liberal Cambridge, Massachusetts, but was driven out after a grassroots campaign opposed it for traffic and safety reasons, even though these issues had not arisen during the fifty years another prep school occupied the same building. Then there's the well-known, predominantly white New York City private school that distributed an anonymous questionnaire to its parents. Large numbers supported black-white friendships and goodwill scholarships to attract some minorities to the school. Everyone felt good about those findings. But when the survey revealed that almost nine in ten parents would not be comfortable with interracial dating among the kids, the parents collectively expressed outrage. Who could feel this way, who are these bigots among us, they asked with righteous indignation.[16]

Perhaps the most intriguing evidence of our desire to appear more integrated than we are can be seen in the many surveys showing that 60 to almost 90 percent of whites claim to have a close, personal friend who is black. Now think about how we make close friends. It's usually with someone who lives nearby, someone we went to school with, someone whose kids are in the same class, or someone in the same profession, at the same status or socioeconomic level. How often do blacks and whites share these factors? Certainly not on suburban Long Island, home to approximately 200,000 blacks but where the chance of white people encountering a black living in their neighborhood is less than three percent.[17] In fact, nearly half of all the counties in the United States have fewer than 250 blacks, and in areas where large numbers of blacks live, very rarely are the neighborhoods genuinely mixed. Nor is the workplace much different. Almost half of Americans work in small businesses, which tend to be the least racially mixed. And studies show that blacks and whites in the same workplace rarely hold jobs of equivalent status. There is also plenty of research showing that blacks and whites rarely socialize together and have only limited contact with one another in any venue outside of work and public transportation. So where do we become such close friends?

A closer look at the friendship numbers reveals an even more startling fact: If three quarters of whites have close black friends, then every black person in America—including the isolated underclass locked in inner cities and the substantial number of blacks who say they don't have any meaningful contact or friendships with whites—will on average be close friends with five or six white people. Or put it another way: there would have to be about 160 million blacks in America, not the 30 million who live here today, if every black were to have one close white friend. A 1992 *Boston Globe* survey of Massachusetts youth found that if whites and blacks were telling the truth about their interracial dating habits, "then each black person would have had to date an average of nine white people."[18] To be generous, let's call it highly improbable, a product of our desire to be absolved of racism and our will to believe we are tolerant and good. As a black character in the John Grisham film *A Time to Kill* says ruefully in response to his white lawyer's affirmation that the two are friends: "We ain't no friends, Jake. We on different sides of the line. I ain't never seen you in my part of town. I bet you don't even know where I live. Our daughters, Jake, they ain't never gonna play together."

The dissonance between professed racial attitudes and actual racial reality should come as no surprise. Ever since the 1960s, as society began to shun overt bigotry and applaud gestures of racial tolerance, social scientists have found whites to exaggerate their contact with and support for blacks. As with any norm, people understandably want to be seen as conforming to it—in this case, they are evincing society's antiracist and tolerant attitudes.

In exit polls after elections, for example, more whites say they vote for black candidates than actually do. One study compared the different responses offered when the phone survey interviewer could be clearly identified as white or black. On topics such as racially mixed schools, friendships with blacks, and who's to blame for current black problems, white survey respondents who were interviewed by blacks consistently provided a more liberal or integrationist response than whites who were interviewed by whites.[19] It could be that some whites simply know the socially acceptable answers and don't want to be perceived as prejudiced even to strangers on the phone. Others might truly believe their answers reflect their realities—and in some cases they do. But even when they do, many times those realities are plainly misleading. One poll, for example, reported the apparent good news that a majority of whites say they live near blacks. But if one black family lives in a neighborhood of fifty families, every single white—100 percent—can make that claim. So can all the remaining whites who live in neighborhoods undergoing racial change. Not only does such a snapshot fail to tell the whole story, but in this case it perpetuates an illusion. The point here is not to deny the credibility of all polls, many of which can be useful in comparing black and white attitudes, but merely to show how powerfully the integration illusion defines our perceptions and self-image. Call it racial civility, decorous integration, or the politeness conspiracy—the bottom line is that our professed attitudes, symbols, and public expressions masquerade as integrated when our lives clearly are not. And what people say is less important than what they do.

Once we strip away the rhetoric and symbolism of integration, we are left with a society only marginally less divided than it was on that hot August day when a quarter of a million Americans descended on Washington for the great civil rights march of 1963. The barriers then were legal segregation and the complete violation of the rights of America's black citizens. The barriers today create a different type of separation—behavioral, social, residential, and psychological—but it is an abiding and resilient separation nonetheless.

This is not to deny or in any way diminish the extraordinary racial progress of the past generation, most evident in the civil rights movement's breathtaking elimination of blatant and legal discrimination, in the eight thousand blacks who now hold public office, and in the economic and educational mobility of the black middle class. For a black population nearly illiterate half a century ago to have nearly the same high school completion rate as whites today—that is remarkable progress. For a Deep South black population dispossessed and disenfranchised less than four decades ago to see black police chiefs, county commissioners, state legislators and members of Congress today—that is remarkable progress. For a black population with few roads to the middle class just a generation ago to see some of its families, when given the opportunity, equaling or exceeding the earnings of white neighbors—that is remarkable progress. Nearly forty years ago a third of all working black women were domestics; today about one in ten female professionals, technical workers, or managers is black. That too is progress. And it is progress when a black man talking with a white woman no longer has to fear the hooded lynch mob. While we should not sugarcoat this progress—indeed there remain stubborn obstacles to full black opportunity and overwhelming economic disparities between blacks and whites—we must acknowledge it as real and tangible evidence that America is desegregating. But we are simply not integrating.

The reality is that blacks and whites today are not much closer to living together, learning together, relaxing together, praying together, and playing together than they were a generation ago. The law might bring people together, but in the matters of choice blacks and whites are simply going their own ways. As a University of Illinois at Chicago study showed, middle-class black and white families go to museums, concerts, churches, and zoos, but rarely the same ones; they have the same interests but lead parallel, separate lives.[20] Even the many white Americans who appreciate and admire black cultural contributions, particularly in music, will rarely experience them in predominantly black venues. We have some racial interaction at work during the day, but almost complete separation after dark.

This resistance to integration is certainly not new. Many of us like to think of the early 1960s as a time untainted by white backlash, black nationalism, and the controversies over busing and affirmative action, when we had a chance to overcome the color line and build an integrated America. But as early as 1963, even as the civil rights movement was ending legal segregation, *Newsweek* noted that white enthusiasm for civil rights ceased with the prospect of a black neighbor next door: "For the future, the crisis point will come if and when the irresistible force of Negro protest meets the immovable object of white intractability."[21] Indeed, the civil rights movement faced its greatest problems when it took the promise of integration literally and asked—or expected—whites throughout the country to comply. White flight away from encroaching black neighborhoods had already begun in the 1950s, and as far as whites were concerned, there was no turning back. "We're not racists, believe me," said a national leader of the Elks in 1971, in a notorious refrain that could be and is repeated anywhere, anytime, by almost anyone. "It's a hard thing to define, but we feel we're a private organization and we have the right to admit who we want in our lodge."[22] A generation later these words are rarely spoken in public, but the sentiment behind them remains intransigent and strong.

Nor are whites the only ones exercising racial choice. Increasingly, blacks—tired of the incessant daily reminders that they are black and not merely people—are viewing whites with distrust and concluding that true integration is an unworkable and unrealistic ideal. Not only are more and more blacks choosing to live in predominantly black communities, but they are affirming their distinctiveness by participating enthusiastically in separate social institutions, seeking out black cultural experiences and entertainment, choosing to attend historically black colleges and universities, and building parallel cultural traditions such as Kwanzaa, a black festival celebrated around Christmas time.

Black Americans know they can never be completely isolated from whites—for practical purposes it would be difficult to earn a living—and many blacks would reject that option as antithetical to the integration ideal they still hold. But just as the economic walls are tumbling down, enabling millions of blacks to realize their American Dream, the psychological and social walls are rising up. During the Cold War the United States would counter Soviet propaganda by saying there was more to people's lives than economic security, that what made us human was the dignity of the free and unfettered individual able to live without insult, wariness, and fear. That same yearning for human dignity was proclaimed by black marchers during the civil rights years when they held up signs that said simply I AM A MAN—and it echoes to-day when a Yale law professor could say without irony that he "felt safer and more comfortable" sitting with black prison inmates "than I do in the faculty lounge at Yale."[23] Economic status goes only so far in life. If this intangible but very real sense of human dignity is unattainable in mixed company, inward is where blacks will turn. The black American search to be merely individuals in society, free and unfettered by the burden of race, was the driving idea behind integration. That true integration seems unreach-able does not mean the idea behind it has gone away—indeed it is the soul of black America today. Yet the search to transcend race is increasingly manifested in the desire, whenever possible, to be apart from whites.

If there is any doubt that the integration of blacks and whites is not working and may never work, it is instructive to compare blacks with the two other most prominent ethnic groups who also share the "minority" label, Hispanics and Asians. Because of comparable levels of poverty and disadvantage today, the plight of Asians and especially Hispanics is often equated with that of blacks. Government equal-opportunity laws make few dis-tinctions among these groups, and they are often compared in terms of their educational, economic, and political achievements. But to lump them together based on a snapshot of today's eco-nomic circumstances is to overlook the more compelling evi-dence that these two recent immigrant groups are assimilating in ways that blacks have never been able to integrate. Indeed, it is a grievous error to lump blacks indiscriminately with Hispan-ics and Asians because it ignores the profoundly different rela-tionships each has with the current American majority. Blacks are not immigrants and never have been, and the black experi-ence is fundamentally at odds with the immigrant experience in America.

A hundred fifty years ago the unmeltable ethnics, besides blacks, were the Irish and the Germans, and a century ago they were the Italian, Jews, Poles, and Russians. All were vilified, excluded, abused, and discriminated against and were portrayed at times as less than human, and always as less desirable than the Anglo-Saxon majority. All have assimilated, except for blacks. If the current assimilation patterns of Hispanics and Asians continue, it will be no different today. On the basis of housing patterns, social interaction, educational achievement, English-language acquisition, and small-business development, today's immigrants are acting no differently from those who preceded them. According to an economist at the Rand Corporation, the economic status of third-generation Hispanics and Asians today typically mirrors that of whites.[24] Or as sociologist Todd Gitlin observes in his book *The Twilight of Common Dreams*, "As citizens, leaving aside tastes in food and music, many if not most second- and especially third-generation Hispanics are indistinguishable from the grandchildren of Italian, Irish, or Polish immigrants."[25] Perhaps not surprisingly, West Indians are the one immigrant group that seems to assimilate less as they become second- and third-generation Americans. They simply become black.[26]

Politicians are almost intrinsically incapable of projecting anything more than today's bumper-sticker slogans into the future, so it is no surprise that a staple of political speeches these days is the end of the white majority by the middle of next century and the rise of a multicultural America. Listen carefully and it sounds hauntingly similar to what politicians warned of a hundred years ago, the only difference being that today's leaders say it with equanimity rather than fear. The politicians were wrong then and they probably will be wrong today. Just as today's majority, through the absorption of yesterday's immigrants, is ethnically different from the Anglo majority of last century, the majority of the next century will absorb today's immigrants and look different from the majority today. But it will still be a majority, and blacks will still be on the outside looking in. It has been the case throughout American history that a second-generation immigrant becomes an American while an eighth-generation black is still a black. Comedian Richard Pryor used to joke that the first citizenship lesson taught to new immigrants was the correct pronunciation of the word "nigger." Ethnic boundaries remain porous for immigrants but virtually impermeable for blacks. "As to this country being a melting pot," wrote Supreme Court Justice Thurgood Marshall in 1978, "either the Negro did not get in the pot or he did not get melted down."[27]

Because they speak most convincingly to the degree of intimacy the majority is willing to have with another group, the two most accurate measures of assimilation are residential integration and intermarriage. On each count the comparison between blacks and both Hispanics and Asians is chilling. According to a 1989 *Time* magazine article, an Hispanic or Asian-American with a third-grade education is more likely to live in an integrated neighborhood than a black with a Ph.D. In their groundbreaking book on racial housing patterns, *American Apartheid,* Douglas Massey and Nancy Denton note that in Los Angeles, "The *poorest* Hispanics were less segregated than the *most affluent* blacks," a pattern they saw repeated throughout the United States. *USA Today* analyzed the 1990 census and reported that blacks were highly segregated in thirty-one of the forty-seven metropolitan areas where they made up at least 20 percent of the residents, a pattern evident in only two of thirty-three areas that were at least 20 percent Hispanic. The newspaper found that the residential isolation of Hispanics and Asians falls when their incomes rise, which is not the case with blacks. Nor is poverty the decisive cause of residential isolation in America, as the immigrant poor, while still relatively isolated, tend to be more mobile and less walled off than many blacks. One study of the Washington metropolitan area found that "black poverty is highly concentrated, while white and Hispanic poverty is highly dispersed." A map of the area shows poor whites and Hispanics scattered throughout the region's suburban neighborhoods, whereas black poverty is concentrated in the city. In general, the isolation of Hispanics tends to be a first- or second-generation phenomenon that dissipates over time. Interestingly, the only Hispanic group that seems to remain residentially isolated are black Hispanics. According to one Census Bureau official, at the current rate of integration it could take as long as fifty years for black residential isolation to fall to the current level of Hispanic isolation. Presumably it would take even longer if we factored out the artificially high isolation of new Hispanic immigrants.[28]

Much attention has been paid to a recent up-tick in black-white intermarriage rates, but again that must be put in its proper perspective. Yes, there are high-profile black Americans like Diana Ross, James Earl Jones, Clarence Thomas, Charles Barkley, and Cuba Gooding, Jr., who have nonblack spouses. And yes, it is not unusual to see an interracial couple strolling in a trendy urban neighborhood. But by no means are these signs of imminent integration and national color-blindness. As with so many other examples of the integration illusion, intermarriage is yet another case of less than meets the eye. Census Bureau statistics show that about four percent of all married blacks in the primary marrying years of twenty-five to thirty-four are married to non-Hispanic whites and about two percent are married to Hispanics, Asians, and Native Americans—which means that fully 94 percent of blacks who marry are marrying other blacks. Now compare the black six percent intermarriage rate with the 35 percent for native-born Hispanics and the 50 percent for native-born Asians. Although there are almost as many Hispanics as blacks in America, whites marry Hispanics at about seven times the rate they marry blacks. As with housing, Hispanics and Asians are following the typical immigrant pattern for intermarriage, which is reflected in the estimated 52 percent intermarriage rate for Jews, the greater than 80 percent rate for Polish Americans, the 73 percent rate for Italian Americans, and the 65 percent rate for Japanese Americans. As demographer Paul Spickard commented in 1993, "Almost no white American extended family exists today without at least one member who has married across what two generations ago would have been thought an unbridgeable gap." With minor exceptions, the only unbridgeable gap seems to be black and white.[29]

Of course, those who find even a glimmer of hope in the six percent black intermarriage rate must also take into account the relatively low number of marriages among blacks. Nonblacks are about 50 percent more likely to be married than blacks, and nonblack children are more than twice as likely to be living with both parents than black children. The intermarriage statistics most certainly do not take into account out-of-wedlock unions, of which a large number are between blacks. A comparison that included these unions would likely yield a much lower interracial rate for blacks. Furthermore, as University of Michigan demographer Reynolds Farley has pointed out, a significant number of intermarriages are among blacks and whites who have served in the military, which is so unlike the rest of America in its compulsory enforcement of racial integration that it barely resembles mainstream society. White women who served in the military are seven times more likely to marry black men than white women who never served; white men are three times more likely to marry black women. Exclude those with military service and the intermarriage numbers decline by about 20 percent. For black Americans, it is integration that creates intermarriage, not the other way around.

Integration rejection is also reflected in the status of interracial marriages and particularly in the identity of the children born to them. Black and white married couples generally have a difficult time with their white relatives and are frequently embraced only among the black side of the family. The social strain on them is so great that even Colin Powell felt "uneasy" at his son's engagement to a white woman: "The older generation knows what the younger generation may still have to learn."[30] It is no surprise that the children of these unions frequently identify themselves as black. Children with one white parent and one Japanese, Korean, Chinese, or Asian Indian parent will usually identify themselves as white. That cannot be said when the non-white parent is black; then, the children are usually black.[31] A survey to determine how many people would check a mixed race category on the census found that no more than 2.7 percent and as few as 0.7 percent of blacks would identify themselves as anything but black. Even those with some black ancestry who claim a mixed designation have a hard time not being labeled black. The "one drop of blood" rule that prohibited anyone with a trace of black blood from calling himself white may not be discussed much in public these days, but its influence remains very real in the way we look at anyone with a black ancestor. Celebrated golfer Tiger Woods—who is an eighth white, an eighth American Indian, a quarter Chinese, a quarter Thai, and a quarter black—has tried to label himself mixed, selecting the Asian designation on forms and even calling himself a "Cablinasian" (a combina-

tion of Caucasian, black, Indian, and Asian) to express his diverse
ancestry. But the public still sees him as black, and some even
equate him with Jackie Robinson. "There are still golf courses in
the United States that I cannot play because of the color of my
skin," Woods said on the Nike ad introducing him as Nike's
newest spokesman. When Woods' fellow golfer Fuzzy Zoeller
made his infamous "little boy" racial slur, his joke pictured Woods
eating not lo mein but stereotypical black food, fried chicken and
collard greens.

Among Western countries, the wholesale rejection of black-
white intimacy appears unique to the United States. In Britain,
where African slavery never existed and most blacks are either recent arrivals or are descended from immigrants, intermarriage is
considerably more common. Almost one third of the married or
cohabiting blacks in Britain under the age of thirty-four have
white partners, a percentage similar to the Hispanic intermarriage rate in the United States. The number is even higher
among West Indians born in Britain, approximately 40 percent
(50 percent for men, 33 percent for women).[32] Even here in
America it was fairly common for blacks and whites to have intimate contact, but that was way before slavery shaped and dis-
torted the entire relationship between blacks and whites. "Up to
and perhaps through the 1660s, it is difficult to document any in-
disputably racist feeling about miscegenation," writes historian
Edmund Morgan.[33] Racial integration may be a thoroughly
American ideal, but its failure is steeped thoroughly in the
American experience.

This is a book with a broken heart, for it is with little joy or enthusiasm that we reach our conclusions. "I look back," said a
somber Kenneth Clark in 1990 upon concluding that America
may never reach his ideal of true integration, "and I shudder and
say, 'Oh God, you really were as naïve as some people said you
were.' "[34] It pains us, as believers in true integration, as Americans who still cling personally to the ideal, to paint this portrait
of a divided country. But we also believe it is best for America to
face the truth and cease pretending that the integration myth has
anything to do with the racial reality. As a people we have been
less than honest with ourselves about race for so long that this

lack of honesty is now compounding the problems brought about by our nation's original sin. For blacks, the integration ideal has come to serve as a constant and frustrating reminder of what is not now and may never be possible in America. For whites, it has become a convenient ideological salve, a substitute for participation in a real and honest reckoning about race. If integration is not—and never was—a realistic goal for American society, perhaps we are better off forsaking it as a goal altogether.

To the minority of Americans who continue to pursue real rather than symbolic integration, whether it be through one-on-one interaction or common cause in the community, we hope you don't give up. All the lives you touch will be truly enriched. You are true racial heroes. To those who participate in discussion groups about race and genuinely attempt other interracial connections, even as you still live separate lives, at least you're trying to bridge the gap. To the black and white pioneers who truly have close friendships with one another, who feel equally comfortable in predominantly black or white groups, who travel between the two worlds and are genuinely color-blind without any racial pretext, you are the rarest among us.

Unless there is a profound and remarkable transformation in this country, however, unless the peculiar nature of race relations undergoes fundamental change, let us not have any illusions that the vast majority of Americans will ever become truly color-blind. The sooner we acknowledge the permanence of the color line in American life, the sooner we strip away the fictional integration behind which the majority hides, the sooner we can begin an honest accounting of our racial divide and develop an alternative vision of our collective future. It is time to make the best of what we have rather than pretend we are building an Eden when we truly cannot.

It is said that a nation needs myths to make progress, that without myths our aspirations are truly lowered. Let us not give up on the ideal, the argument goes, let us rededicate ourselves to it. But some myths can actually thwart progress, particularly when the very success of promoting the myth becomes a convenient way to avoid addressing the real problem. Such is the sad and ironic case with integration.

Even with the failure of integration, we do not foresee any racial cataclysm or a coming race war in America. Wrath and hatred may always brew among the most dispossessed blacks and the most embittered whites, and resentment may be the octane of both black and white extremists and rabble-rousers. But except for the occasional manifestation of public rage, open hostility between blacks and whites is a more marginal issue today than it was thirty years ago. It is more accurate to say that the vast majority of black Americans and white Americans simply coexist in separate realms, interacting when necessary and occasionally crossing over, but ultimately retreating to our different worlds, perhaps like the French and Flemish in Belgium, or the French, Germans and Italians in Switzerland. "It's more innocent than it looks," an Indianapolis high school student told the NBC show *Dateline* when describing the separate black and white tables in the cafeteria at lunchtime, and indeed it may be. The races do not have to hate each other to be divided, and indeed we can be very cordial about it. To say we are racially separated is to state a fact, nothing more, nothing less. Nor is it pointing fingers to say it is a result of history, custom, culture, choice, resentment, prejudice, and fear. It's just the way it is. Like it or not, perhaps the best we can expect is what Booker T. Washington advocated a century ago: "In all things that are purely social we can be as separate as the fingers, yet one as the hand in all things essential to mutual progress." Perhaps we must put our energies into achieving some of the objectives we thought would be realized with integration, such as improving black access to educational and economic opportunity, and addressing the corrosive idea of black inferiority that continues to be internalized by so many blacks and whites. Tackling these challenges will ultimately make our coexistence much more peaceful and mutually gratifying.

Failure is not a word that sits comfortably with most Americans. National leaders who speak of limits—such as Jimmy Carter—are usually dispatched and defeated. America is a nation that prides itself on conquering every challenge, a nation founded not on geography or ethnicity but on ideals and promises that for over two centuries we have worked so hard to meet. We see ourselves as different, the exception and not the rule, number one in everything.

"There's never been a challenge we've ever faced we haven't been able to overcome," President Clinton once said. To suggest that America is not capable of fulfilling one of its most cherished ideals—one so central to our self-image—will no doubt be met with outcry and resistance. To say we are no better than Belgium or Switzerland strikes at the very heart of a national identity built on this sense of American exceptionalism. Certainly no politician seeking reelection or high approval ratings will ever utter these words.

Indeed, one of our nation's proudest and most remarkable achievements is how we have embraced, welcomed, and united an extraordinary number of nationalities, religions, and ethnic groups, making one out of many, *e pluribus unum.* It is a feat replicated by no other nation. Surely, we will hear, there is no reason why we cannot enlarge the melting pot to include blacks. "That is the unfinished work of our times," President Clinton said in his June 1997 speech on race relations, "to lift the burden of race and redeem the promise of America." Our racial problem can be fixed—all we need is to roll up our sleeves and resolve to do it. Former senator Bill Bradley, a true voice of racial idealism, said, "There is a significant majority of people out there who want to deal with this and put it behind us."[35]

Given this can-do, fix-it, put-it-behind-us mentality, we were not surprised that a number of publishers who expressed interest in our book wanted to know what our plan was to solve the problem we were identifying, as if they could market it as a how-to manual for race relations. We responded that if we knew what to do we would be receiving the Nobel Peace Prize in Stockholm, not sitting in their editorial offices in New York. As we went through this ritual with almost every publisher, we became more convinced that the futile search for the magic bullet has deepened our national frustration and contributed to the fraying of our racial nerves. Unmet expectations tend to intensify disappointment. Perhaps our nation is so tense and defensive about race because our failure to integrate holds up a mirror to the fallibility of our national experiment, implying that we are not so different or exceptional after all, that we are less than the sum of our ideals. It is not an image of ourselves we want to acknowledge or see.

What makes the failure of integration even more tragic is that blacks may be the most American of all ethnic groups, people who have worked hard, played by all the rules, and deferred gratification literally for centuries. Our current focus on the pathologies of many blacks has made us overlook the extraordinary forbearance most blacks have shown in their pursuit of the American Dream. Immigrants who didn't like the United States were able to go back home. About a third of European immigrants who arrived at the turn of the century returned home overseas to families and communities. Blacks have never had that option. Their survival, endurance, and transcendence are at the very root of what it means to be an American.[36]

It began with slavery, when they were sold as chattel and separated from loved ones, and received no compensation for their sweat and labor. After slavery, blacks never received the forty acres and a mule promised them for their years of denial. For generations, many in the South were forced into sharecropping and tenant-farming arrangements that replicated slavery without the chains and left most blacks penniless despite back-breaking work—the same conditions many immigrants fled when they came to America. Although a ray of hope came when many blacks moved north for factory work during World War I, they were thrown out of jobs once the white soldiers returned. After the great black migration to Northern cities that took place following World War II, it wasn't long before entry-level manufacturing jobs moved to the exclusively white suburbs and, in an economic twist of fate, disappeared altogether. Those blacks with the means were and in some cases still are denied the homes and neighborhoods of their choice. Today blacks are as religious, socially conservative, and patriotic as any other ethnic group, with a deep belief in the goodness and inclusiveness of American society and, despite the popular perception that blacks blame whites for their problems, a willingness to shoulder a large amount of responsibility for the present condition of their brethren.[37] Values supposedly matter in America, but if black people have these values and are still not fully welcomed into the mainstream, it is fair for them finally to ask whether anything they do will ever make a difference.

To concede failure does not dishonor the great and noble lives that have been sacrificed for the integration ideal; rather we must thank them for giving it their best and forcing the question of whether society was or ever will be ready to live up to this ideal. That we are not now ready and never have been should give us pause, because an America without the integration illusion must ask what that means for the future of this unique and remarkable country.

CHAPTER TWO

A Day in the Life of Two Americas, Part 1: Living, Learning, Working Apart

Some people simply call it "the box." It's usually a large cardboard box found hidden away in a walk-in closet or down in the basement next to the washing machine. It contains diplomas, artwork, books, music, and especially all the family photos—anything that can identify the family as black. If a black family living in a predominantly white neighborhood wants to sell their house, they are often advised by friends or their real estate agent to put everything identifiably black—any vestige of who they are—in the box. Otherwise, white people may not buy the house.

For understandable reasons, real estate agents are often unwilling to acknowledge this practice. Nor are black homeowners very effusive about something so tinged with shame and regret. But walk into an open house any Saturday or Sunday, and if there are no family photos or mementos around, rest assured they're in the box. It happened once to the man who would become the highest-ranking civil rights official in America, former Assistant Attorney General Deval Patrick: "Yes. Actually, one time in one city, and I'll leave it at that. The realtor asked my wife and me to put all of our family photos away." It happened to a *Wall Street Journal* editor, who, after his house was appraised significantly below market value, decided not only to replace all the family photos with those of his white secretary but asked her and her blond son to be in the house when a new appraiser came by. The strategy worked. Black families are also advised to clear out when prospective white buyers want to see the house. Too many times a white family will drive up to a house, see the black homeowner working in the garden or garage, and quickly drive away.[1]

The box is a very small part of the daily commerce between blacks and whites, and its use is by nature limited to the relatively rare black family living in an overwhelmingly white community. But as a metaphor for race relations it looms very large, because it shows the lengths to which many whites will go to avoid intimate contact with anything black, and the degree to which blacks accept and grudgingly accommodate this reality. For blacks to succeed in the predominantly white world, they must—figuratively—carry this box around with them every day.

On a typical day in America, the lives of blacks and whites may intersect, but rarely do they integrate. In the matters most intimate and important to our lives—our neighborhoods, schools, work, faith, entertainment, and social life—we either go separate ways or, when forced together, follow what seems like a shadow dance of polite interaction. This by no means denies the real and meaningful contacts between some blacks and whites, but these instances are infrequent enough to be the conspicuous exceptions that prove the rule. Black and white Americans wake up in separate neighborhoods, send their kids off to separate schools, listen to different radio stations during the morning commute, briefly interact on the job but rarely as equals, return to their own communities after work, socialize in separate environments, and watch different television shows before going to sleep and starting the same process all over again. This is a day in the life of two Americas.

Separate Neighborhoods

Most days begin the same for everyone, with the fresh morning air and the hustle to get out for work. But for black and white Americans, our lives begin to diverge after that. Chances are that a black family leaving home in the morning will see other black faces leaving their homes, and that a white family will see almost exclusively whites. Where we live defines so much of our lives—how we get to work, where our kids go to school, where we shop, whom we chat with, and who our friends will be. And where we live is more often than not determined by race.

About a third of all black Americans live in neighborhoods that are 90 percent or more black, and most other blacks live in neighborhoods disproportionately or predominantly black. Scholars Douglas Massey and Nancy Denton write in their book *American Apartheid* that "blacks remain the most spatially isolated population in U.S. history."[2] The isolation of blacks in central cities is as well documented as it is tragic. As Massey and Denton have pointed out, many blacks in these areas would have to go clear across town simply to find a white family. In cities like Chicago, Detroit, New York, Cleveland, St. Louis and Birmingham, blacks and whites are as divided and in some cases more divided than they were 40 years ago. Most whites lead parallel lives, living in virtually all-white neighborhoods, though often with a smattering of Hispanics and Asians. We may live in a nominally multiracial society, but millions upon millions of white Americans have no regular contact in their neighborhoods with blacks.

Years ago the suburbs were seen as the integration panacea, fresh fields for color-blind Americans to live together. More Americans now live in suburbs than anywhere else. But with the rise of black suburban migration over the last generation—close to a third of all blacks now live in the suburbs—the same pattern of separation has taken hold there as well. Most typical is the white suburb that stays virtually all white, the established black suburb that becomes more black, or the previously white suburb that in due time becomes all black once the color line has been broken. Very few suburbs boast a stable racial balance similar to the mix of middle-class blacks and whites in the metropolitan area, and even in these communities, residents still tend to cluster by race.

Consider the case of Bloomfield, Connecticut, which in 1971 was honored as an All-American City by *Look* magazine and the National Municipal League for its commitment to racial harmony and integrated schools. A small town with barely two thousand inhabitants, Bloomfield sits outside Hartford in pristine New England splendor, complete with a town green, church steeples, and well-appointed single-family homes. But with each passing year, Bloomfield has slowly become less and less white, and more and more black, first five percent black, then 10, then 20, and now nearing 50. First to change were the public schools, which by 1996 were nearly 85 percent black, despite a lingering white majority in town. It won't be long before the actual population follows suit. While many communities in the 1960s turned from all white to all black in a matter of months and years, today the transformation is more gradual. But it is a transformation nonetheless. Bloomfield is indeed an all-American city.

Bloomfield may be different from most communities because it tries to maintain a certain degree of integration, but it is no different in the inexorable residential process taking place there. It is a process that occurs in almost any region of the country where there is a substantial enough black population for whites to feel potentially threatened. The first harbinger of change in a community is the public school—much like the proverbial canary in the coal mine. As black students begin to populate the schools in more than token amounts, white flight from the schools begins to accelerate. White families either send their children to private schools or move out altogether—usually to an established white community or to a new development they call "a nice place to raise kids." In this beginning stage, the number of blacks in public schools is always higher than the number of blacks in the community. Usually the black and white neighbors are cordial and will stop each other to talk and say hello. As years go by and white families move out, few white families will move in. In some communities not a single white person will move in after the first black person calls the area home. Blocks and neighborhoods soon become racially identifiable. Eventually the only whites in the community are those who can't afford to move out, those with no children in school—empty-nesters—or those who can afford private school. Ultimately the remaining whites move out and the community turns predominantly black. This process is not always evident from the beginning, as the presence of one or two black families is often celebrated by most white neighbors as evidence of tolerance and diversity rather than feared as a sign of change. But once the welcome mat is put out for blacks, all it takes is a few white families to worry and move away and a few black families to take their place, and the domino effect begins.

Call it black humor if you wish, but the joke among blacks living in neighborhoods like these is to ask each other what the most popular vehicle is among the remaining white residents. The answer is a U-Haul. Humor is certainly a defense against disappointment, as it is indeed dispiriting to see neighbors move simply because of the color of one's skin. Study after study has shown that blacks would prefer to live in well-integrated neighborhoods between one-third and two-thirds black. All-black and especially all-white neighborhoods are the least desirable locations.[3] The reason is simple: a well-integrated neighborhood would be black enough to buffer against prejudice and isolation, but diverse enough to expose their children to people of all backgrounds. The problem for blacks is that a neighborhood that appears integrated will attract more blacks, which then accelerates white flight and the changeover to a predominantly black neighborhood. And so what many hail as racially mixed neighborhoods are actually neighborhoods undergoing racial transition. Seeing this, a number of blacks have simply stopped trying to integrate and are increasingly opting for identifiably black communities.

Whites see it very differently. Although public opinion surveys show considerable white support for residential integration, what actually happens in the neighborhoods is quite the opposite. If whites could be guaranteed that the number of blacks in their neighborhood would not rise above, say, five or six percent, few would move. But there are no such guarantees, so the white discomfort level begins to rise with each new black face on the block, and the neighborhood begins to tip. With the image of black crime and urban blight so formidable and pervasive, middle-class whites don't want to take what they perceive as a risk. It doesn't seem to matter if the new black residents have equal-status jobs or higher incomes. Whites still move away. It doesn't matter if the schools remain good, if crime doesn't increase, or if home values continue to rise. Whites still say the neighborhood will eventually go bad. Nor does it matter that homes in all-white areas tend to cost more than homes in racially diverse neighborhoods. Whites will pay the extra. For most whites, integration really means managed tokenism, and anything beyond that evokes anxiety and fear.

Take a tour of America and you will see how this process has played out in every possible way. In Chicago, nineteen census tracts flipped from predominantly white to predominantly black during the 1980s. Near Detroit, whites describe neighbors who have moved three or four times just to stay ahead of black families. In suburban Prince George's County, Maryland, the first American county where income and education levels rose as the area turned majority black, the white population dropped from 85 percent in 1970 to 31 percent in 1997; and according to the 1990 census, more than half of the county's census tracts are at least 70 percent white or 70 percent black, with at least ten communities more than 90 percent black. Fast-growing Atlanta has identifiably white suburban counties—Gwinnett, Rockdale, Dade, Whitfield, and Cobb—and counties increasingly populated by blacks—DeKalb and Fulton. The middle-class Atlanta neighborhood of Cascade Heights, home to former mayor Andrew Young and civil rights leader Joseph Lowery, was mixed a generation ago but is virtually all black today. Long Island, considered the nation's first suburb, is home to the nation's most affluent black population, but two thirds of Long Island's neighborhoods are less than one percent black, half of those have no blacks at all, and 95 percent of Nassau County's black residents live in five percent of the census tracts. On the other side of Manhattan, in three contiguous New Jersey towns—Tenafly, Englewood Cliffs, and Englewood—the first two are less than one percent black while the third is nearly 40 percent black but has virtually no whites in the public schools. It's no different in the Pittsburgh area, where three-fourths of the white population live in neighborhoods 90 percent or more white, and more than a third of black home buyers in the early 1990s purchased in just twenty black-dominated census tracts. The booming Charlotte-Mecklenburg area is often held up as an example of peaceful integration in the South, but there as well housing is divided, with some communities virtually all black and others, including some brand-new developments, virtually all white. In all-white Metairie, Louisiana, near New Orleans, one researcher found that about a third of all residents moved there to escape blacks.[4]

Nor is this phenomenon limited to those with the means to move. Even people without many choices make a choice when race is involved. Public housing throughout the nation is notoriously divided. In Montgomery County, Maryland, poor whites "have often given up their places on the public housing lists" to avoid being placed in a predominantly black housing cluster, according to the *Washington Post*. Chautauqua Street on the north side of Pittsburgh was home to almost ninety lower-middle-class white families in 1968, but is 80 percent black now. With no trace of irony, a reporter for the *Pittsburgh Post-Gazette* said, "The integration of Chautauqua Street has been a harmonious, trouble-free process."[5]

Three fairly recent phenomena reinforce the residential separation of the races. First is the rapid growth of the gated community, where an estimated four million Americans—mostly white—currently live. With private security guards, visitor passes, locked entry gates, and tightly run residential associations, these communities have become, according to a 1995 article in the *Yale Law Journal*, "homogeneous enclaves undisturbed by the undesirably different." For many of these communities, the residential association serves as community gatekeeper and is often "a powerful tool for segregation," according to the *Yale Law Journal* article. One gated community described itself in marketing materials as a place that makes you "secure within the boundaries of your own neighborhood." It's unclear how much irony was intended when the gated communities on South Carolina's Hilton Head Island were officially called "plantations," but the message of most gated communities is clear to blacks: these are walled-off, peaceful oases for whites, and no matter how much you've accomplished in life, you are not welcome as a purchaser or guest.[6]

Whereas gated communities enable white Americans to live in isolation close to the city, the second phenomenon sees whites exiting the city to more distant suburbs and outlying communities relatively far from the urban core—so-called exurbs—that are attracting high-tech industries and an increasing number of residents. States especially popular for this white exodus are Nevada, Idaho, Utah, Colorado, and Washington. Between 1990 and 1994, more than one million Americans left the suburbs for these exurbs, and the trend is growing rapidly. The search for a more basic, pastoral life is nothing new in American history, so it is perfectly possible to ascribe this phenomenon to a desire for innocence, peace, and simplicity. But it would be naïve not to acknowledge that part of what whites want to escape is proximity to blacks. As one Utah executive candidly explained: "One thing people don't want to worry about is race relations. Companies think if they go to a neighborhood where everyone is like me, it makes it easier. It takes away from stress. People want to remove some of the variables of their lives."[7]

The third phenomenon reinforcing separation is the stabilization and growth of identifiably black middle-class communities, which are increasingly becoming the neighborhoods of choice for upwardly mobile blacks who want a secure place to raise families and are tired of rejection by whites. These are often urban enclaves or inner-ring suburbs just outside the city that years ago housed the first wave of white suburban migrants but have long since turned predominantly black. In Chicago, for example, nearly nine in ten black middle-class households with incomes above $35,000 live in predominantly black neighborhoods in just two parts of town, a pattern also found in other cities with a substantial black middle-class population.[8] Many blacks are also setting down roots deeper into the suburbs and moving to predominantly black communities such as Mitchellville outside Washington, D.C., Brook Glen outside Atlanta, and Rolling Oaks outside Miami. Builders in these areas understand what's going on and market these communities specifically to blacks. As *Los Angeles Times* reporter Sam Fulwood III writes in his compelling autobiography: "Without fully comprehending why, I was smitten by the model home with its subtle, subliminal persuasions aimed at racial pride and feelings of estrangement from white neighborhoods. . . . Indeed, I had never before seen a model home that featured decorations aimed at middle-income black buyers. The book with Dr. King's image on the cover was one item . . . on the bookshelf along with storybooks and a black-faced rag doll."[9]

Marketing isn't the only reason this is happening. It's a matter of living with dignity and respect. "We're flocking to mostly black suburbs partly because we still can't readily integrate with white society," said an editor of the black-oriented magazine *Emerge*. "We work in these corporations, law firms, hospitals, what have you, but we see what the limitations are. You also want to make sure your children can function without the stings of racism penetrating them all the time. . . . If I locked myself out of my house one night in a mostly white neighborhood, my neighbor might hesitate to open his door because of the color of my skin. That happened to me recently. But in an all-black area, I'd merely be inconveniencing my neighbors. They'd let me in."[10]

Unfortunately, one phenomenon that has not changed is plain old housing bias. Years ago blacks as prominent as baseball star Willie Mays or distinguished historian John Hope Franklin could not even buy a house in many neighborhoods and had no legal protections against blatant housing discrimination. That was all supposed to change with passage of the Fair Housing Act of 1968, and to a great extent it did. Blacks wishing to move into a community now had a legal weapon with which to protect themselves. The nefarious real estate practice of blockbusting—in which agents found an all-white block, deliberately sold a home to a black family, instilled fear in the remaining whites, and then reaped profits from panic home selling—has all but disappeared. The great hope of the housing reformers was that these changes would free up housing sales to blacks, curtail white flight, and eventually lead to a residentially integrated America. But what happened instead is that the bias was driven underground, made more subtle, and used artfully rather than blatantly to perpetuate the divided housing patterns already in place. Rarely do we see nowadays the flagrant abuse such as the real estate appraiser's handbook popular in the 1970s that ranked nationalities according to their effect on the local housing market, with English, Germans and Scandinavians on top and blacks on the bottom.[11] More common is a deceptive real estate practice called steering.

Imagine you are a black person looking to buy a home. You find an area you like but learn from the real estate agent or builder that there are no available homes left in your price range. That area happens to be all white. The agent then shows you a number of other homes, all in racially mixed or predominantly black neighborhoods, and encourages you to buy there. Whether you know it or not, you have just been the target of steering, which is supposed to be illegal but thrives throughout the industry. It doesn't matter if you are solidly middle-class or if you spent years in the military serving the country. As local governments discover when they send people out to test the problem, blacks are steered to black or mixed neighborhoods, and whites are steered to white neighborhoods.[12]

The agents are often more subtle than simply showing black buyers homes in black neighborhoods. They might show the black family homes in a white area, but only ones that are out of the family's price range so that the purchasers steer themselves to a more affordable—more black—area. Or the realtor might try to dampen interest by telling the family they must first be cleared by a mortgage company before they could see any homes. Brokers who violate the unwritten rules of this game have been threatened by colleagues, according to the testimony of one Long Island agent. Whites are steered as well, particularly when they show interest in an affordable but mixed neighborhood. The message is often communicated in the common code of racial steering: "The neighborhood is changing and you won't feel comfortable there," whites are told. Builders selling new homes in all-white areas have a large stake in steering, as they know that white families will be less inclined to buy if the first few families in the development are black. One agent was told by a developer to delay and prevent a black family's purchase "by any means necessary." The real estate industry defends itself against the charge of steering by saying the only color that matters to agents is green. "Ninety-eight percent of all buyers are self-steering," said one realtor. But regardless of whether the buyer or the broker does the steering, the end result is a nation of homeowners divided by race.[13]

Nor is steering limited to buying a home. The rental woes of black Americans are well documented and widespread. Rental brokers describe how their jobs depend on their ability to screen out blacks. Some large rental agencies try to train agents to recognize a black person on the phone. One interracial couple, both attorneys, got a friendly reception over the phone from a New York City co-op, but after the black husband showed up to meet the building's board, their application was denied. Indeed, a frequent frustration among blacks is to be told the apartment is available over the phone but was just rented by the time they show up. Agencies that send white and black testers report that whites are quoted lower rents, offered more incentives, shown more units, and never told the apartment has been rented when

it actually hasn't been. Blacks are often steered to other neighborhoods or to a particular building quietly designated for
blacks. A federal study found that 60 to 90 percent of housing
units shown to whites are not made available to blacks. We like
to think it's the exception when the Department of Justice files
a housing-discrimination complaint, as it did against a three-
hundred-unit Akron, Ohio, building that had never rented to a
black American—or when a leasing company is sued for renting
only three out of a thousand units to blacks. But they are merely
the most obvious examples in a nation whose neighborhoods follow the color line.[14]

Of course, not all bias is manifested as clinically as a rental application denied. Some white Americans who don't want any
blacks in their neighborhoods will simply act it out in hateful
ways. These folks may comprise a tiny minority of whites, but
their influence is large. Lorraine Hansberry wrote her stirring
play *A Raisin in the Sun* in 1959, but her tale of a black family's
move into a resentful white neighborhood continues to echo
loudly today. BULLETS GREET NEW OWNERS was the headline describing a June 1997 incident near Atlanta, and a July 1996 article about Cleveland's largest suburb, 99 percent white Parma, was
headlined CROSS IN YARD SCARES OFF MAN WHO SUED FOR HOME.
There are cases of arson and firebombing, of garbage tossed on
the porch, of racial epithets scrawled over the house, of windows
shot out, of water pumped into the basement, of ketchup poured
on the front steps to look like blood, of black homes needing
twenty-four-hour police protection. These incidents sometimes
backfire because they clearly violate America's antiracist norm.
But they also work. While some black families stick it out, others
leave, and many more will hesitate before moving in.

Perhaps more troubling still is when the harassment comes
from the people charged with upholding the law, the police. Rare
is the black man living in or passing through a predominantly
white neighborhood who has never been given the once-over by
police. In Dearborn, Michigan, a city only five percent black and
not known for its racial welcome mat, black motorists received
more than 27 percent of the traffic summonses issued in 1996. A
police check can involve being pulled over and questioned, being
followed until you've left the community, or having the police car

slow down and drive close by as you walk on the sidewalk. Black men have even been questioned in their own yards and driveways or just a block from their homes. Some cases have ended in tragedy, which is why black parents often warn their sons to act respectfully in these situations and not to make sudden moves. But usually it all passes without further incident, with the police often justifying their action by saying they were looking for someone who fit that general description.

To the black men involved, however, it sears the memory and creates a general feeling of unease about their welcome in such a community. It has happened to musician Wynton Marsalis, actor Blair Underwood, prosecutor Christopher Darden, and journalist William Raspberry. In one widely reported case, the tall and clean-shaven son of a well-known black businessman was detained even though the alleged suspect was of average height with a mustache. After one such incident, a young journalist wrote, "To almost all cops and most of society, I am a criminal who happens not to have committed his first crime." A Long Island lawyer said that despite his degrees from Columbia and Harvard, "I end up just another black guy, outside his car with his hands up." When Harvard professor Henry Louis Gates, Jr., moved to Lexington, Massachusetts, he actually went to the local police station to introduce himself and say he would be driving and walking in town and would not appreciate being pulled over. To the black citizens of our country, the message comes through loud and clear: stay out of this neighborhood and go back to where you belong.[15]

What's so poignant about the entire phenomenon of residential separation is that the vast majority of Americans, black and white, would probably make good neighbors if they only gave it a chance. Sustained personal interaction is always the best inoculation against distrust and fear. But try as we might, the result almost always ends up the same. Even in some of those rare communities known for aggressively maintaining a degree of integration—such as Shaker Heights near Cleveland, Oak Park near Chicago, Freeport on Long Island, and Mount Airy near Philadelphia—the centrifugal forces seem to play themselves out to one degree or another. Blacks and whites might gravitate toward different ends of town, for example, or the overall white population might begin to dwindle, especially as some white residents see that integration means more than tokenism. "Don't we have a black-a-block program?" a white resident asked the Oak Park community relations director. Research on these communities indicates less social integration than the overall residency figures suggest, with blacks and whites patronizing different stores and interaction generally limited to casual contact. Children who spend time together when young tend to drift apart with adolescence and dating. In most cases, whites eventually flee the public schools, which then turn disproportionately or predominantly black, at which point the interracial glue holding these communities together begins to decompose.[16]

One community that has decided to make integration a priority is Matteson, Illinois, a well-appointed town of 12,800 that has spent about $100,000 on advertising to stabilize its population mix and lure white home buyers. A typical ad features a white schoolteacher with a racially diverse group of students, an old-fashioned porch, and an American flag—a Norman Rockwell scene in black and white. It may be a futile effort. Matteson's white population has declined precipitously since 1980, dropping by almost half, while its black population rose from 12 percent in 1980 to 44 percent in 1990 to an estimated 55 percent in 1997. A town that was almost exclusively white a generation ago is projected to be 60 percent black and 37 percent white in 2002. Certainly whites cannot be leaving because the neighborhood is in decline. Matteson is an attractive community of middle- and upper-middle-class homes, and during the same 1980s that saw about a third of its whites flee, the town's median income rose by 73 percent. Crime has not increased, schools have maintained the same standards, and home prices have continued to rise; the only change is the skin color of its residents. But as a withering 1997 NBC television documentary on Matteson showed, whites are somehow convinced that crime is up and the schools are getting worse, and they are moving out to predominantly white neighborhoods with the rationale that they only want a good place to raise kids. Despite Matteson's efforts to attract whites, few are moving in. One scholar who researched the fate of these mixed communities has been forced to conclude that efforts like

Matteson's may simply not work: "In sum, it is not clear whether integrated neighborhoods can be maintained."[17]

Perhaps the most destructive aspect of integration's failure is the message it sends to our children, a message that encodes the behavior for future generations. "We just want to keep this neighborhood. . . . We don't want this to become black," a ten-year-old white boy told the *Cleveland Plain Dealer*. "They can have everywhere else, we don't care. Just leave us this neighborhood. Is that too much to ask?" The newspaper then interviewed a twelve-year-old black child, who described how white youngsters in the adjoining neighborhood "yell things at us and tell us to go back home." The child said, "We know we can't go over there. They don't want us. . . . Why do they do that to us?"[18]

Separate Schools

It may be the most honest public high school in America. Just off Interstate 55 in the northwest corner of Mississippi is Hernando High School. Actually, it is two high schools in one building. There are black and white principals, black and white class presidents, black and white yearbook honors, and a black and white Mr. and Miss Hernando High. The students share the school's facilities and resources, but behave as separate student bodies. Like many Mississippi schools, Hernando lost most of its white students soon after the school was desegregated. But unlike other schools, Hernando gained many of them back after the district created the dual school structure, and it is now 70 percent white. In many ways Hernando offends our integrationist sensibilities, deeply so. It has recently made news because one student decided to challenge the status quo. But strip away the dual administrative layers and Hernando resembles countless other desegregated high schools throughout the country. Their administrators may not be as candid as Hernando's, and the racial division may not be quite as bald-faced, but the reality is pervasive nonetheless: two student worlds in one building, intersecting but not integrating.

On a typical day in America black and white parents pack lunches for their kids, send them off to school, and hope with all their hearts that their children receive a quality education. But the similarity largely ends there. Just as our neighborhoods are separated by race, so too are our schools. Millions of black children attend schools with few or no whites. Millions more white children attend schools with few or no blacks. Whites rarely constitute more than 15 percent of the students in our nation's largest urban school districts, and most of the time they attend predominantly white schools in their own corner of the city. In the South, nearly two-thirds of blacks attend majority-black schools, a proportion that has remained about the same for twenty-five years. Kansas City has spent nearly $2 billion in a court-ordered effort to rebuild and integrate the public schools. There are magnet schools now with broadcast studios, state-of-the-art computers, Olympic-sized swimming pools, and even a planetarium—but few whites. In Prince George's County, Maryland, where 62 percent of the residents are black, but about 80 percent of the schoolchildren are, integration has meant busing black students from 95 percent–black schools to schools only 70 percent black, ostensibly to achieve a better racial balance. The county also holds a number of seats empty in its well-regarded magnet schools in the vain hope that white youngsters will take the spots reserved for them, even if it means keeping hundreds of frustrated black students on waiting lists. One cash-poor district in South Carolina spent one million dollars to expand an all-white elementary school rather than send white students to a predominantly black school that was one-third empty and only 800 yards away. It is a litany that can go on and on.[19]

The situation isn't much better in racially mixed schools, though the separation is less obvious, more subtle. Students attending the same school are sometimes as divided as students attending separate schools. We like to think of racially balanced schools as integrated, but they are not. Race simply becomes the central organizing principle at these schools, often determining the social and educational lives of the students. Youngsters of both races may pass each other and even talk a bit in the hall, but their contact in the lunchroom, the classroom, and the schoolyard is frequently defined by race. These schools differ from Hernando only in that they do not have the dual administrative structure that makes the separation blatant. After almost three decades of busing, magnet schools, court orders, reassignment plans, and even state troopers guarding schoolhouse doors, America's public schools are barely more integrated than they were a generation ago. And while the rare success story deserves applause, the trend toward separation, according to Harvard's Project on School Desegregation, is in fact getting worse.[20]

When the civil rights movement broke the back of segregation, most people assumed that putting black and white students together at school would help us solve the nation's racial divide. It hasn't happened that way. The good news is that through grade school, younger kids tend to get along well in mixed settings. They are indeed color-blind. But it begins to break down soon after that. For students who attend racially mixed schools, the social separation of the races usually begins in middle school and all but ossifies by high school, when students become acutely aware of what it means to—as they put it—act one's color. Black kids who spend time with whites are accused of "acting white" or "bleaching out." White kids who hang out with blacks are derided as "wiggers" and "wannabes." Most evident is the invisible seating chart that divides cafeterias by race. "At lunch we're around the people that we want to be with," said a black high school girl during a focus group discussion of black teenage girls in Montgomery County, Maryland, and all the other girls in the group nodded in agreement.

But the separation is not just a lunchtime phenomenon. It filters to almost every aspect of school life. In some schools there are bathrooms blacks use and bathrooms whites use. In other schools the two groups use and congregate around different school entrances. Black kids wear Morehouse and Spelman sweatshirts, whites wear shirts from Harvard and Yale. Given the choice, blacks and whites often choose separate buses when going on field trips, separate sections of the stands when watching the basketball team, and even separate parts of the classroom in which to sit. School clubs and extracurricular activities, ranging from the drama club to the yearbook staff to the environmental club, rarely are mixed beyond the token member of the other race. As we will discuss in more detail later in this chapter, even high school sports teams, widely seen as the great racial leveler, have begun to divide by race, with blacks involved more in basketball, football, and sprinting while whites tend to play tennis, soccer, baseball and field hockey, and run cross-country.

Even when schools attempt to address racially relevant issues or celebrate Black History Month, the racial division festers under the programmatic veneer. While black students often express a proprietary attitude toward these events, white students quietly express their alienation. A Kansas City school that decided to have a "racial harmony day" on Martin Luther King's birthday was met with open resistance from black students who wanted the day devoted solely to King. A black history lecture in a Pittsburgh area school attracted enthusiastic black students but not a single white. Seating at Black History Month school assemblies is often divided by race, as is the level of interest. When given the chance to speak confidentially, as in a focus group, white students will complain about a Black History Month curriculum that includes books like Richard Wright's *Black Boy* or the film *Raisin in the Sun*, or express resentment at blacks who act "righteous" and "snobby" during the month. "They expect us to kiss their feet," said one white student in a focus group. Black students in these confidential settings say they are tired of educating white peers about black culture and often express anger that some whites provocatively call for a white history month.[21]

Most students from racially mixed schools make no integration pretense after school because they don't really have to—they rarely see each other. If black and white kids get together, it's often when schoolwork is involved, little more. Groups that are not all white or all black usually have only one white or one black, seldom more. Interracial dating is rare, especially between black girls and white boys, and some of the most socially isolated children in America are black girls attending predominantly white high schools. For the sake of appearing racially tolerant, kids might say there's enough interracial dating, but probe further—as in a focus group—and the charade begins to fall away.

Music is another dividing line, with blacks tending toward rap or hip-hop and whites toward rock. Even when music crosses over and white kids listen to urban sounds, which is not uncommon, the closest most get to blacks is by watching *MTV Jams* in the comfort of their suburban homes, and when dancing is involved, the parties still tend to be all black or all white. The months of

April, May, and June rarely pass without a news story on a student body that's holding two proms, one for blacks and one for whites. Although there are plenty of instances of true interracial friendship among young blacks and whites, these are still atypical. Most of the time the two worlds simply coexist in relative peace, while any tensions are kept under the surface. But not always. In one small Indiana town, a small breach of the dividing line was so threatening that the largely white high school nearly erupted when a group of white girls began dressing in urban hip-hop style. Act your color, they were told. One reporter who visited the town found a sweet irony when the same angry white students who threatened the girls were busy dancing with their classmates to the rhythm of gangsta rapper Dr. Dre.[22]

What concerns educators is not necessarily the social divide but the pull it is having on the academic performance of blacks. So intense is the sense of alienation and separation felt among many young blacks that anyone perceived as "acting white" is frequently stigmatized, belittled, and ostracized—and "acting white" often includes academic success. Black students tell of camouflaging their schoolwork, of rarely talking with peers about their studies, and of never sharing their grades with friends. Some blacks even report avoiding honors courses for fear of the resulting social isolation. And while it is true that young people of all races exert peer pressure against academic achievement— no one wants to be called teacher's pet, brown nose, or nerd—in the case of blacks the stigma has become racialized. For many blacks a refusal to "act white"—expressed as an anti-achievement ethic—has become a point of racial pride.

Perhaps even more alarming is that self-destructive attitudes may be partially spawned by the unintentional if not insidious practice of tracking black students into classes that isolate them from whites and create a culture of low expectations. Various studies suggest that tracking begins as early as kindergarten and first grade, when five- or six-year-olds are labeled gifted, average, or below average—and intensifies in middle school and beyond. "It was horrendous to automatically relegate a kindergarten kid to one of those low-level sections and to leave them there forever," said a white superintendent from rural southwest Georgia who has been threatened for his stance against racial tracking.

In racially mixed schools, honors and accelerated classes tend to be mostly white, and special-education, basic-skills, and vocational classes tend to be mostly black. For example, in one Cleveland suburb blacks make up only 10 percent of the advanced-placement classes, even though the school district overall is 50 percent black. Some school districts have found that even regular classes tend to be racially imbalanced, as if the students were assigned by race even though no such policy was in place. A College Board study found that black students are steered away from college preparatory courses—geometry, algebra and laboratory sciences—and into the less demanding "general" track, in which math consists of consumer arithmetic and foreign languages and science are rarely taught. According to the College Board's president, black eighth-graders with testing levels and grades similar to whites "were being shunted into remedial courses in high school." One federal magistrate found the racial tracking in Rockford, Illinois, so disturbing that he said it raised "discrimination to an art form." It is not unusual to hear a story like the one told by Harvard Law School professor Christopher Edley, Jr., who was so astonished by an elementary school's classification of his son that he spent $2,000 on tests that proved the school woefully wrong and then put his son in a private school in midyear.[23]

While some observers suggest that white students are tracked into predominantly white honors classes as a way to stem further white flight from racially mixed public schools, the practice of racial tracking is so widespread and apparent that we must assume no more than an ingrained and unconscious bias is at work. How else could a well-regarded teacher choose a white student over a black student for the gifted class when the two had identical test scores, grades, and attitudes? How else could some schools routinely hand white parents information packets on gifted classes and black parents information on regular classes? It has gotten to the point that white kids express surprise when they find out their black peers get good grades. In the end, whether tracking creates or merely reinforces separation, the result is the same: even blacks and whites who attend the same schools very rarely integrate in the classroom. This fact alone may help to explain why some black leaders are now rethinking the traditional focus on integration and are instead calling for a greater emphasis on school quality, regardless of the racial mix.[24]

The situation does not improve when the kids go off to college. It actually intensifies. We used to think that the great integration experiment would flourish in a college environment of reason, inquiry, and camaraderie. But inside the ivy halls things are no different from the outside. To begin with, there are still many schools that remain virtually all black or all white. In the South, three in five black freshmen attend historically black institutions while flagship state universities remain overwhelmingly and disproportionately white. There is not even an illusion of integration on these campuses.[25] Elsewhere, the vast majority of black college students attend majority-white institutions. A look at most of these schools will reveal an earnest effort to bridge the racial divide. There are multicultural centers, civility weeks, diversity programs, Black History Month celebrations, and race relations training sessions for dorm counselors. Yet the divide persists at almost every level of these institutions.

Despite all the diversity and brotherhood programs, they didn't prevent an administrator at the State University of New York at Oneonta from providing police with a list of black male students after a seventy-seven-year-old woman said she had been attacked by a black man with a knife in her home near the campus. Nor do they make it any more palatable for black scholars who are stopped and questioned by campus security guards, or for black students who, more often than educators like to admit, hear racially inappropriate remarks from faculty. Racial harmony programs also seem irrelevant when black students protest a white professor who wants to teach a black studies course, or even boycott a black professor who is not deemed "ideologically black." Schools that try to push for more integrated residence halls are sometimes met with protests by black students who say their very survival at the university depends on having a place to live—a support system—where they feel comfortable among peers. At Cornell, students rallied against one such housing plan, vowing to fight against what a black student leader described as "racial attitudes and white supremacy" at the university.[26]

To be fair to the colleges and universities, the separation begins long before the students set foot on campus, so even the most well-intentioned program is bound to run up against the divided reality. Coming from separate neighborhoods and schools, most college students have little personal exposure to people of other races, particularly as peers. Students who truly believe they are not prejudiced and seek out friends from the other race often find that the racial separation of college life will pull them apart. Press attention focuses on incidents like a fraternity's mock slave auction or a sorority's black-face show or the scrawling of racist graffiti on a building or a fraternity's requiring pledges to get pictures of themselves kissing a black woman from another college. But more common is the quiet separation that takes place, the dual college experience of blacks and whites. As one Northwestern University graduate told *Newsweek*, "I don't remember any overt racial hostilities. You need a certain amount of *contact* to have hostilities."[27]

The campus separation is evident the day the freshmen move in. Residence-hall directors tell countless war stories of white parents and students who ask to change rooms immediately upon seeing a black roommate. Such incidents symbolize the overall residential patterns on many campuses, as white students choose to live with white housemates and black students tend to concentrate in a specific dorm or side of campus or choose to live in a black theme house. Racial separation is also reflected in a school's dining hall, where Dr. King's "table of brotherhood" is a rare phenomenon. One university administrator decided to track how many times black and white students sat down together at the dining center. Not until the eleventh day did an interracial pair finally eat together. Look almost anywhere else on campus— fraternities, sororities, parties, dances, social gatherings, student clubs—and the same separation pattern is evident day after day. Indeed some of the strongest and longest-lasting bonds among blacks are created in black fraternities and sororities. Even when black and white students should be together, blacks stand with blacks and whites stand with whites, as happened in a unity rally to improve race relations at the University of Iowa. In some cases black students hold separate graduation processions and ceremonies. One Georgetown University student wrote in *Essence*, "There was dialogue and talk of inclusiveness, but for all intents and purposes, socially, Blacks and Whites didn't really mix."[28]

Let us not underestimate the pulls and tensions many under-graduates feel. Remember, many of these students are still teen-agers, on their own for the first time, caught up like any other young person in the search for an identity and image. For black students, it is no easy assignment to be thrust into a majority-white and not always friendly environment where they are expected by some to integrate and by others to separate, particu-larly when they perhaps have a part-time job on top of their stud-ies. It is no surprise that many assume a posture of protest and independence from whites that is often manifested when middle-class black kids adopt street styles and black student groups invite speakers whom whites will find threatening, such as Louis Far-rakhan. It shouldn't be surprising if black students, who are often asked to represent their race in campus meetings and in class-room discussions, will seek a retreat from being black by sur-rounding themselves with blacks.

To white students accustomed to predominantly white settings, even to the most well-meaning black assertiveness on campus can be jarring. Since whites are the majority, they usually don't think of life in racial terms. So when confronted with black stu-dents whose status as minorities forces them to think that way, whites react defensively and ask why blacks have an "attitude," why they have to keep raising the racial issue. The result is a spi-raling separation that, contrary to the hopes and dreams of par-ents and college administrators, seems not to improve but to worsen as the years pass. And while there are plenty of black-white friendships on campuses, the social pressures to separate are so strong that some students describe these friendships as contraband, something that needs to be hidden from their race peers. It is no wonder that black interest in historically black in-stitutions has been on the rise. "I have to deal with racism the rest of my life," one student told the *New York Times*. "Why should I deal with that in college?" When *Black Enterprise* magazine asked readers in 1995 if they preferred a predominantly black college for their children, 60 percent said yes.[29]

To describe the lack of integration at every level of American education is not to enter any public policy debate about the extent to which we desegregate our public schools. While some all-black schools have certainly shown outstanding results, there is also plenty of evidence to support the notion that black students in desegregated high schools perform better, primarily because they have access to more academic resources and broader career networks than blacks in racially isolated schools. But wherever public policy leads, let us have no illusions that desegregating a school will lead to an integrated school environment. Whether in the public schools or the hallowed halls of higher education, blacks and whites either attend separate institutions or attend the same institutions separately.

Separate at Work

Race influences America's workday even before anyone opens up the plant or the office in the morning. It begins the moment we walk out the front door, when we glance around and see people who look like us also heading to work. In large metropolitan areas, mass transit use tends to be overwhelmingly minority, and when it isn't, whites and blacks either get on at different stops or take bus and subway routes that originate and pass through racially separate neighborhoods. Most Americans travel to work by car, so it might be safe to assume we all share the identically stressful commuting experience. After all, we may come from different parts of town, but we still merge onto the same highway and put up with the same bad drivers and standstill traffic. Yet even then there are differences. The commuting story is a common one among blacks, who describe how their drive is fueled by the sounds of jazz, gospel, or urban contemporary music until just a few blocks from work, when they turn down the volume and prepare themselves mentally to face yet another day as the very visible minority in the office. Much like putting all the family photos in the box when selling their home, blacks feel they must hide a part of themselves simply to get by in the predominantly white work world.

We like to think of the workplace as the most integrated part of America. Although there are plenty of businesses that employ few if any blacks—and thus there are millions of white Americans who never work with a black person—the workplace is still where blacks and whites are most exposed to each other and, in varying degrees, make daily contact with each other. Because blacks and whites who work together must depend on each other to make a product or finalize a sale, rarely is overt racial tension tolerated. Interaction uncommon outside work happens regularly here. But just as with mixed neighborhoods and schools, there is much less integration at work than meets the eye, for it is in the workplace that we most confuse racial intersection with racial integration. Nowhere is the integration illusion more at work than at work.

It would be difficult to dispute the statement that the American workplace is a white world, if for no other reason than whites are in the majority and hold most of the executive and decision-making positions in the country. To many whites, race is an intrusion into the workplace, an annoying distraction on the job. Racial issues can involve piles of bothersome paperwork, thankless amounts of politicking, unwarranted risk taking, and emotions ranging from resentment to guilt that few people want to deal with when they're at work. Having blacks around also means you have to watch what you say lest it be taken the wrong way. It would be so much easier to hire that friend of a neighborhood friend who's working in another department or company—you're certain he or she would do a good job—but sometimes you just have to go with the black applicant even if you have hidden doubts about his or her competence.

White supervisors tend to address these concerns by treating black employees as problems to be managed instead of members of the team. If "the problem" is managed reasonably well—if, say, a diversity program is put in place or the black employee exceeds expectations and is given a promotion—then whites perceive it as a job well done and deserving of praise. No one can say that most companies aren't making at least some effort to address racial issues. Some studies report that almost three out of four major corporations have instituted some type of diversity program. Almost all large companies have an affirmative action officer and an outreach program in place. Little wonder that surveys show that as many as nine in ten whites, both employees and managers, routinely rate race relations excellent or good in their workplace or business.[30]

One common way to manage "the problem" is to promote a black employee to a high-visibility position in the organization. The message sent is clear and unequivocal: we believe in diversity and we're not prejudiced here. But various studies, including one by the Federal Glass Ceiling Commission whose members were appointed by President Bush, show that the few minorities in senior management positions tend to be concentrated in such soft and low-budget positions as human resources, minority affairs, community relations, and administration—rarely in the core decision-making and profit-generating areas of production, sales, and marketing. A very visible example is the National Basketball Association (NBA), where blacks make up about half of the community relations directors but less than 10 percent of the vice presidents, and not one chief financial officer is black. A black female executive at Grand Metropolitan PLC told *Black Enterprise* magazine, "It took my breath away to go into a meeting of the most senior level executives in my corporation and realize that I was the only black person at this level."[31]

Putting black executives in high-profile but not very significant positions serves a number of corporate needs. One is for public consumption to portray a corporate image of diversity and tolerance, very important in a society that wants to see itself as integrated. It's the same reason why companies display black faces prominently in their publications, out of all proportion to the number of black employees working there. The highly publicized Texaco discrimination lawsuit revealed a case in point: of the 2,029 senior managers employed at Texaco in 1994, a mere 23 were black, but that didn't stop the company from distributing a brochure on Texaco's "vision and values" that featured three blacks among the nine employees pictured on the cover. Another reason to have prominent if not consequential black employees is to help the company compete for business, particularly when affirmative action laws or other diversity imperatives apply. One mid-sized public relations firm whose only black employee was a secretary gave her a temporary new title and named her as a possible account executive in a proposal to a potential black client. Wall Street firms are notorious for hiring few black investment bankers, but when they do it's often because they want to win some underwriting business from diversity-minded state and city governments; rarely are blacks hired for the more powerful and lucrative positions in corporate finance and arbitrage, areas in which all the clients tend to be white. As *Business Week* noted in 1991, "Many companies hire just enough minority workers to satisfy the government and protect themselves against discrimination suits." Blacks clearly understand these employment conditions and wonder if they will ever be considered part of the team, which might explain why blacks working in predominantly white companies leave jobs more frequently than their white coworkers, and why so many blacks are opting out of these companies altogether to start their own business.[32]

Of course, not all white employers are so cynical, and most of those that are will either deny or evade this description of their hiring motives. But that is why lawsuits can be so helpful in stripping away the integration fiction and taking us behind the closed doors of corporate America. In the recent Texaco case and one involving the electronics retailer Circuit City, white supervisors were reported to have called their prominent black employees "porch monkeys," which in more polite company means window dressing. And Texaco is just the "tip of the iceberg" among corporations, said Texaco's CEO.[33]

So unaccustomed are white Americans to seeing blacks as equals or superiors at work that black executives and professionals have almost come to expect being mistaken for file clerks, paralegals, and administrative aides. In his book *The Rage of a Privileged Class*, journalist Ellis Cose vividly describes an incident almost any black can relate to, in which a black senior partner at a law firm was treated disdainfully by a patronizing young white associate before the office officially opened one morning. Presuming the black man to be someone who didn't belong there, the associate first asked officiously if he could help, and then demanded in a "loud and decidedly colder tone, 'May I help you?' "[34] Black supervisors who visit work sites with white assistants never cease to be stupefied that the client or customer initially directs most of the questions to the white assistants, assuming them to be in charge until advised otherwise. Hollywood had fun with these assumptions in the film *The Associate*, which features actress Whoopi Goldberg as an investment banker who invented a white associate so that people would take her firm seriously. He—actually she—goes on to build a financial powerhouse.

As grating as it may be for the black professional, white surprise at seeing a black equal or supervisor at work certainly has a strong foundation in reality. It is not uncommon for most blacks in an organization or business to work around the edges of an office in subordinate roles—in the mailroom, as a clerk, in human resources, in the steno pool, or as a uniformed delivery person. One black lawyer who engaged in heated negotiations with another black lawyer as their white staffs looked on described the occasion as so uncommon that "I got this chill up my spine." A *Business Week* reporter wrote in 1994 that white resentment at affirmative action is somewhat overblown given that "the impact of diversity programs, even in the companies that have them, is still limited." The statistics bear this out. About 90 percent of the supervisors and managers in one study had not a single black colleague of equal job status and responsibility at work. Applying this criterion to all workers, the same study found that nearly 60 percent worked in jobs that were completely segregated by race, and another 30 percent were almost completely segregated.[35]

Some occupations are virtually all white. Advertising, the industry that controls our public and commercial images, is less than two percent black, and the percentage dips even further when you exclude employees at black-oriented firms and only count blacks at the mainstream agencies. As of 1990, according to the *National Law Journal*, the 250 largest law firms had 23,195 partners, only 210 of them black. Sales representatives, engineers, physicians, college professors—all high-profile fields, all with a minuscule number of blacks. Since most black adults work, their underrepresentation in some fields means overrepresentation in others. Disproportionately black fields include nursing aides, licensed practical nurses, social workers, data-entry clerks, janitors, and baggage porters. Blacks and whites might work in the same hospital, hotel, office building, law firm or airport, and they might say hello to each other every day, but rarely do they work together as equals. They simply inhabit two separate workplace worlds.[36]

It would be easy to attribute our separation at work to the

myopia and prejudice of conservative white men who hire only in their own image, but the problem is more endemic than that. In a welcome bit of self-critical journalism, a columnist for the left-of-center *Nation* admitted in 1995 that only one nonwhite had served on the magazine's editorial staff in the thirteen years she'd been there, despite a complete turnover during that time. And *The Nation* is not alone among major liberal publications, most of which have all-white editorial staffs or just a token number of blacks. According to *Village Voice* writer James Ledbetter, hip *Rolling Stone* had no black writers or editors as of 1995, and in the 700 issues of the magazine since 1967, only one cover story was penned by a black writer. Mainstream women's magazines, consumer and financial publications, and other entertainment magazines are not much different.[37]

Indeed, the so-called liberal media establishment resembles Texaco much more than its leaders would like to admit. Despite all the high-profile anchors and reporters on television news and all the black celebrities who flash across the screen, few blacks hold positions of responsibility in the media. In all of Hollywood, only about fifty black writers regularly get work, and less than three percent of the members in the West Coast writers and directors guilds are black. Not a single black writer ever worked on *The Jeffersons*, the highly rated black sitcom of the 1970s and 1980s. Although the proportion of black writers is somewhat better on black-oriented sitcoms today, rarely does a black writer work on a *Seinfeld* or *Friends*, shows that have a predominantly white audience. As for blacks in decision-making roles in the major studios, *People* magazine put it this way: "About the only black faces getting near Hollywood's executive suites are studio security." On the East Coast, where publishing reigns, the story line is much the same. Rare is the black acquisitions editor at a major publishing house, the person who finds the authors and bids on the books. The *Village Voice*'s Ledbetter writes that he has attended at least two hundred publishing parties—a staple of the publishing network—but rarely sees blacks: "I can say with confidence that there have been fewer than ten occasions on which there were more than five black people in the room. On many, many occasions, there were precisely two black people in the room—often the same two."[38]

The news business is no different. As of 1996, there were only four black general managers in America's TV newsrooms. In New York, the most diverse city in the world, only three blacks have served as news directors since the inception of television nearly half a century ago. Almost half of America's daily newspapers have no blacks in their newsrooms, and the number of black reporters at mainstream dailies hovers under five percent, not much different from two decades ago. In only a few papers, among them *USA Today* and the *Washington Post*, are there enough black reporters and editors to make the newsroom appear mixed, but even then there is evidence of strained relations and isolation among blacks. Some black reporters have even been asked by white editors if they can be objective covering the black community, a question never asked of whites covering predominantly white neighborhoods. "You need to be a reporter first and a black person second," is what some editors have been known to say, oblivious to the irony of giving this advice only to blacks. *Los Angeles Times* reporter Sam Fulwood III says there is a double standard for black reporters: "My source building is not as easy and as comfortable as theirs. . . . I know that people that I can be easy and comfortable with, when I bring them back into the newsroom in my stories or as sources, there's a resistance to take them seriously because they may be black." One area we would reasonably expect to be integrated is sports journalism, but again the same pattern plays out. As of 1996, there were only ten black sports columnists in newspapers with a circulation of at least 175,000 people, and only eight black sports editors in all of our nation's dailies. At *Sports Illustrated*, of thirty-one senior writers in 1996, only one was black.[39]

In a truly color-blind society, employers choosing among equally qualified job candidates might still prefer the worker whose background and mannerisms most resemble theirs, but skin color should not make a difference. Thankfully, gone are the days when blacks were told out front not even to apply for jobs. But the sad truth is that hiring by skin color remains alive and well in America today. It's just more subtle, more hidden now. When equally qualified blacks and whites seek employment through job-referral agencies and the whites are usually chosen for interviews, there is no way for the black candidate to know who got the job and why. ABC's *Prime Time Live* secretly taped an employment service to see how it handled identically credentialed black and white twenty-eight-year-olds; absent this test, how would anyone know that the agency lectured only blacks about laziness? Certainly there would be no reason for a white job applicant to wonder why there was no such lecture. Study after study confirms what blacks have known all along: that their race often works against them even when employers are presented with otherwise similar job applicants. It happens in every sector of the economy, from manufacturing to banking to insurance and beyond. Sometimes it is plain old prejudice at work, as plenty of whites continue to believe that blacks are either lazy or not as competent and intelligent as whites. There are still too many employees like the former human resources director at Circuit City, who said that the company's black retail sales associates were not "the kind of people" he would hire for jobs at corporate headquarters. But there are also plenty of employers who don't have such raw thoughts or would never act on them. They just say they want a person on the job who will fit in most comfortably. That person is almost always someone like them, and that means white. Since it's difficult to know where comfort ends and prejudice begins, it may simply be irrelevant whether an employer is bigoted or just looking for a good fit. The result is the same.[40]

Perhaps nowhere is the racial divide more disappointing than in the ranks of police officers and firefighters, whom so many children dream of emulating when they grow up. One would think that racial boundaries would dissolve in jobs requiring such a high degree of trust and intimacy. That is certainly the popular image, nourished by Hollywood dramas that depict interracial collegiality among the people in blue, who rarely talk about race. But the real world is very different. When a deputy police chief in Dallas wanted to break up the longstanding pattern of all-white and all-black partnerships by forming what he called salt-and-pepper teams, eight officers filed grievances and effectively blocked the idea. "This is creating a racial problem where before there was none," said one white officer without intending any irony. A New York State judicial commission found New York City's lower courts to be so filled with racial tension that black and white court officers informally segregated themselves into different locker rooms. One white Chicago police supervisor told author Studs Terkel that he was so offended by incidents of antiblack bigotry in the station house that he reprimanded three roll calls about it, only to be labeled a "nigger lover" and become the subject of a union grievance filed by some of the white officers.[41]

In many cases the problem for blacks is getting hired in the first place. Police and fire jobs tend to be very clubby and people are often recruited through friendships and word of mouth, which means the forces rarely will be integrated. On suburban Long Island, home to nearly 200,000 blacks, the police force in 1990 had only 130 blacks out of 5,545 officers. The *Pittsburgh Post-Gazette* reported in 1996 that most of the 283 police agencies in the six-county Pittsburgh area have no black officers. One community 23 percent black has no black officers, while another community, 53 percent black, has only four blacks among forty-two officers. Until a successful employment discrimination suit was filed against Palm Beach Gardens, Florida, the police department routinely threw applications from blacks in the garbage and refused to advertise job openings in order to limit the number of blacks applying. It's no different at our fire stations, where blacks represent less than two percent of all firefighters nationwide, and less than one percent of all volunteer firefighters. According to the newspaper *Newsday*, Long Island's fire departments are so racially divided and impervious to change that most majority-black communities have virtually no black firefighters, while one racially mixed community has an all-black fire department that has been unable to recruit whites onto the force. "Even within integrated fire departments," writes *Newsday*, "minority firefighters often are concentrated in some companies, while others remain all white." Los Angeles has an unwritten policy of prohibiting more than one black firefighter per four-person engine company as a way to prevent self-segregation and deter white flight.[42]

The phenomenon of hiring people who look like you is not restricted to whites. Research indicates that blacks will tend to choose blacks from among equally qualified candidates.[43] If you walk through the halls of Congress, you will see that the predominantly white offices of white legislators are matched by the predominantly black offices of black legislators. But the problem is that whites make most of the job decisions and constitute the vast majority of employees in America, and thus it is blacks who must navigate, often alone, in the predominantly white and far-from-color-blind work world. For black employees, that means carrying an extra burden every day in which they see no alternative but to be wary of the seeming goodwill of their white coworkers. What whites see as a chip on the shoulder, blacks see as an appropriate defense.

It's not just the blatant incidents that create this wariness—the comments about watermelon, or the fake job application circulating around the office that asks how many words a black candidate can "jive" per minute. More corrosive are the subtle assumptions so many whites hold, especially the presumption against a black colleague's competence and work habits. For blacks it happens too often to be written off merely as a coincidence. There are black attorneys in law firms who are replaced on an account or relegated to research responsibilities after white clients speak with the firm's managing partner. There are the hiring processes in which the special writing test seems to be waived only for whites. There are the meetings in which the black participant's ideas are greeted with silence or furrowed brows, which sends a message to the black worker and his or her white colleagues. There is the well-documented attitude among whites that black-owned subcontractors will not provide quality work. It may well be that a particular black attorney isn't doing a good job, or a black job applicant has no other way to demonstrate writing skills, or a black meeting participant is saying something off the point, or a black-owned business does indeed do poor work. But how is a black worker to know what is valid and what is prejudice? It is a terrible bind for both whites and blacks that further reinforces the distance between them.[44]

Compounding the problem for black workers is the feeling that they are suspended between two worlds. Their livelihood is tied to a white work world that claims to want them but does not always welcome them. This is a world in which you can do a good job but still not have access to the connections and networks available to whites that often determine real upward mobility. This is the world of social events after work—of business mingled with pleasure—in which there are often more blacks serving drinks than attending as guests. This is the world of deals made while people golf at country clubs that do not accept black members. "How can people Monday through Friday claim that they can fairly evaluate and promote minorities on a color-blind basis [but] on Saturday and Sunday run off to a club that actually discriminates?" asked black author Lawrence Otis Graham. But then there is the other world, the world of black identity that many blacks repress on the job for fear of further distancing themselves from their white colleagues and supervisors. And so blacks advise each other not to lunch together too frequently or congregate at the office too much—you don't want colleagues to think you're not a team player—and black executives are told to avoid Afrocentric themes in the office and instead to express themselves more subtly through color schemes or small sculptures.[45]

For black workers, these many pulls and tugs have a cumulative effect above and beyond the normal stress of making ends meet, leading to what one study called a higher tendency to feel "burned out" and a greater likelihood to change jobs.[46] The same surveys in which whites report positive race relations at work find most blacks adamantly disagreeing. Ironically, it may be that the pressure to get along during work pushes people further apart after work. Who wants to carry racial stress beyond five o'clock? Many Americans may work in a racially mixed environment, but it is hard to escape the conclusion that America at work seems to be going through the motions of integration without ever achieving it.

CHAPTER THREE

A Day in the Life of Two Americas, Part 2: Praying, Playing, Entertaining Apart

Separated Socially

In western Ohio next to Interstate 75 sits the city of Lima, with a population of about 45,000, nearly one quarter of them black. Right after the 1992 Rodney King verdict, rumors of imminent unrest spread throughout town. Child-care centers closed their doors, the court building shortened its hours, and businesses drew up contingency plans to board up their windows. Mayor David Berger decided to hold a press conference to plead for calm, and invited a dozen prominent black and white clergy to stand at his side. But to the mayor's surprise, the black ministers and the white ministers did not know each other. So he had to spend fifteen minutes introducing them. "I was just really struck by the fact that I had to introduce the clergy to one another," Berger said. "And this is a small town."[1] To his credit, Berger has since worked closely with Lima's religious community to bridge some of the racial gap in town. But what he discovered that day in 1992 could be found in almost any community throughout the land, and it is yet another parable about America's racial divide. We are one of the most religious countries in the western world, yet in this nation of regular churchgoers, most blacks and most whites pray separately to the same God. Even as we transcend the temporal, we remain earthly bound by the color line that holds us apart.

It is said that the most segregated hour in America is on Sunday morning between eleven and noon. Nearly nine in ten black church members nationwide belong to black denominations, such as the African Methodist Episcopal church and the National Baptist Convention. Likewise, most whites never see a black face in the pews on Sunday. The Unitarian Universalist church, one of the most liberal Christian denominations today and the spiritual home of the great nineteenth-century abolitionists William Lloyd Garrison and Theodore Parker, is about 98 percent white. Other mainstream Protestant denominations—Lutherans, United Methodists, Presbyterians, Episcopalians, Southern Baptists—are also predominantly white, as is the Catholic church in America. The very devout Jimmy Carter faced considerable embarrassment when he became president in 1977 because his Southern Baptist congregation, the Plains Baptist Church, resisted the pressure to welcome black worshipers; Carter and others subsequently founded another church where blacks were welcome. Even when blacks affiliate with a predominantly white denomination, they tend to cluster in their own churches.[2]

Deeply uncomfortable with their divided pews, many churches and denominations have made an extra effort to reach out. Indeed, most religious leaders adhere to a gospel of inclusion, and the national offices of the mainstream white denominations have made a valiant effort to integrate their staffs. Black and white Pentecostal organizations merged into one office in 1994, and there has been talk of merger between the black and white Methodist groups. In communities across America, there are infrequent but heart-warming examples of all-white and all-black churches holding interracial services around Easter or the Martin Luther King holiday. "This is the way it should look every Sunday," said one minister during an interracial King holiday service.[3] But it doesn't. His 550-member congregation has only one black. As welcome as these sentiments and initiatives may be, they matter little where it really counts. With rare exceptions, our churches—the center of communal, spiritual and social life for so many Americans—reflect and reinforce America's divide between blacks and whites.

The Plaza Methodist Church in Charlotte, North Carolina, found this out the hard way. An all-white church for years, it started losing members as more and more blacks began to move to the neighborhood. Acknowledging the new demographics, church elders set out to attract new members and build an integrated congregation. In 1994 they appointed a new pastor who was committed to this vision. He happened to be black—a former college football star comfortable in a racially mixed environment. Sadly, some white church members refused to shake his hand when he first arrived. Nearly every white member soon left the church. Of course, not every racially diverse church immediately witnesses white flight, and a few are able to maintain mixed congregations. But even in these rare instances, the color line still intrudes. In Beaumont, Texas, black and white United Methodist congregations, each with declining memberships, decided to merge into one church, the first such merger in East Texas. Although the new church lost some members, many stayed on, but only because the church decided to hold two separate services on Sunday morning, one for blacks and one for whites. Certainly, it is possible to attribute the racial separation at church to different styles of worship, but that tells only part of the story, for it is also the social environment of a church or other house of worship that draws people to it. One racially mixed Philadelphia church, for example, discovered that its singles events drew only whites or blacks but rarely both together.[4]

For blacks who live in mostly white suburbs, the black church has become somewhat of a refuge, a place of comfort to combat feelings of social isolation, even if it means driving downtown or to another suburb to get to one. Nor is church the only all-black social environment that black suburbanites seek out. If there is no all-black Scout troop where they live, many will take their kids to one in the city. National organizations such as the Links, Deltas, Alphas, Twigs, Carousels, Boule, and Jack and Jill of America provide black adults with a social venue for themselves and their children.[5] This black suburban effort to maintain a black social context is a manifestation of the larger social separation between blacks and whites. In metropolitan areas that offer black-oriented plays, museums, and concerts, blacks will go in large numbers but whites will seldom attend. Where arts programming tends either to ignore black culture or cater mostly to whites, some blacks will participate but at numbers significantly lower than their percentage of the population. After work, blacks congregate at mostly black clubs, whites at mostly white clubs; people self-select on the basis of the music being played. Sometimes these clubs are on the same block, or across the street from each other, but they might as well be miles apart. Depending on the music, some clubs in Washington, D.C., are predominantly black one night, predominantly white the next. One all-white Virginia college-town club that wanted to stay that way stopped playing soul and rap music after blacks began crowding in; it produced the desired result.[6]

This social separation is often a matter of choice. As in every other part of society, whites are more comfortable among whites, and blacks are more comfortable among blacks. Whites who deal with racial issues during the workday want to be free of them afterward. Blacks who wear a mask at the workplace don't want to keep it on any longer than necessary. "The game is over," said a black female patron of a black club who was interviewed by the *Washington Post*. "You don't want to be stared at now."[7] And while there are examples of crossover, particularly in some areas of youth music and the performing arts, black and white cultures in their various forms have a powerful pull on their own constituencies.

But choice and culture are not always the determining factors. Plain old prejudice is also part of the mix. The highly publicized case of Denny's restaurant chain shows the managerial gymnastics some establishments will perform to stay all white. Denny's managers were instructed to ignore blacks waiting to be seated, to say that no tables were available, to seat the black group but not to serve them, or to require identification, a cover charge, or prepayment of the meal. In some cases black patrons were seated only in certain areas, and in one California region the managers were told to declare a "blackout" if too many blacks attempted to eat there. Denny's eventually settled the discrimination lawsuit filed against it. Then there was the case of the Holiday Spa fitness company. Government agencies often will hire black and white testers to ensure that an establishment doesn't discriminate, but for years Holiday Spa used testers to make sure that its fitness centers did discriminate. The company simply believed that its white patrons didn't want black people sweating next to them. Fitness companies in general are known to steer blacks to clubs in black neighborhoods, to tell them only about the most expensive memberships, or to say they accept only cash, no checks. There's also the case of the Buffalo mall that tried to minimize black patronage by refusing to allow buses from the black side of town onto mall property, a policy that was changed only after a black teenager was killed while crossing a seven-lane highway on the way to a fast-food job in the mall.[8]

The social separation filters down to the most basic levels of our lives. The chatter and gossip at hairdressers and barbershops is the stuff of everyday life in America, and once again these tend to be separated by race. At barber school, white students are taught on white or straight hair, black students on black or kinky hair. A suburban Washington woman sued the department store Bloomingdale's in 1996 for refusing her a wash and dry because of her "black hair." In Corning, New York, where there were only "white" barbershops, Corning Inc. even recruited a black barber as a way of making its black employees feel more at home.[9]

At the doctor's office the same separation is often found. Although there are not enough black doctors in America to make the separation as complete as in the barbershop, a study of California's black doctors found that a majority of their patients are black. Graduates of Howard and Meharry medical schools, which produce a quarter of all black doctors in America, are five times more likely to practice in predominantly black rural and inner-city areas than the typical white medical school graduate. White physicians who don't serve the white middle class are more likely to serve poor white areas rather than affluent black neighborhoods. Many black physicians report that it is still difficult to gain access to white hospitals. Reaction was so strong to a proposed merger between two Nashville hospitals, one of which served mostly black patients and the other mainly whites, that 85 percent of the white hospital's staff said they would quit rather than move, and it was widely assumed that most of the white patients would not go to the black hospital. The presumption of black incompetence appears to influence whites in medicine just as it does in the workplace. Heart surgeon Julius Garvey, son of the black nationalist leader Marcus Garvey, describes how white patients who come to his office turn around and walk out after finding out that he is the doctor. Or as journalist Nicholas Lemann wrote in an article on one of the black doctors whose admission to medical school brought about the famous *Bakke* Supreme Court case on affirmative action, "The idea that, as an obstetrician-gynecologist, he could build a practice on the west side of Los Angeles based on middle-class white women is a joke."[10]

One might think that vacationing is a color-blind pleasure we all share, but again race enters the equation. Although many black seaside resort communities declined in popularity after desegregation, others stayed strong, among them the black resorts of Oak Bluffs, on Martha's Vineyard, and Sag Harbor, on Long Island. The Michigan county that houses the black resort town of Idlewild has the third-highest percentage of blacks in the state and the highest population of blacks sixty-five and older in the Lower Peninsula. Black college students often vacation together; Daytona Beach's Black College Reunion, Atlanta's Freaknik, the Penn Relays in Philadelphia, the Black College Weekend near Richmond and the Essence Jazz Festival together attract an estimated 200,000 black students from colleges and universities around the country and have become annual rituals similar to Florida's spring break for white students. One summer holiday trend in the black community is to hold a black family reunion for an extended network of relatives who gather in one locale and tour the area together. Race also influences the world's greatest party, Mardi Gras in New Orleans, as the big floats, costumes and masks hide a divided reality of racially separated krewes (the term for the float organizations behind the big parade) and their exclusive functions and balls.[11]

For many blacks, the decision on where to vacation often comes down to whether a place will be "color comfortable," as the magazine *American Demographics* put it. Popular historian Richard Shenkman writes that "the crowds at most of our big, famous national shrines are overwhelmingly white"—largely because blacks rarely find their American experience in the history. "At Colonial Williamsburg (the shrine)," Shenkman noted in a 1996 article, "they didn't even admit until a few years ago that slavery existed." One reporter who did a story on Ocean City, Maryland, found that blacks "feel out of place there." The reporter walked a twenty-block stretch of beach in mid-July and counted only sixty-four black faces. "It was possible to walk for several minutes before seeing a single one," she wrote. Yet the Baltimore-Washington metropolitan region, which feeds Ocean City most of its summertime tourists, is about one-quarter black.[12]

One of the saddest ironies of our social separation is how we celebrate the one day dedicated to the dream of racial integration, the Martin Luther King holiday. Don't celebrate it only as a "black holiday," Coretta Scott King, Dr. King's widow, has repeatedly pleaded. But despite the occasional interracial service or gathering, Mrs. King's fear has largely been confirmed. According to a 1997 study by the Bureau of National Affairs, only seven percent of America's manufacturers and 16 percent of nonmanufacturing businesses other than banks observe the holiday with a paid day off. As for the rest, it's an optional holiday—"If you're black," observed an *Atlanta Constitution* editorial, "you can take the day off." One informal survey of Detroit-area school districts found that the larger the black student population, the more likely the schools will either close or hold a major program. The annual youth assembly organized by the Martin Luther King Federal Holiday Commission attracts young people from all over the country, but almost all of them are black. In general, King holiday community meetings and parades tend to have few white participants. For example, among the 15,000 spectators at Houston's 1996 Martin Luther King Holiday parade there was only a sprinkling of whites. Perhaps the best that can be said is that we honor the integration ideal separately.[13]

Separate Sports

"Of all the things we do in America," observed newsman Ted Koppel on his late-night news show, *Nightline*, "few are as thoroughly integrated as the games we play and watch." The sports arena, according to conventional wisdom, is the one true manifestation of the great American melting pot. Indeed, anecdotes and surveys both show how athletes at all levels have forged interracial friendships through sports. Two of America's most racially progressive white politicians, Republican Jack Kemp and Democrat Bill Bradley, are former professional athletes. "Day in and day out we [whites and blacks] lived together, ate together, rode buses together, talked together, laughed together, and, of course, played together," said Bradley in a 1991 speech on race relations. Gone are the days when baseball had no black players and basketball teams limited the number of blacks that could be on the court at the same time. For black Americans, athletics provides the one true opportunity in which merit cannot be diminished or trumped by prejudice.[14]

And so it is all the more dispiriting to see that the same forces of separation at work in the rest of society are subtly at work in sports as well. The demographics of sports are beginning to divide up according to race. Baseball is increasingly becoming nonblack. Basketball and football are already predominantly black. Ice hockey, field hockey, and tennis are virtually all white, soccer tends to be Hispanic and white, and boxing is almost entirely Hispanic and black. No black has ever been a member of the U.S. Olympic swimming team, and not a single black American participated in the 1996 U.S. Olympic diving trials. Track events involving speed are almost all black, while long-distance running is mostly white. Despite all the publicity over the Tiger Woods phenomenon in golf, barely three percent of all golfers in America are black. These trends are evident at every level of sports, from high school to the professional leagues. In 1996, the Kansas City Junior Blades ice hockey organization had one black youth among five hundred kids, not much different from the five blacks among nearly seven hundred professional ice hockey players in the National Hockey League.

The increasing separation is most evident—and most poignant—in our national pastime, baseball. One major league baseball scout predicted that blacks might soon disappear from the sport altogether. Subtract the hyperbole and it's clear he's on to something. In 1980, blacks made up nearly one quarter of all major league baseball players. By opening day of the 1997 season, that number had dropped to just over 15 percent; by comparison, the National Basketball Association is 80 percent black and the National Football League, 67 percent black. In 1996 two major league baseball teams, the Minnesota Twins and the Philadelphia

Phillies, spent significant parts of the season without a black on the team. Whereas blacks have received nearly two-thirds of all Division I men's college basketball scholarships and about half of the football scholarships throughout the 1990s, only about seven percent of the baseball scholarships have gone to blacks. The 1996 U.S. Olympic baseball team had only one black player. Fan interest among blacks also seems to be waning, as the enthusiasm that greeted baseball in the era of the old Negro League has since dissipated. Former commissioner Bowie Kuhn has been quoted as saying that stadiums have become "a white man's place to be," and attendance numbers seem to confirm it. The major leagues estimate that blacks purchase only about five percent of all game tickets, although individual team reports suggest an even lower number. The Chicago White Sox, despite aggressive marketing to the black community, estimate that blacks account for only two percent of ticket sales, and an independent audit commissioned by the St. Louis Cardinals found that blacks account for only 2.8 percent of the team's attendance. Nor does the future seem any brighter, as young blacks are showing little interest in the game and baseball is often treated as an orphan sport in many predominantly black high schools. Little League is mostly a white suburban or rural institution, and despite a recent effort by the major leagues to infuse some resources and enthusiasm into urban baseball, little long-term change is expected. As one *Washington Post* reporter found when interviewing a group of nineteen black youths at the site of Jackie Robinson's former ballpark, Ebbets Field, only one could name a major league player while all were fully fluent in the personalities and dynamics of professional basketball.[15]

To call baseball a "racist sport," as one black player did in 1992, may be a harsh or unwarranted judgment. What may be at work instead is the same racial self-selection process that leads blacks and whites to different clubs and social environments once the workday is over. Whether motivated by prejudice, a need for comfort, or a desire to be around one's racial peers, the end result is the same. Blacks are gravitating to some sports, whites to others. Most white parents who push their children into soccer, tennis, swimming, or hockey, and most black parents who boost

track or basketball, are not making these choices consciously because of race. Neither are the teenagers in racially mixed schools
who play on racially defined intramural teams or varsity sports.
They are merely accommodating their lives to a culture influenced and in many ways determined by race. One *USA Today*
writer found that few white Americans currently compete in the
800-meter race, compared to 1970, when the top ten 800-meter
runners were white. He also found that whites who are running
today have a slower time than the whites two decades ago. It
couldn't be that whites are slower today, he reasoned. It must
be that whites from junior high on up are taking their talent
elsewhere.[16]

The racial separation in sports becomes even more fascinating
when one looks at the way positions are divided within racially
mixed sports. What happens is a phenomenon called stacking,
which the leading expert in the sociology of sports, Richard
Lapchick of Northeastern University's Center for the Study of
Sport in Society, defines as "positional segregation." In 1996,
blacks made up more than 50 percent of all major league outfielders but only seven percent of the pitchers and one percent of
the catchers. During the 1995 professional football season, only
nine percent of the quarterbacks were black, but about 90 percent of running backs, wide receivers and safeties, and 100
percent of the cornerbacks were black. Whites were disproportionately represented on the offensive line, blacks on the defensive
line. *USA Today* analyzed its All-USA high school football teams
from 1982 to 1991 and found that all the running backs and almost nine in ten receivers and defensive backs were black, while
whites made up 78 percent of the quarterbacks and offensive
linemen and 94 percent of the kickers and punters. "A wide receiver, five-foot-nine, a white guy, it's really not something you'd
look at going in the NFL," one University of Iowa football star
said about himself. There is also evidence that when black football players move up the ranks through high school and college,
they are shifted to positions where blacks predominate: quarterbacks are moved to what are considered speed positions and
offensive linemen are retooled for defense.[17]

Is prejudice at work here? Lapchick cites the "widely held
belief" that coaches and managers "either consciously or sub-

consciously" make selections by race. Blacks are put in positions requiring speed, athletic ability and quickness, while whites are slotted according to thinking, leadership, and intelligence. This is certainly the attitude reflected in the notorious comment by former Los Angeles Dodger executive Al Campanis, who in 1987 said that blacks "may not have some of the necessities to be, let's say, a field manager or a general manager," and pointed to the lack of black quarterbacks and pitchers as proof. A slightly more benign explanation for stacking could be that whites and blacks are more comfortable working most intimately with people of their own race. In baseball, pitchers will work more closely with catchers than with outfielders, just as offensive and defensive squads in football spend most of the time among themselves. A conceivable but less likely reason is that these numbers reflect a random division of interests that happens to manifest itself by race. Whatever the reason, benign or benighted, it shows once again that a racially mixed environment does not mean a racially integrated environment.[18]

It's also unclear whether the sporting environment is as color-blind and racially harmonious as its boosters claim. Certainly, the more that black and white players separate themselves into different sports, the less opportunity they will have to build inter-racial ties. As for the fans, we've come to expect arenas full of whites cheering their black ballplayers, but one 1988 study should give us pause because it concludes that changing from an all-black to an all-white professional basketball team would increase attendance by 3,000 to 4,000 fans per game. Other troubling events suggest a sporting culture not much more enlightened than the rest of society. There was a white New York Yankees executive who called the black youngsters from the neighborhood around Yankee Stadium "monkeys." There was the enthusiastic welcome accorded white golfer Fuzzy Zoeller in his first appearance after he had disparaged Tiger Woods racially—according to the Associated Press, "Zoeller was cheered as he walked the course yesterday, with fans lining up to have him sign visors, programs and admissions tickets." There are the occasional news reports of racial epithets being traded during games between predominantly black and predominantly white high school teams: Janesville, Wisconsin, players called their opponents "nigger" and "white nigger"; a white Chicago Catholic school crowd shouted racial insults at the opposing basketball team; in east Texas, parents shouted "niggers" as they watched their sons lose to a black junior high school team. Incidents like these—as well as the continuing prevalence of racial stereotypes in sports— led scholar John Hoberman, in his book *Darwin's Athletes*, to conclude that there is a "racialized universe of everyday encounters" in sports that "receives far less attention than the highly public and officially deracialized theater of professional and collegiate sport, which white administrators present as an oasis of racial harmony."[19]

Even if we treat the hateful incidents as blemishes and not typical, America's athletes are far from operating in a racially integrated world. The image we prefer to hold is captured in the photos of black and white players embracing each other after victories and consoling each other after losses. But the racial dynamics of a mixed sports team are much more complicated than that. That players depend on each other to win does not mean they have overcome the color line. "Race can tear a team up," said one women's basketball coach. Athletes do not like to talk about it, but there is evidence of racial tensions on many teams. Furthermore, a lack of overt tension does not equal harmony, since black and white players usually keep their distance off the field. Among university athletes, teammates tend to room and socialize according to race. During recruiting visits to campuses, most coaches accede to the racial pull and pair black recruits with black players and white recruits with whites. At predominantly white schools, particularly those with a small black enrollment, studies of black athletes show that when the cheering stops and they walk off the court, large numbers of them feel isolated from other students and racially isolated in general. Even Bill Bradley acknowledged that his black and white pro teammates had different friends in every town; one of Bradley's black contemporaries said, "The truth is, black and white players go their separate ways after games. We meet up again at practice the next day."[20] What the players say is not too different from what black and white workers say about each other: We get along fine when we play, and we don't really dislike their lifestyle, but ours is different and we just don't have that much in common. In short, black and white teamwork during the game rarely translates to camaraderie beyond the game. The athletes intersect but rarely integrate.

Finally, there's the one question perennially posed by the pundits: Why do so many young blacks pursue a sports career when the odds of becoming even a benchwarmer in the pros are so slim? Sure, we all like sports, but why take it so seriously? Wouldn't it be better to subordinate sports to education and build a firm foundation for the future? These questions, though well intended, miss the larger point of how sports is uniquely tangled up with race in America. For many black Americans, sports plays a special role in life that most whites will never begin to comprehend. To most white Americans, it is simply an article of faith that the American Dream is within reach if you work hard and take control of your life. But that has never been the case for most blacks. The idea of taking control, of choosing your future, seems alien in a nation that has so rarely allowed blacks that option. No matter how hard you worked or how good you were at what you did, it mattered little under the thumb of slavery, Jim Crow, or discrimination. What was yours could be taken from you or denied by someone else. The one exception is and has been sports. Former NBA star Chet Walker writes: "Soaring over an opponent, driving in at him, then *looking* at him to say 'I crushed you'—that's control. Perhaps the only place a young black player can feel it."[21] From the playground to the local YMCA to the professional arena, sports ceases to be a game and becomes almost a mission. This may explain why young blacks have gravitated to two sports that require this type of intensity, basketball and football. The man, as so many blacks call whites, cannot deny, reverse, or devalue the slam dunk or the crushing tackle. They are decisive, final evidence of control—perhaps for some young blacks their only taste of the satisfaction that for so many Americans comes naturally upon achieving their American Dream.

Separate Experiences

In 1959 a white journalist named John Howard Griffin took six Psorlen pills a day to darken his skin so he could pass for black and see whether life in the South was really different for those on the other side of the color line. What he reported became a legend during the civil rights era. As he traveled through the South, routine experiences he took for granted as a white American became ordeals for him as a black. Finding a toilet, a place to eat, a bed for the night, a store to cash his check—all tested his patience and weary body. Just looking at a white actress on a movie poster elicited a nerve-racking threat. Griffin's book, *Black Like Me*, became a national best-seller because it exposed the basic indignities of black life during segregation.

Things have changed profoundly since then. The malignant and dehumanizing institution of legal segregation is now a memory. Blacks no longer live under the oppressive daily burden of Jim Crow, the law no longer tolerates discrimination, and the climate of fear that could turn a conversation with a white woman into a death sentence no longer exists.

In 1994, thirty-five years after Griffin's journey, a twenty-year-old white student from the University of Maryland, Joshua Solomon, decided to undertake the same experiment to see how much had really changed. The Psorlen pills made him look black. His plan was to live as a black for an entire college semester, but two days into it he decided to stop. Even without WHITES ONLY signs or segregated establishments the message was clear: you're not welcome here. Though his dress and demeanor were the same as when he was white, restaurants made him wait despite having open tables, storekeepers treated him rudely and followed him around, car doors were locked and women rushed away when he passed, and whites ignored him when he asked them for help. "I just couldn't take being constantly pounded with hate," he wrote. "It never seems to stop."[22]

It is entirely possible that a white person who deliberately makes himself black may be looking for a racial dimension to an incident when in some cases it does not exist. All of us, black and white, confront from time to time the indignities of mere living. Perhaps many blacks overreact and make race an issue when it doesn't belong. Perhaps blacks are not "constantly pounded with hate." Perhaps. But it would be hard to argue that daily life for black Americans is not influenced, altered, and tarnished by the small but disquieting slights of race. For many blacks the daily ordeal of racial insensitivity builds up. Over time it feels like a death by a thousand cuts. Former assistant attorney general Deval Patrick calls it the "indignity du jour."[23] Whites who never live through the inconvenience and degradation of being black in America don't fully understand how profoundly different the black daily experience is from theirs.

In a day in the life of two Americas, the mere prospect of hailing a cab, going to a store, eating at a restaurant, taking an elevator, or driving the interstate takes on entirely different meanings for blacks and whites. "I remember coming from a meeting with the president of the United States in the Oval Office, out on Pennsylvania Avenue one night and not being able to get a cab," says Patrick. "And I don't mean not getting a cab because it was raining and there were a lot of people competing. I mean cabs that would fly by me but stop for the person who was dressed like me, someone standing down the street a ways, someone who was white."[24] It is hard to find a black person, especially a black man, who has not experienced some variation on this theme. Some resort to guerrilla tactics, such as asking a white pedestrian to hail the cab while hiding behind a tree until the cab stops. Some call ahead or walk to a hotel. Some never get the cab and walk as their anger wells up. Cab drivers might respond that they fear crime or that they don't want to push the odds of driving through a rough neighborhood just for one fare. Regardless of the reason, the result is the same, and it's something few whites will ever go through in their lives.

Unpleasant experiences in stores are also commonplace to most blacks, from being watched by store security to being asked for additional identification when paying by credit card to being either tailed or ignored but not helped by sales clerks. One *Wall Street Journal* editor was told that the store would not allow him to return the sweater he had bought an hour before without a dry-cleaning ticket. A young black man shopping at an Eddie Bauer store was stripped of his shirt and told to come back with his receipt because no one at the store believed he had bought it there the day before. One bookstore manager called a woman's bank to make sure she had enough money in her checking account to cover her $137 purchase, even though company policy only required an address check and a white customer making a similar purchase that day faced no such call. Some stores will steer black customers to the inexpensive clothes, while others will declare unasked that the store has no lay-away policy. In expensive shops the salespeople will conspicuously announce the cost of an item when a black patron is eyeing it, assuming the customer cannot afford it. One upscale mall in Washington, D.C., actually kicked out a group of teenagers, seven blacks and one white, claiming the mall barred teens during school hours unless accompanied by an adult, which somehow didn't apply to groups of white teens shopping there.[25]

It is common knowledge that sales clerks and store security are told to keep their eye on blacks in the store. Some stores avoid the problem altogether by refusing to stock black-oriented items, such as black hair-care products. And woe to the black customer who wants to return an item without the proper receipt. When one Los Angeles police detective tried to return a wedding gift of expensive china, he learned from a colleague that the department store called all the other stores to see if it had been stolen. Blacks tell each other that if you want to bring an item back into the store, be sure to have the original bag so as not to be accused of stealing. Indeed, some blacks have begun to adopt a defensive shopping strategy of their own, such as carrying briefcases or wearing designer clothes when they go out shopping to give the impression of being affluent shoppers. Black parents will often tell their kids not to touch small items on display counters to avoid being accused of shoplifting. So racially charged is the shopping experience that it has influenced where blacks go to shop. Consumer research shows that both blacks and whites choose stores first based on price. The number two reason for whites is availability of merchandise; for blacks it is respect.[26]

Driving is also fraught with unpleasant possibilities, which is why many blacks call the experience "driving while black." We've already discussed the way police pull over black motorists passing through predominantly white neighborhoods. Perhaps more jarring is this statistic from Maryland: out of 823 cars state troopers searched on Interstate 95 between January 1995 and September 1996, 73 percent (600) were driven by blacks, even though blacks made up only 17 percent of the motorists on the highway during that time. ABC's *Nightline* interviewed black police officers from Miami who described how they have been pulled over for no reason when driving in another part of the state; even after identifying themselves as police they were still given a hard time. Evidence like this illustrates the profoundly different relationship that blacks and whites have with the police. To most whites the police work with them, but to many blacks the police seem to work against them. A 1995 Louis Harris survey found that more than half of all black teens say that they or their friends have been questioned by police at least once or twice. As one report on black high-achieving high school students put it, "Almost every black male told of hostility from the police. They related stories of being stopped while driving, being pulled over in malls, and being singled out when there were many more white kids around. They have no trust in the police."[27]

What is so corrosive for blacks is that there is no escaping these racial indignities. No matter how much you've accomplished, no matter how wealthy you may be, no matter how many people you may employ, presumptions are made about you that are based solely on the color of your skin. For successful blacks, writes author Ellis Cose, "the moment never arrives when race can be treated as a total irrelevancy. Instead, too often it is the only relevant factor defining our existence." The supermodel Iman doesn't ask but is told how much an item costs in an expensive store. The former press secretary to first lady Barbara Bush is presumed to be a sales clerk by other customers at an upscale boutique. A Boston Celtic basketball player is forced at gunpoint onto the sidewalk by police after a bank teller says he resembles a robbery suspect. Baseball great Henry Aaron is seated in a restaurant near six white women, all of whom pick up their purses and hold them nervously on their laps. A newspaper columnist emptying his mailbox—wearing linen trousers and dress shoes—is asked how much he would charge to mow someone's lawn. A professor is presumed to be the hostess in a faculty dining room and is asked about seating. Outside hotels, prominent black executives are mistaken for parking valets or chauffeurs. White women exit elevators when black men in business suits enter. Among blacks not served at Denny's were a federal judge, secret service agents, and a military couple. When a black psychologist who was walking on a sidewalk glanced at the Bill Cosby book a white woman was holding, she considered it enough of a provocation to race across the street, tightly clutching her purse.[28]

The fact that even the most successful blacks must deal with this jarring racial reality is not lost on every other black in America, who cannot but wonder whether they will ever be able to escape the trials of race. For whites—most of whom never think twice about driving the highway, shopping at the mall, eating at a restaurant, entering an elevator, or walking around their block—there is no parallel experience. It is yet another wedge that drives us apart.

Separate Media

In the typical American household the television is on about seven hours a day. With the exception of sleeping, the average American over the course of a year spends more time watching television than doing any other activity, including eating, working, or going to school. And when we're not watching television, we're often listening to radio or reading a magazine. The media have become the town square of modern American life, the locus of our culture and the marketplace where we acquire our sensibilities and ideas.

Over the past few decades, however, this town square has begun to change. Although not very visible at first, a new and very different configuration has been reshaping the American media landscape. It is called *segmentation*, or *narrowcasting*, and in practical terms it means that the media no longer pretend to reach a general audience but are instead geared to the needs and desires of particular demographic groups. Largely in response to the targeted needs of advertisers, media segmentation has begun to divide audiences according to lifestyle, ethnicity, gender, and age. While there's nothing new to the notion that demographics drive the news, as the publishers of women's magazines learned to their great financial benefit more than a century ago, segmentation is no longer the exception—it is the rule. And nowhere is this segmentation more evident than in the increasingly divergent media choices of blacks and whites. It's not that black and white Americans don't share similar media habits: We all watch television, listen to radio, go to movies, and read magazines. But when given the choice, we watch different television, listen to different radio, go to different movies, and read different magazines. When we relax, we relax differently. Even on the media town square, we rarely gather together.

The change is most pronounced on television only because it is our most dominant medium. During the 1996–97 television season, according to a report by the advertising agency BBDO, only one of the top twenty shows for black households, *Monday Night Football*, ranked among the top twenty for whites.[29] Besides football, not a single top ten show among blacks ranked better than sixtieth for whites. Most top-ranked black shows—*Living Single, New York Undercover, Martin, Moesha,* and *Malcolm & Eddie*—are among the least-watched shows for whites. Likewise, many top-ranked white shows—such as *Seinfeld, Friends, Suddenly Susan,* and *Frasier*—ranked toward the bottom for blacks. Among the highly ranked shows for whites, only a few, like the well-regarded *ER*, attract a reasonably strong black audience, largely because of well-developed black characters. But shows with a black character who has no life outside of his relationship with whites, such as the mid-1990s sitcom *Dave's World*, have little drawing power among blacks. The deep divide in our media culture can be further gleaned from research reports issued by the Simmons Market Research Bureau. *Black Entertainment Television* and sitcoms such as *Living Single* and *Martin* are watched by almost 40 percent of all black adults but only about three percent of white adults. Seventeen percent of blacks but only one percent of whites watched *The Wayans Bros.* On these black-oriented shows, the T-shirts feature Morgan State or Xavier, the plots unfold at catfish cookouts and black family reunions, references are made to such black writers as Zora Neale Hurston and Richard Wright, and the background music has an urban contemporary beat. Rarely do these themes appear on white-oriented shows.

Perhaps the greatest irony of *The Cosby Show*, which was designed for a broad audience and took great pride in its crossover appeal, is that it spawned a new generation of black-oriented shows that only blacks tend to watch. These shows received a boost because the three upstart networks—first Fox, and then WB and UPN—used them to carve out a prime-time presence among blacks. Out of the top twenty shows for blacks during the 1996–97 season, twelve were on these three networks. NBC, the network that brought us *The Cosby Show*, did not have a single black-oriented show that year. Increasingly we are not even watching the same networks. Some observers point to the hopeful sign that there is more crossover among teenagers, but again that may simply be a result of the paucity of shows aimed at teens and the fact that nearly half of the youth-oriented shows that do air are currently made up of largely black casts. When two similar shows with strong youth appeal went head to head in 1995, *Living Single* hit the top of the black teen rankings and sank to the bottom of the white teen rankings, the exact opposite of its competitor show, *Friends*.

Those who regret this trend point to the fact that blacks and whites had many more shows in common up to the mid-1980s. But it is misguided to assume we've somehow lost a common culture. For years blacks had few if any programs that resonated with their lives, and they watched the available white-oriented shows almost by default. The recent changes reflect the increased availability of choices for blacks. The cultural schism was always there, just waiting for the programming to reveal it.

The fact that whites and blacks watch different shows doesn't mean that white-oriented programs never include a black character or two as part of the plot. Far from it. Dramas such as *ER*, *Chicago Hope*, *Homicide*, and *NYPD Blue* all have a strong black presence, and some sitcoms include a secondary character played by a black actor. This formula has also proved successful in the movies, which increasingly feature racially mixed casts. Denzel Washington, Sidney Poitier, Cuba Gooding Jr., Whoopi Goldberg, James Earl Jones, Whitney Houston, Will Smith, Laurence Fishburne, Samuel Jackson, and Morgan Freeman are by now very familiar and reassuring faces to whites. But just as in television, very rarely will a film built on a black theme or protagonist garner a substantial white audience. For *Waiting to Exhale*, a well-regarded film about four black women, 20th Century-Fox spent millions of dollars on promotion and opened it on 1,300 screens nationwide with the goal of attracting a large crossover audience, particularly among women. It didn't. Although some crossover took place, a majority of the people who saw the film were black women. One 20th Century-Fox executive said, "We spent weeks and weeks trying to get middle white America to buy into this movie. We never succeeded." The same could be said of a long list of critically acclaimed films like it, including the Civil War film *Glory*, *The Preacher's Wife* starring Denzel Washington and Whitney Houston, the family drama *Soul Food*, and Spike Lee's *Malcolm X*. Harvey Weinstein, the president of Miramax Films, observed, "If you want to see prejudice at work, make an all black movie." Little wonder that one of the most recent trends in the film industry is simply to make black films for black audiences and not to worry any longer about crossover sales.[30]

Racial segmentation also characterizes the way we listen to radio and read magazines. Because both of these media generally survive on niche audiences and highly targeted advertising strategies, they cannot afford to blunt their core appeal. The allure of a radio station is especially linked to the music it plays, which is often rooted in the memory and experience of its audience. Because memory and experience are so racially divided in America, it is no surprise that radio is highly segmented by race. As a result, while there is some black and white crossover on the radio dial, the typical black American listens to urban contemporary, rhythm and blues, gospel, and jazz, while the typical white American listens to album rock, classic rock, rock'n'roll oldies, easy listening, and country music.

Consider the case of country, which garners one-fourth of the radio market and one-sixth of the record market today. Although some old-timers in the country scene acknowledge a debt to black music, for the most part this genre is completely white. With the exception of Charley Pride, there are no major black country artists, virtually no black country songwriters, and barely a handful of black backup musicians. According to the former country editor of *Billboard*, "Country these days is fundamentally based on the white experience." It is, as Bruce Feiler, the author of a forthcoming book on country music, observed, "the largest segregated corner of American music today."[31] Needless to say, country music has a negligible black audience. Turn the dial from country and you might accidentally hit an urban contemporary or hip-hop station, but unfortunately proximity on the radio dial means little. Statistics from the Simmons Market Research Bureau show that almost 40 percent of all black listeners tune to urban contemporary radio, compared to less than three percent of white listeners. When all black-oriented radio formats are combined, some estimate that black radio reaches almost every black teenager and adult in the land.[32]

What is so important about radio is its role as a community resource and voice. If television provides the entertainment in our town square, radio serves as both grapevine and bulletin board. Divided radio audiences mean we share neither the same information nor the context to put it in. A *Washington Post* radio critic compared two Washington area oldies stations, one catering to an audience almost 90 percent white and the other to an audience almost 90 percent black. Although the two playlists shared some of the same songs, especially Motown tunes, it was clear they had different audiences in mind and did not consider themselves competitors. Most striking was the way they provided community information, each announcing events targeted to the counties in which their respective audiences live.[33]

Just as segmented are the magazines we read. Magazines such as *Cosmopolitan, Vanity Fair, Good Housekeeping, Fortune, Reader's Digest, Rolling Stone,* and *The Atlantic* are targeted primarily to whites, while *Essence, Emerge, Ebony, Jet,* and *Black Enterprise* are read almost exclusively by blacks. In a typical month, more than half of all black adults read *Ebony* and about one third read *Essence. Jet* is in the hands of four in ten black adults during a typical week. Less than one in a hundred whites reads these magazines.[34] A magazine like *Vogue* is caught in somewhat of a dilemma: although about 15 percent of its readers are black, the core readership and targeted advertising audience is white. When *Vogue* puts a black model on the cover, newsstand sales decline. "In terms of fashion magazines," wrote *Vogue*'s editor, "it is a fact of life that the color of a model's skin . . . dramatically affects newsstand sales." A 1991 study found that less than two percent of the magazine's advertising models were black.[35] So *Vogue*'s readers end up seeing few black images and little about the lives of blacks, leaving the magazine's black readership with their noses pressed to the glass as they stand outside the party looking in. Then there's the example of *Washingtonian*, one of the many metropolitan magazines published throughout the country that appeal to the upscale side of the middle class. Although the Washington region is about one-fourth black and has a larger black middle class than any other region in America, *Washingtonian*'s targeted readership is decidedly white. As a result, blacks are not very visible in the magazine, even though it is purported to be about a metropolitan area with a large black population. Of 899 feature articles between 1990 and 1996, only 33 had black-oriented subjects, and of these only five covered social and lifestyle issues; the rest were on high-profile topics like politics, sports, entertainment, and the media.[36] To magazine publishers, editorial content is simply a reflection of the advertising base, which itself is a reflection of our racially segmented society.

Perhaps the only medium with an integrated audience is the American daily newspaper. But even here segmentation pressures are seeping in. "There's a dirty little secret in all newspapers," a *New York Times* editor once said. "The advertisers we cater to are not thrilled when you sign up a bunch of readers in some poverty area for home delivery."[37] Some large newspapers now publish editions or sections targeted to specific and often racially distinct parts of their circulation area. Racial demographics even influenced coverage of the O. J. Simpson trial, according to *Los Angeles Times* media reporter David Shaw, who found that the papers with the fewest number of Simpson stories were in metropolitan areas with the lowest number of blacks. Racial targeting is also evident on the editorial pages, where black columnists are often the only ones writing about racial issues.[38] In May 1997, the month before President Clinton's widely anticipated speech announcing a presidential initiative on race, we tracked the columns of four prominent black columnists and three prominent white columnists; race was the subject of only one in thirty-three columns by the white writers compared to nine of thirty-three by the blacks.[39]

Among black readers, distrust of mainstream newspapers is so high—particularly in the way their lives and communities are portrayed—that many turn to black-owned weekly newspapers as sources of information. In a 1987 article published in the *Colum-*

bia Journalism Review, one writer who compared "mainstream" and black-owned media in Boston found "one crucial difference" between the two: "stories about education, city government, community and cultural events, and the arts, as well as profiles of educators and entrepreneurs, all appeared much more frequently in the black news media." When reporting news on Boston's two predominantly black neighborhoods, the mainstream press offered almost exclusively negative news, with 59 percent of the articles emphasizing crime; the black-owned press painted a different picture, describing these black communities as eager for educational advancement, entrepreneurial achievement, and solutions to their problems.[40]

The evidence does not indicate that newspapers will segment themselves the way other media have. For economic reasons alone, it simply won't happen. But there are enough indications to suggest that there is more black and white to newspapers than the newsprint.

Finally, to those who say that the mass media is nothing more than an excuse for advertising—that television shows are merely the seven minutes between commercials—it is no surprise that the same pattern found throughout the media is also found in the ads. Indeed it would be shocking to find otherwise, given that advertising imperatives have largely driven the segmentation of America's media. Ads on black-oriented television shows tend to be much more black than ads on white-oriented shows. On episodes of the black-oriented shows *Martin* and *Sister, Sister*, blacks played prominent roles in around half the ads and in some cases most of the ads in which people were shown. Many of the ads for the televised celebration of *Ebony*'s fiftieth anniversary featured black families, shoppers, drivers, and celebrities. The producers might have done well to air exclusively black-oriented ads: research indicates that although blacks have acclimated themselves to a predominantly white commercial culture, they respond very favorably to ads that are targeted specifically to them, and are predisposed to products and stores that speak to their ethnicity, tastes, and lives—more so than any other non-white ethnic group.[41] When Pillsbury wanted to sell more of its Hungry Jack products to black consumers, the company learned that its white lumberjack logo had no relevance to blacks. So it eliminated the lumberjack and developed a campaign around a black family eating together with the slogan, "You look hungry, Jack." The McDonald's famous "breakfast club" campaign of the 1980s, featuring a group of young black professionals talking at breakfast, helped make the fast-food chain a leader among blacks. Seeing a black consumer market with nearly $500 billion in purchasing power, advertisers and their clients are rapidly responding.

Not unexpectedly, ads in the white-oriented media tend to be predominantly but by no means exclusively white. Ads in magazines are significantly more white than ads on television, according to a 1991 study of twenty-seven national magazines by the New York City Department of Consumer Affairs, largely because magazines are much more prone to have racially targeted audiences. That study found blacks in only 4.5 percent of the ads, and a large proportion of these blacks were athletes, musicians, children, and recipients of philanthropy.[42]

Television is not as thoroughly a segmented medium, and so the advertising industry has been more responsive to diversity concerns and the growing black consumer market. It also costs a lot to produce a television ad, so sponsors try to reach as many groups as possible without diluting the ad's effectiveness. As a result, the advertising industry has been making commercial images on television much more racially inclusive than in years past. It is rare for a television show not to have some ads that feature a minority face or two, although that does happen. In two episodes of the fairly popular show *Coach*, the first episode had one ad that included a black, but the second had none. In general, while TV ads for the mainstream audience infrequently show an all-black or predominantly black cast, whites do not seem uncomfortable with commercials featuring a black celebrity or a black actor or two as part of a predominantly white group. The whole thing is a balancing act, as some advertising executives admit that a product seen as "too black" might find its sales plummet among whites. It is also worth noting that a number of black-owned advertising agencies have done a thriving business on ads targeted to the black consumer, but are rarely asked to pitch a campaign for a more general audience. With advertising as with almost everything else involving beauty, status, sophistication, and intimacy, the black image is a hard sell among American whites.

So yes, America has changed. No longer are there separate water fountains for blacks and whites. But in their place are the separate water coolers that we stand around while we discuss the different shows we saw on television the night before.

CHAPTER FOUR

The Motown Metaphor and the Promised Land of the 1960s

The Motown Metaphor

The millions of white Baby Boomers who grew up dancing to the Temptations and Supremes had reason enough to believe that a new age of racial integration was in the works. The early 1960s Motown sound was energetic, cheerful, innocent, and black, the perfect anthem for a civil rights era that would conquer prejudice and draw blacks and whites together in soulful harmony. That whites could move to the rhythm of soul symbolized the imminent unity of the two races and the elimination of all the artificial barriers that had kept us apart. Forget the static of politics—it was on the dance floor that whites were opening their arms to blacks and their culture. So certain did integration seem that *Billboard* magazine discontinued its black rhythm and blues chart in late 1963, merging it with the predominantly white pop singles chart. In retrospect, we think back to Motown as an unspoiled music that, for a short moment in history, brought us together without tension or fear. The 1983 benchmark film about white Baby Boomers, *The Big Chill,* used the Motown sound as a nostalgic counterpoint to the larger theme about the loss of sixties idealism. If only the Motown spirit had stayed alive.

But just as with almost everything else about race, there's more to the Motown phenomenon than meets the nostalgic eye. In January 1965, just fourteen months after dropping its black rhythm and blues chart, a chagrined *Billboard* reinstated it, acknowledging that the Motown crossover was an anomaly and that blacks and whites generally listened to separate radio stations and music. Most of the soul artists who sold well among blacks barely scratched the mainstream pop chart, and white groups were all but invisible on the black chart. In 1967, Chicago's black soul station WVON, which reached 90 percent of Chicago's black households each week, had 774 different records on its playlists, and all but ten of them were by blacks. White pop stations rarely if ever played such popular black soul artists as Joe Tex, Ben E. King, Arthur Connelly, The Parliaments, Percy Sledge, Sam and Dave, The Impressions, or Jackie Wilson, though some of these artists sold millions of records to blacks. In fact, the soul artists most popular among whites found a somewhat less favorable reception among blacks. The Supremes, for example, had more number one hits on the mainstream pop chart than on the black soul chart.[1] Even in the age of Motown, radio played in black and white.

Call it the Motown metaphor for American race relations, an early version of the integration illusion. Many Americans both black and white like to think of the early to mid-sixties as a time driven by ideals, fueled by hope, and uncluttered by the racial end-game of today's politics and culture. We like to think of it as an era when blacks and whites reached out to each other in common cause and made integration possible. We long for the friction-free crossover of the Motown nation. But beyond the reach of the civil rights movement, outside the range of Motown's alluring harmonies, something very different was happening in the United States. At the very same time the heroic civil rights movement was defeating legal segregation, during the same triumphal days of the 1963 March on Washington and the enactment of civil rights legislation against racial discrimination, the contours of today's racially separated America were beginning to take shape. By the time President Johnson signed the landmark Voting Rights Act in the summer of 1965, racial patterns in housing, education, behavior, and culture had made real integration all but unattainable.

To think that racial integration was taking place or was even possible during the civil rights years is to project the idealism of the movement onto the rest of the nation. "As I stood at the Lincoln Memorial on August 28, 1963, preparing to give my speech to the 250,000 gathered," recalled Congressman John Lewis, "I could actually imagine our building an interracial democracy."[2] But integration was as much a distant dream then as it is today. Perhaps the saddest irony of the civil rights era is that true integration was becoming less likely in society just as desegregation was beginning to prevail in the law. The result is that black and white Americans would learn to accommodate one another in the public spheres that required interaction, but would remain distant in the private spheres that involved choice and any form of intimacy. As the sixties progressed, we would intersect more economically, politically, and symbolically. Fewer and fewer whites would object to working near blacks, seeing blacks on television, or sitting next to a black person on a bus, at the lunch counter, or in the movie theater. But in the things that mattered most in our lives—the spheres of home, school, status, family, community, and friendship—integration was not about to happen. As *Newsweek* described white attitudes toward blacks in 1966, "The closer the Negro gets, in his advance from lunch counters to jobs to schools, the more whites tend to worry—and they worry most about integrated housing."[3] The color line was not erased in the 1960s; it was merely redrawn.

There is a conventional wisdom about the 1960s that most writers and commentators follow. The story line is this: we came close, very close, to solving America's racial dilemma completely in the mid-sixties, until a number of factors stalled our progress and undermined the consensus. Great strides were made toward integration, according to this view, but unfortunately we now live with a bitter aftertaste. This version fits with the popular tendency to look at the early 1960s through the romance and nostalgia of Camelot and King, an innocent time when the great civil rights struggles united the black and white majority in America. We had a teachable moment for racial harmony, the story goes, and we squandered it. To liberals, blame for our current problems falls squarely on President Nixon's parochial and cynical strategy to build a silent majority from racial resentment and to draw discontented George Wallace voters into the Republican party—the southern strategy. It was a strategy that, liberals say,

Ronald Reagan turned into a fine art. To conservatives, the villains include the black nationalists who fueled racial discontent and the liberal social engineers who rationalized violent crime and foisted divisive policies like busing, affirmative action, and group rights on well-meaning middle-class whites, deeply embittering them. To be sure, this type of finger-pointing is as much about present agendas as past events, but this fact should not obscure the similarity between the liberal and conservative points of view: that we had a chance to put this racial thing behind us if people had only put the national interest ahead of their special interest.

The trouble is, this view is not wholly accurate. The fact that some of us dreamed of integrating does not mean it was ever close to happening. The civil rights movement ended legal segregation in America. It created unprecedented opportunities for black political power and economic mobility. It established a social norm that no longer tolerated or condoned overt discrimination and bigotry. It was no doubt a crowning moment in American history, justifiably embraced and celebrated today by people of every political stripe. But it simply couldn't build an integrated America. As much as we like to blame the southern strategy, the silent majority, affirmative action, busing, race riots, multiculturalism, black power, or the precipitous rise of inner-city violent crime for poisoning the "beloved community," the evidence shows that the infrastructure of a separated America had already been established by the time any of these factors even entered the realm of race relations. The racially divided urban and suburban housing patterns of today were set in place in the early sixties. So were the dynamics around desegregated schooling. Even the way we now interact and perceive each other was foreshadowed then. In November 1964, only four months after Congress passed the 1964 Civil Rights Act outlawing discrimination in employment, government programs, and public accommodations—a law whose purpose, as President Johnson stated, "is not to divide, but to end divisions"—the people of California, by a resounding two-to-one margin, approved a constitutional amendment for their state that overturned an open housing law and effectively allowed racial discrimination in housing. We may get misty-eyed when we think back to Martin Luther

King's remarkable speech at the 1963 March on Washington, but barely two months later, Bower Hawthorne, the editor of two Minneapolis papers, the *Star* and *Tribune*, said, "We're getting increasing complaints from our readers that we are overplaying the integration story. Some of our white readers are getting tired of reading so much about it."⁴ We can accuse Nixon, Reagan, limousine liberals, black leaders, urban ethnics, or the social engineers of sowing discord, but they were merely acting out roles that in many ways already had been written for them in the early sixties. To those who decry what they see as the balkanization of America by racial preferences today, the truth is that the boundary lines of today's balkanization were shaped long before racial preferences even became an issue. To those who fret over what they see as resegregation today, the sad truth is that there was never an integration from which to resegregate.

In fact, the 1960s seems like an echo chamber for today's excuses, rationales, attitudes, and illusions. "Until the time of the O.J. trial and verdict, I wasn't a racist. I am now," one man told the *Washington Post* in 1995. "People who weren't prejudiced before, are now," a Seattle mechanic told *Newsweek* in 1966 after a summer of black protests.⁵ Today most whites blame black leaders for pressing black demands too hard, stirring up racial enmity and undermining racial comity. It was the same as far back as the early sixties, before race riots and affirmative action, as whites condemned blacks for moving too fast, for not appreciating the progress already made, for undermining the goodwill of moderate whites, and for shattering a mythic sense of racial harmony. "It is just creating racial animosity where none existed before," one opponent of a New York school desegregation plan that did not involve busing said in 1964. "The forced integration of the races in Washington brought about strife and chaos where before there had been understanding and harmony," a southern congressman said in 1963. Or as one white author, a self-described advocate for racial equality, wrote in an 1963 essay for *U.S. News & World Report*, "The emotional excesses which now characterize our racial revolution could hamper rather than hasten the integration of the Negro in our society. Of all the plans for demonstrations now contemplated, none would be more disastrous than the march of thousands of Negroes upon Washing-

ton in August."[6] White Americans needed to justify back then—
just as they do today—why they felt animosity toward blacks and
why our nation has veered from its ideal of racial understanding.
To most whites the answer was and is clear: things would have
been fine had the blacks not pushed too far.

There is an eerie and almost startling consistency to the integration illusion as expressed almost four decades ago and today.
White Americans today back integrated housing in theory but resist it in their neighborhoods, just as they did in 1963 when they
told pollsters they supported equal rights in housing as long
as those equal rights didn't apply next door. Whites today say
they want blacks to have equal job opportunities, but overwhelmingly reject affirmative action as unfair. In 1964—before affirmative action even existed, before employment discrimination was
outlawed—whites also supported better job opportunities for
blacks but, according to the pollster Louis Harris, increasingly
resented that "Negroes are getting a better break than their
own fathers and grandfathers received as immigrant outsiders."[7]
Today whites tell pollsters how much they support school integration, and then move from the neighborhood when more than
a few black children enter the local school. In 1963, a Harris poll
found that more than three-fourths of all whites said they would
send their own children to integrated schools. "Whites are now
ready to make this a reality," wrote *Newsweek* at the time.[8] History,
of course, records otherwise. In an incident that would be comi-
cal were it not so sad, a black man happened to be walking on the
Brooklyn Bridge on a snowy day in March 1964 at the same time
that 15,000 whites were marching across the bridge to protest the
desegregation of their local schools. "Put him in the middle,"
one march leader yelled through a bullhorn, and so he was hur-
riedly drawn into the crowd and given a placard before he was
able to get away. Back then, even the angriest desegregation opponents wanted their ranks to appear integrated.

As the sixties progressed, the head of the NAACP, Roy Wilkins,
found the disconnection between white attitudes and behaviors
increasingly frustrating for blacks. Whites "have the idea that 'because I don't hate the Negro, he is my friend and I am his friend.'
But there is a lot of difference between not hating a man and let-
ting him live in your neighborhood or have a good job," said

Wilkins in a 1967 interview. For many whites, integration was styl-
ish as long as it took place somewhere else. Northern whites
championed blacks as noble victims in the early 1960s, but only
when the injustice was clear and was fought in the South. "It's so
'popular' to be a Negro these days that no white party is a success
without one," a black leader from Washington, D.C., said in
1963. But as soon as black concerns collided with the racial ambi-
guities of everyday life in the North, and as soon as blacks began
to express their frustrations more adamantly, whites increasingly
lost interest in the cause and began to view blacks as tiresome and
troublesome interlopers. "Black people have stopped being chic,"
observed black leader Julian Bond in 1973.[9] From the 1960s on-
ward, one hears a recurring theme among white Americans: we
are people of goodwill, we get along with blacks, we want nothing
but the best for them and we've already done a lot, so why are
they so angry, why do they keep making unreasonable demands,
and why are they pitting themselves against us? What do these
people want, anyway?

Just as it does now, the integration illusion governed relations between the races during the 1960s. How else could a Tennessee woman tell a reporter in the same breath back in 1963 that
the black woman who kept the local church nursery "is a real good
friend; we all love her dearly"—but then say she wouldn't want
this good friend living next door because "it would lower the standard of the neighborhood." How else could a Queens, New York,
parent say in 1964 that "this is a liberal neighborhood. We don't
object to Negroes or to integration. We believe in civil rights"—
and then lead an angry demonstration against a plan to pair her
all-white elementary school with an all-black school just six blocks
away. How else could an Indiana worker claim, "I wouldn't get too
upset if Negroes moved into this neighborhood"—and then add,
"but I'd try to move to an area without them."[10] It is a refrain with
multiple variations that we have heard countless times since. In a
very sad way, America since the sixties would move little beyond
Newsweek's 1963 description of the state of racial integration.
"The average white American . . . knows [the Negro] as a shoe-
shine boy, postman, waiter, janitor, porter, ballplayer, entertainer,

gardener, chauffeur—but not as a friend. He sees the Negro often, everywhere; but the Negro remains a stranger."[11]

No More Than a Dream

Most portraits of 1950s America are painted with broad brushstrokes about the Cold War, the Silent Generation, the domesticated housewife, the traditional family, the gleaming new consumer economy, and the alienated Beatniks. But perhaps no phenomenon of the fifties had a more lasting and seminal impact than the rapid suburbanization of America that began after World War II and accelerated throughout the fifties and sixties. In a demographic shift almost as momentous as the rise of industrialism in the mid-nineteenth century and the wave of European immigration in the early twentieth century, nearly one in six Americans—more than 28 million Americans, 97 percent of whom were white—moved to the suburbs between 1950 and 1966.[12] The housing patterns set during these years have transformed us into a nation of homeowners, so that now more Americans live in suburbs than anywhere else. The asphalt roads and housing developments that were carved out of potato fields and virgin countryside created a new type of community that would profoundly influence our culture, economy, politics, and social relations.

It is tempting to look at this suburban exodus as a white reaction to the great migration of nearly five million southern blacks to northern cities during the same period. But particularly when looking at the years immediately after World War II, such an analysis would be far too simplistic. It is important to remember that Americans were just emerging from nearly two decades of depression and war. For many Americans, the GI Bill made owning a home affordable, the postwar economy made it possible, and the baby boom made it desirable. Suburban housing developments with names like Rolling Hills, Windsor Forest, Island Trees, and Oak Grove beckoned Americans seeking a better life with the promise of a new sense of community built in an idyllic family setting away from the stress and pace of the city. Nor was it just the appeal of a picket fence that drew people to the suburbs.

According to one estimate, suburban areas received as much as 80 percent of the new jobs in manufacturing, retail and wholesale trade, and selected services after 1948.[13] There were plenty of rational, nonracial reasons for Americans to pack up the family for greener surroundings.

Nevertheless, race was an important factor driving suburban growth, and it grew increasingly significant as black and white lives began to collide first in the cities and then in the initial tier of inner-ring suburbs. Between 1950 and 1960, as the black population rose quickly and substantially in most American cities, white emigration swelled the surrounding suburbs, many of which nearly doubled in population during that time. In some urban neighborhoods, it was only a matter of months between the time the first black family moved in and the last white family moved out. As housing patterns in some well-appointed neighborhoods of Washington, D.C., made clear, it didn't seem to matter that the black people moving in were solidly middle-class in search of upscale homes and manicured lawns—the whites still moved out. In his book *Blockbusting in Baltimore*, W. Edward Orser of the University of Maryland–Baltimore County describes how one west Baltimore census tract shifted block by block over two decades, turning from 6,662 whites and 13 blacks in 1950 to 9,276 blacks and 841 whites in 1970. Whites in an adjoining census tract didn't feel the pressure until the 1960s, but when they did they too moved out en masse, dwindling from 8,708 in 1960 to 390 in 1970. By the mid-1960s, three Chicago blocks would tip from mostly white to mostly black each week. What blacks called an evacuation, whites called an exodus to the suburbs. Whether the white flight was spurred on by plain old white prejudice or by blockbusting real estate agents who preyed on—and reaped profits from—white fears of declining neighborhoods, the bottom line is the same: wherever blacks moved in, whites quickly moved out. By 1963, the conservative *U.S. News & World Report* noted with alarm that "Negroes live in one part of town, whites in another. When Negroes move into a white neighborhood or into a predominantly white school, many whites move out—often all the way out of the city into the still-white suburbs. The result is new segregation, rather than integration."[14]

Whether or not a white family fled to the suburbs because of race, they could virtually be guaranteed an all-white community once there. According to one estimate based on Census Bureau figures, the suburban white population increased by almost 1.8 million a year between 1960 and 1966, while the number of suburban blacks grew at a much slower pace during these formative suburban years, by only about 37,000 per year.[15] Some of the reasons for this, at least initially, seem fairly benign. Many blacks simply didn't have the resources to buy a house and make the move. Blacks migrating from the South moved primarily to the cities, where they joined family members and not unreasonably expected to find jobs. In the 1950s and early 1960s, most factories remained close to the urban hub. The economy's flight to the suburbs had yet to be a widely noticed national phenomenon, and blacks very rationally went to the places that seemed to hold the greatest promise for employment.

But just in case blacks with the money and resources wanted to set down suburban roots, whites used every means possible to make sure those roots weren't planted in their communities. Long Island's Levittown was the first great American suburb of the postwar years, a dream come true for the emerging American middle class who wanted a house of their own, a plot of land, modern appliances, and a relatively short commute to work. For many veterans, a house in Levittown didn't even require a down payment, just a $100 deposit that was refunded at closing. The mortgage interest rate was so low that most families in the early years paid only about $57 a month on a thirty-year loan. By 1960, Levittown boasted more than 65,000 residents, about a third of them under age ten. And one other thing: 99.9 percent were white. Clause 25 of Levittown's original 1947 purchase agreement prohibited use or occupancy "by any person other than members of the Caucasian race," except for "domestic servants." It also proscribed resales to blacks. Although restrictive covenants like this were struck down by the Supreme Court in 1948, prospective black purchasers—including many World War II veterans hoping to use their GI Bill benefits—continued to be turned away. "I have come to know that if we sell one house to a Negro family, then 90 or 95 percent of our white customers will not buy into the community," said builder William Levitt. "That is their attitude, not ours. . . . As a company our position is simply this: We can solve a housing problem, or we can try to solve a racial problem, but we cannot combine the two." The tone and tenor of this community—indeed of all the suburbs—had been set. By 1990, only 118 blacks called Levittown home.[16]

Black veterans who couldn't buy in Levittown found a special welcome only a few miles away in the Long Island community of Wyandanch, which increasingly became known as a major black suburb in New York. Blacks pursuing their suburban dream in the 1950s and 1960s generally moved to all-black communities like Wyandanch, most of which were suburban towns outside the central city that already had turned black, or to inner-ring suburbs adjacent to the city that were being deserted by whites. Even in communities with open-housing laws, many blacks preferred not to endure the stress of being racial pioneers and instead opted for black areas where they would be welcome and comfortable. Acknowledging this, Martin Luther King once said that if the quality of housing improved, "many white people would be surprised at how many Negroes would choose to live among themselves." In fact, demand for housing in Wyandanch had grown so much by the mid-fifties that a developer tried to expand the community and build a new development geared primarily to blacks. The problem was that the new development, although physically an extension of Wyandanch, was legally part of an adjoining all-white town called Babylon. In 1959, Babylon completely rezoned the area under consideration from residential to industrial, stopping the project and creating a buffer zone for its residents. "There is no prejudice in this town," Babylon's town supervisor said—they just wanted to attract industry and reduce taxes, he explained.[17] Four years before Martin Luther King's plea for brotherhood at the March on Washington, residential integration had been stopped cold on this part of Long Island, and it wasn't long before the same script played out in suburbs throughout the rest of the country.

When one looks back on those years, it is hard to find anyone connected with housing who in some way wasn't involved in building this residentially divided America. The real estate industry in particular played a central role, either by protecting all-white areas from potential black homebuyers or by hastening neighborhood turnover through the odious practice of blockbusting. Countless realtors got rich by purchasing homes from panicked whites and then selling them at a profit to blacks. Until 1950, the real estate professional code of ethics warned agents not to be "instrumental in introducing into a neighborhood . . . members of any race, nationality, or individual whose presence will be clearly detrimental to property values in that neighborhood."[18] The code may have changed in 1950, but not the ethic.

It wasn't only the realtors who kept blacks from white areas during these crucial years. In addition, mortgage lenders refused home loans to blacks. And if it wasn't the mortgage lenders, it was the government, which at every level placed obstacles in the way of integration. Until the late 1960s, the Federal Housing Administration promoted racially restrictive neighborhoods by refusing to insure loans for black families moving into white areas. Local and state governments reinforced racial separation in the cities—and kept black areas from engulfing white areas—by building highways between black and white neighborhoods or by razing black neighborhoods under the guise of "urban renewal" and relocating the displaced residents to massive, all-black public housing projects that had none of the stores, jobs, or amenities of their former neighborhoods.[19]

Finally, when nothing else kept the races apart in the fifties and sixties, the people themselves did. Many whites either didn't want to be near blacks, or truly believed that a black family in their neighborhood meant increasing crime and decreasing property values. Whether accurate or self-fulfilling, whether built on facts or prejudices, this fear for family and pocketbook drove whites to construct literal and figurative walls around their communities. Evidence that property values rose in middle-class black neighborhoods during the 1950s, or that black middle-class families also wanted safe neighborhoods and good schools, didn't seem to matter.[20] Whites didn't want blacks around and didn't want to take the risk, just as they don't want to today. As early as the late 1950s, many whites would legitimately point to deteriorating inner cities as proof that they were right in clearing out, unconcerned with the sociological explanation that their wholesale desertion of the cities stripped the remaining blacks of an institutional and economic base on which to build. And so they became willing partners with real estate agents in refusing to sell or rent to blacks. In liberal-minded cities like Berkeley, California, and Seattle and Tacoma, Washington, they used the referendum process in the early 1960s to defeat, by large margins, local open-housing laws. They voted one Michigan governor out of office in 1962 because he championed a rule to forbid real estate agents from practicing racial discrimination. According to a 1964 Harris Poll, white suburbanites bristled at any comparison with the South and called themselves racial moderates—yet believed that blacks were getting "too uppity," thought "that Negroes must be kept in their place," and found nothing wrong with refusing to sell a house to a black.[21]

Blacks clearly understood that they were not wanted and increasingly began to suspect the protestations of tolerance by self-proclaimed suburban moderates. As their economic choices grew and they began their own suburban exodus, it was to predominantly black communities they moved. Between 1958 and 1966, according to the Michigan Civil Rights Commission, fewer than sixty black families moved to all-white areas in the state. The residential color line had been drawn, and black suburbs would become a fact of American life just like the white ones that preceded them. Ultimately, civil rights leaders would acknowledge that real integration was an empty promise unless something could be done to move blacks into all-white suburban neighborhoods.[22]

By 1966, when the nation woke up to this issue and turned its eyes to Chicago as thousands of whites angrily jeered and threw rocks, bottles, and bricks at an open-housing march led by Martin Luther King, the residential die had already been cast throughout much of the nation. Inner cities had become black, most other urban neighborhoods were separated by race, the black middle class had found their own suburban havens, and the rest of the suburbs—where an increasing number of Americans would live in the years ahead—had become "white sanctuaries," as *U.S. News & World Report* described them in 1963.[23] To blame this residential landscape solely on prejudice and residential discrimination is to overlook the many factors that combined and conspired to create it, such as the postwar rise of suburbia, the black emigration to northern cities, and the difference in black and white economic circumstances. But regardless of the cause, the end result is the same: racially divided neighborhoods that have become self-protective enclaves, clear about who they are and whom they welcome.

If there was a leading factor that compelled white families to move and move fast, it was the fear of having their children sit in the same classroom as blacks. White flight was especially rapid in cities that desegregated their schools in the mid-1950s, such as Washington, Baltimore, St. Louis, and Kansas City. Moving-van activity in New York City seemed to correlate with every new initiative to desegregate the schools. Then as now, the public schools served as a bellwether of residential change. In a pattern that has become ingrained today, white families with school-age children would either move out altogether or put their kids in private schools, leaving the public schools much more black than the populations they served. Washington, D.C., in the early 1960s was 54 percent black, but its schools were nearly 90 percent black; St. Louis was 29 percent black, but its schools were 60 percent black; Philadelphia was 26 percent black, its schools, 56 percent black. By 1965, the number of white students in Chicago attending private schools almost equaled the number attending public schools; all but 10 percent of the city's black grade school children attended all-black schools; and one fourth of the city's public elementary schools were all or almost all black while two-thirds were all or almost all white. In 1963 in Englewood, New Jersey—a city of 28,000 residents of whom one-quarter were black, a small enough proportion to imagine a reasonable racial mix in the classroom—there were three elementary schools, one all black, another predominantly black, and a third almost all white.[24]

Individual schools fared no better. In Baltimore, every one of the nine all-white schools that were required to integrate in 1954 had become all black just seven years later. Roosevelt High School in northwest Washington, D.C., had 747 whites and no blacks in 1953, the year before desegregation; 634 whites and 518 blacks in 1955, the second year of desegregation; and 19 whites and 1,319 blacks in 1963, the tenth year of desegregation. White parents in Milwaukee even protested when some black children were transferred temporarily to white schools in 1963 while schools in predominantly black neighborhoods were being rebuilt. Years before busing roiled the educational waters, the pattern of school separation had been set.[25]

In the South, what garnered headlines in the years after the Supreme Court's 1954 *Brown* v. *Board of Education* decision was the way white politicians stood in the schoolhouse doors and the way southern white parents deserted the public schools for hundreds of all-white private academies. The most famous incident occurred in Prince Edward County, Virginia, where the white residents chose to shut down the public schools rather than desegregate them. The standoff lasted for five years, until the Supreme Court ordered the public schools reopened in 1964, during which time all the white children attended a newly created private school and the black children went without schooling until a privately financed school was opened for them in 1963. Given this white southern resistance, it is all the more remarkable that the percentage of southern blacks attending majority-white schools increased from nearly zero in the 1950s to about 35 percent in 1972, and peaked at more than 40 percent in the late 1980s. For almost three decades it has remained consistently higher than the percentages in the Northeast and Midwest. Though this evidence still shows remaining widespread racial separation, with most blacks attending predominantly black schools, the change is striking enough to support the notion that we were on the way toward an integrated America in the sixties, at least in a repentant South, until the racial extremists and opportunists thwarted our progress.

But the story is much more complicated than that. The South had never been as residentially divided as the North, because middle-class southern whites were accustomed to having their black gardeners, nannies, and domestic workers—their "help"—live nearby. Under segregation in the South, school integration wasn't an issue for whites because the neighboring black children were simply bused across town to all-black schools. But that all changed after the 1954 *Brown* decision, leaving southern whites with the difficult challenge of preventing a racial mix in schools that drew from a racially mixed population. Unlike the North in the fifties and early sixties, the South had few suburbs to which whites could flee. Instead, the white South borrowed a number of creative tactics that some northern cities had used to stall deseg-regation, and adapted them to their peculiar circumstances.

In an illuminating 1994 article on southern school desegre-gation that appeared in the education journal *Phi Delta Kappan*, Virginia educator Forrest R. White writes, "Suddenly the race was on to rezone, rebuild, and redevelop the cities in an all-out effort to create well-defined color barriers between neighborhoods, to isolate black populations, to demolish mixed-race areas, to relo-cate integrated schools, and otherwise to create an even more segregated society than had existed before *Brown*." Charlottes-ville, Virginia, carefully drew school zone lines in 1958 so that one black zone covered almost all the black kids who had hoped to attend a previously all-white school. Norfolk, Virginia, used ur-ban renewal as an excuse to bulldoze not the rundown buildings in the slums but the homes of middle-class black families whose children would have integrated the all-white schools. Other cities built highways, parks, and industrial zones to divide blacks and whites, and still others merged with nearby jurisdictions so they could gerrymander their school district lines according to race.[26]

It is fair to say that southern resistance to desegregated schools took many more subtle forms than blocking schoolhouse doors. The residential proximity between southern blacks and whites should have translated to even greater school desegregation over the years, but the white southerners who had benefited from this proximity found ways to minimize its impact on the schools. Today, as southern communities increasingly move toward the racially divided residential patterns of the North and as southern whites and blacks build their own suburban sanctuaries apart from each other, it should be no surprise that southern schools are resegregating at the fastest rate since the *Brown* decision four decades ago.

By the early 1960s, white America had built an effective de-fense against integrated education, just as it had with housing. Southern whites, ironically burdened by a residential propinquity with blacks that had served their interests for years, turned to Rube Goldberg–like measures to hold off full and complete de-segregation. Northern whites simply took to the suburban fron-tier, so much so that by 1965 one urban school official observed,

"We are fast running out of whites to integrate with Negroes." By the mid-1960s, even the most well-meaning urban educators found themselves echoing the sentiments of builder William Levitt, saying that the schools alone could not solve the nation's racial problem. As the Pittsburgh school board wrote in a report it issued in September 1965, "Racial integration is essentially a social and economic problem, not an educational problem. It is a problem that cannot be solved by the schools alone, even through the manipulation of children into a contrived 'balance.'. . . It is important that all of our citizens, Negro and white, comprehend the enormity of this task. As yet, no map has been made to show the integration route."[27]

Educators soon began to concede that the only way to achieve even a modicum of racial balance in the schools was to merge suburban and city school districts, or at least work out cooperative arrangements between them. The U.S. Commission on Civil Rights recommended precisely that in 1967. But proposals in St. Louis, Baltimore, New York and Philadelphia were immediately dashed by the suburban districts. Nor was the resistance limited to working-class and middle-class white suburbanites, as is commonly assumed. That these folks seemed angrier and more vehemently opposed to racially mixed schools reflects the fact that they were the white people most often on the front lines of desegregation policy. Consider wealthy Great Neck, New York, which in 1969 asked its residents to approve a modest proposal to bus about sixty kindergarten, first-grade, and second-grade black schoolchildren from nearby Queens into its schools. The plan wouldn't cost local taxpayers any money, and no more than three black children would be assigned to a particular classroom. Great Neck's liberal reputation and financial support for the civil rights movement in the South made the outcome obvious—until the votes were counted. The proposal lost. "Even your best friends who openly support the plan will vote their prejudices once they're behind that curtain," said Viron Jones, the director of Great Neck's NAACP chapter.[28] In 1974, the Supreme Court spared communities like Great Neck any further embarrassment. Its *Milliken* v. *Bradley* decision all but exonerated suburban communities from any responsibility to desegregate urban schools and eliminated any chance that black and white children would not be bound by the residential lines drawn by their parents.

If this nascent pattern of racially divided neighborhoods and schools didn't completely doom the integration dream by the early sixties, a third factor all but guaranteed it. At the very moment the civil rights movement succeeded in outlawing racial discrimination in America, a cruel, ironic, and at first largely unnoticed economic twist of fate befell a considerable segment of black urban America: the urban industrial economy began to fail. The kinds of unskilled and semi-skilled entry-level jobs that had supported the rise of the white middle class began to disappear from urban America just as blacks were legally empowered to claim their fair share of them. The jobs moved to the suburbs, to the Sunbelt and overseas—or vanished altogether as the industrial economy began to change. Now that the law was on their side, the economy wasn't. The resulting rise of the urban underclass defied easy solutions, fed racial stereotypes, reinforced antisocial behaviors among blacks, further divided black and white opinions on how to achieve racial progress, and offered white Americans yet another reason to retreat into their protected suburban enclaves.

The underclass really has its roots in the limited way that urban blacks were able to share in the prosperity of post–World War II America. True, the economy nourished a small but growing black middle class during those years, and many blacks took advantage of the rapid growth in public-sector jobs around the country, but the majority of blacks had at best a tenuous hold on the ladder of economic opportunity. By the sixties, a disproportionate number of blacks had for years been largely excluded from the industrial economy, either by employers who did not want them or by unions that kept them out. Many black workers who moved North in search of factory work during World War II found their jobs evaporate once the white soldiers returned. The experience of blacks stuck in "Negro jobs"—porters, janitors, servants, waiters—contrasted sharply with the experience of immigrant families, whose prospects often improved after a generation.

Particularly onerous were the union restrictions, because they virtually locked large numbers of blacks out of the robust urban economic boom of the post-World War II years. Although some unions, most notably the United Auto Workers, received high marks for racial inclusion in the 1950s, many others resembled the most segregated institutions in the South. The united front that organized labor portrayed at the 1963 March on Washington masked an all-white urban ethnic culture that permeated many unions. Until 1964, the International Association of Machinists allowed its local chapters to keep out blacks. Other unions weren't quite so explicit but practiced exclusion nonetheless. Most renowned for excluding blacks were the building trade and construction unions, which is especially ironic given that they were building the cities that blacks would increasingly occupy and whites would abandon. There were no blacks in New York's 3,200-member Sheet Metal Workers Union in 1963, and only two in Local 2 of the 3,300-member Plumbers Union. Of the Washington, D.C., union locals involved in building the gym at historically black Howard University in 1963, the Plumbers, Sheet Metal Workers and Steamfitters had no blacks, and the Electrical Workers had only three. Between 1953 and 1963, only six blacks completed the five-year apprentice training program to qualify for membership in Chicago Journeymen Plumbers Local 130. Of the 3,900 union apprentices in all trades in the majority-black city of Newark, New Jersey, in 1964, only 14 were black. The Labor Department reported in 1963 that only 300 of the 5,658 skilled journeymen employed on forty-seven federal construction projects that year were black. Blacks who made it into construction jobs were concentrated in the "trowel trades" at the lowest end of the industry's wage scale. Anything beyond that ran into the father-and-son clauses and other devices that unions used to keep jobs within their own ethnic communities.[29] The industrial-based middle class that reshaped America in the 1950s was largely built to the exclusion of blacks.

Although the union movement would soon open its ranks to blacks and antidiscrimination laws would begin to provide legal protections against bias on the job, it was a bit like being invited to the party after the buffet had been picked over and the guests had begun to leave. The declining industrial economy is often viewed as a 1970s problem, for that is when its full impact hit the average American worker, but for urban blacks the job drain began in the late 1950s—just as blacks were starting to make legal headway against employment discrimination—and it never stopped.[30]

Between 1957 and 1966—boom years in the American economy—the number of blacks in the private-sector work force stagnated. The city of Detroit's share of the metropolitan region's manufacturing jobs declined by nearly a third during that time, while St. Louis' share declined by more than 20 percent—numbers almost inversely related to the rising black population in these cities. The drop in retail, service, and wholesale jobs was steep as well.[31] Only in public-sector jobs did blacks see a significant increase. Manufacturing jobs that didn't move to the suburbs often moved overseas. In 1964 a leader of the International Union of Electrical, Radio, and Machine Workers suggested that the union drop the word "Radio" from its name because there were virtually no more radio jobs left in the United States. It wasn't long before shoe workers, steel workers, and garment workers started feeling the pain. Unionized jobs in the private sector began to decline around this time. Other urban jobs simply fell victim to the dynamism of the economy. The railroad industry, a major employer of blacks, all but collapsed in the two decades after World War II. Automation and mechanization further eroded the blue-collar jobs base, the first rung on the middle-class ladder, and led to an increased demand for workers with skills and an education, which many blacks at the time simply didn't have. In 1967 *Newsweek* magazine summed up the plight of inner city blacks: "The Negro arrived with few more marketable assets than a strong back at precisely a period of history when strong backs were becoming obsolescent."[32] Those who say that the cities began to decline when the black middle class moved away miss an important point: The jobs that would have replenished the middle class largely disappeared.

By the mid-1960s, the urban black community was caught in an economic Catch-22: when jobs were plentiful, blacks had only limited access to them; when their access improved, the jobs started to disappear. In 1966, while the overall white unemployment rate hovered around three percent and the overall black rate neared eight percent, inner-city unemployment was already

at the Depression level of around 20 percent and stood significantly higher among black youth. Employed urban blacks were
concentrated in the unskilled and semiskilled jobs that were most
vulnerable to economic vicissitudes, and they worked substantially shorter weeks than did similarly situated whites. As early as
1964, Herbert Hill, labor director for the NAACP, warned that if
these trends weren't reversed, "we're going to have a permanent
black underclass—permanent unemployables."[33]

Meanwhile the white population saw their own lives getting
better and began to wonder why most blacks didn't seem able
to share in the prosperity. The small but growing number of
"showcase Negroes" hired for visible positions in many companies only confirmed what whites suspected all along: the problem
wasn't with society or discrimination but with blacks themselves.
What whites couldn't see—what few people could see—was that
by the time of the greatest civil rights triumphs in the 1960s, before riots, drugs, and violent crime devastated the inner cities,
the stage had already been set for a permanent black underclass
that would provide the perfect excuse for a society unwilling to
integrate. Thus, a visible and conspicuous population of impov-
erished inner city blacks—isolated socially, economically, psychologically, and physically, but menacing precisely because of their
isolation—has served to reinforce white fears, stereotypes and basic assumptions about blacks and has furnished a prime excuse
for whites to move from their homes rather than call a black person their neighbor.

The Roots of White Backlash

Perhaps most jarring about the Boston busing battles in the
1970s were the recurring images of fine, decent, upstanding
middle-American parents with their faces twisted in anger and
rage over the prospect of black children attending their neighborhood schools. How could this have come about?

The genealogy of white backlash has generally been traced to
middle-class resentment against the liberal social policies of the
late 1960s, particularly busing and affirmative action, and to a
generalized fear of black lawlessness that began with the 1965

Watts riot and now shows up in the randomness of violent crime. Implicit in this version is that most whites embraced the apparent gradualism of the early civil rights era and would have remained in the moderate or liberal camp had they not been driven away by social engineering elites and the unshackled, sociologically condoned fury of blacks. Call them what you wish—the angry whites of today, the Reagan Democrats of the eighties, or the Silent Majority of the seventies—but the impression is of decent people who work hard, pay taxes, believe in fairness, and simply think that it's tough enough for everyone so no one deserves a special break. Had the government not tried to impose racial balance in their schools and reverse discrimination in their jobs, and had blacks not demanded special treatment while tearing down the cities, white anger never would have welled up in the late sixties and integration would have proceeded smoothly without all the bitterness and ill will. Or so we are led to believe.

Yet as we have seen in this chapter, many of these same whites voted against real integration with their feet as early as the 1950s, and there was no shortage of overt backlash among self-proclaimed moderates even during the halcyon days of the civil rights era—before affirmative action, race riots, black power and busing supposedly alienated them. Praise for the bedrock fairness of America's middle class is a staple of political rhetoric these days, but the bottom-line is this: from the very beginning of the civil rights movement, from the moment desegregation became the law of the land, most whites were willing to accept and indeed applaud a degree of public interaction with blacks, but drew the line when it came to family, home, social life, school and work—the linchpins of real integration. Whenever and wherever blacks threatened to cross that line, whites first tried to flee and then, tired of running, resisted and fought. "I know people in Chicago who have moved three or four times," said Democratic Representative Roman Pucinski of Illinois in 1966, "and now they are saying, 'I'm not going to move again. I'm going to make my stand here.' " In the same September 9, 1963, issue of *U.S. News & World Report* that reported King's inspiring speech at the March on Washington, the magazine also described both "a sudden growth of resistance to Negro demands in many Northern communities" and "a spreading mood of fear and resentment among white people almost everywhere in the U.S." Three-quarters of the whites in a *Newsweek* poll around that time said "the Negro is moving too fast," and about half of white New Yorkers in a 1964 *New York Times* poll felt that the nonviolent protests—like the ones led by King—were hurting the "Negro's cause." Cleveland's mayor pinned the blame on "extremists" and said that white people "are getting fed up." The word *backlash* itself was coined in the summer of 1963 and reflected a current that had been gaining strength for some years. The contours of today's racially charged politics were clearly evident back then.[34]

Remember, that was 1963, before affirmative action, riots and busing, when King tugged at our collective conscience and our nation supposedly unified behind the integration ideal. The fact that the backlash did not seem as vocal or visceral as it did in Boston a decade later did not mean it was any less compelling or strong. As pollster Louis Harris put it in July of 1964, "the white backlash itself exists, lurking more or less menacingly in the background," and "suburbanites are the strong silent partner to overt anti-Negro sentiment."[35] It is thus fair to ask whether the controversies over affirmative action and busing actually created the current tensions between blacks and whites, as today's conventional wisdom suggests, or if they simply enabled us to rationalize what was already there. As moderate civil rights leader Whitney Young, head of the National Urban League, observed as early as the summer of 1963, "If we're told to give up certain tactics because we might lose our white friends, we can't be so sure that we had those friends to begin with." The Chicago Urban League director, Edwin Berry, put it more bluntly in 1966: the phrase "white backlash" is a misnomer, he said. "It's white front-lash. It's a prejudice that's always been there."[36]

According to most political observers at the time, the typical kitchen table discussion in America in the early 1960s did not center on Russia, Cuba or Vietnam—it centered on race. "I'm not sure that this is a thing that can be reached by public-opinion polls," a prominent Democratic source told *U.S. News & World Report* in 1963. "Many, many people will not express their real feelings because they do not wish to appear to be bigots." A Chicago Republican boss told *Newsweek* the same year, "The key issue is white versus black, and it's much deeper than people realize." Yet in public most moderate politicians remained decorous and cautious, not wanting to violate the new social norm against overt bigotry, not wanting to breach the ethic of goodwill and the illusion of imminent integration. It was "the silent issue," as one politician called it—until people got into the voting booth.[37] All they wanted was a way to express it without appearing prejudiced. As noted earlier, a number of liberal cities—Berkeley, Seattle, Tacoma—as well as the state of California defeated open housing laws by resounding margins in 1963 and 1964. Then actor Ronald Reagan voted with California's majority on this issue, saying that there was no need for the law, that most people were fair and open-minded, and that black charges of housing discrimination were merely "staged attempts to rent homes, when in truth there was no real intention of renting, only causing trouble."[38] Blacks, in other words, were creating the problem and pushing too hard. Other 1963 election results revealed similar sentiments: Kansas City voters came within 1,743 votes of defeating a law that would prohibit discrimination in taverns, stores, amusement parks, and other places of business; resentful white voters in heavily Democratic Philadelphia nearly succeeded in throwing out the incumbent mayor because of his perceived accommodation to blacks; an expected Democratic landslide in Kentucky's gubernatorial race turned into a razor-thin margin of victory after the retiring Democratic governor issued an executive order barring discrimination in establishments under state license. Racial rhetoric was rarely in the forefront of these campaigns, with politicians wrapping their speeches in the more acceptable framework of neighborhood schools, states' rights, freedom of choice, or the right of private individuals, groups, landlords, and business establishments to associate with whomever they wish. But the message was clear.

By spring of 1964 white backlash had become strong enough to embolden Alabama's segregationist governor George Wallace to test the presidential waters and gauge the depth of white resentment outside his native South. Wallace, ever the crafty demagogue with his finger placed firmly on the nation's racial pulse, knew better than to challenge the new national norm against bigotry and base his appeal directly on race. "I am not campaigning as a segregationist," he told overflow audiences throughout the Midwest and West, and he discussed the subject only when someone brought it up. Instead, he tapped into America's traditional distrust of government, blasting federal intrusion into individual and states' rights. "Certainly I wouldn't tell you to segregate or integrate or anything else," he told students at Earlham College in Indiana. "You know more what is right in your state than I do." Through Wallace, the honorable rhetoric of political conservatism had become a cover for racial resentment. In the three key primaries he entered, Wallace received 34 percent of the vote in Wisconsin, 30 percent in Indiana, and 43 percent in Maryland. "I want to be able to say who I can associate with, where I live, where I send my kids to school," a white Milwaukee welder told a reporter who asked why he voted for Wallace. "I don't want a police state with the government telling me what to do."[39] All this occurred before black power, riots, busing, and affirmative action.

In October 1964, one of America's greatest political journalists looked into the crystal ball and wrote a prophetic, searing essay for *Life* magazine on white middle-class resistance to integration. Backlash, observed Theodore H. White, is "as invisible, yet as real, as air pollution." It would probably not show up in the 1964 presidential election results, he wrote, but it "is an unease whose impact will be felt not as much now as over the long range," particularly as whites see increasing black encroachment on their holy trinity of home, school and work. For the Democrats, the long-term peril of a divided party is clear, he noted. The Republican party, "born in racial strife, [must] choose whether it abandons its tradition and becomes the white man's party or refreshes its tradition by designing a program of social harmony." And so he concluded: "Only one political certainty can be stated now which will outlast next month's election: If, at this time when the nation is so rich and strong, both parties ignore the need for constructive answers to the question 'What Do They Want?' then disaster lies ahead—and backlash—the politics of chaos—will carry over, its snap growing in violence from 1964 to 1968 and all the elections beyond, until the question *is* answered."[40]

The pattern had clearly been set for whites by the early 1960s: acceptance of integration in public, rejection of integration in private. Thus we see the genesis of today's integration illusion: the public acclaim for the progress we have made, the importance of integration symbolism, the overt demonstrations of racial harmony, the rejection of blatant bigotry, the abstract support for neighborhood and school integration—all coupled with the continuing resistance to living, learning, playing, and praying together. That we see the same spine-stiffening opposition to real integration in 1963 that we do today should tell us—at least in terms of white willingness—that integration was no more realistic back then than it is now.

The Roots of Black Anger

In the early sixties, blacks also felt a greater wariness of integration than our current myths would have us believe. We like to think of the early sixties as a time of patience and promise, one characterized by the deep and abiding dignity of the civil rights movement and the uplifting dream that the color line could indeed be dissolved. Blacks were portrayed as noble victims, willing to set aside three centuries of frustration for the good of the whole, trusting the good faith of whites, and ready to integrate once whites welcomed them. "The biggest asset that white Americans have is Negro patience," wrote *Newsweek* in 1963.[41] According to this story line, not until the late 1960s did black anger well up: black radicals took over college buildings, the Black Panthers flaunted their guns, black community leaders demanded control over their schools, and the Black Power movement—coddled by elitist white liberals—eclipsed civil rights moderates as the voice of black America and undermined our national consensus.

This tidy division of the sixties into the early era of noble Negroes and the later period of angry blacks fits with the myth that we could have achieved so much more had the purveyors of ill-will and animosity—and their apologists—not gotten in the way. But once again there is more to what happened than what we would like to believe. It is true that the civil rights movement under King was characterized by an extraordinary degree of magnanimity and forbearance. It is true that blacks have faced their tormentors and hardships over the years with remarkable optimism and endurance. And it is true that most blacks expressed a strong desire to integrate. But to mistake the patience of civil rights protests for an absence of deep frustration and anger is to misread the mood of black America at the time. For below the surface of the early civil rights movement, and outside the reach of any civil rights legislation, a strong undercurrent of black frustration and alienation was welling up, one that continues to define black-white relations today. King understood this frustration and harnessed it brilliantly into nonviolent demonstrations. The master tactician in him also knew that manifestations of anger would undermine the sympathy he was cultivating among whites. But he also feared for his ongoing ability to control it. He knew that the disparity between the dream and the reality could shatter the consensus any day, anytime. The Black Power movement of the late 1960s didn't create the anger, but merely gave vent to it.

Consider for a moment what a middle-class black American family was seeing in 1963. Beyond the uplifting images of King at the Lincoln Memorial and civil rights heroes resisting white brutality in the South, they saw the stark realities of black life in a white America. If this family wanted to move to the suburbs, the options were few, and only in black communities. If this family moved near a white block or its children registered in a predominantly white public school, massive white flight took place. This family saw the inner cities becoming more crowded and isolated, their boundaries hardening. Quality union jobs remained largely unattainable, and since 1954 black unemployment was up and the income gap between whites and blacks had barely changed. Another aspect of this family's experience was the great new expectation setter, television, which Theodore White in 1964 described as "a prison with glass walls" for black America, a window into the world that their fellow citizens did not really want them to enter.[42] As much as blacks appreciated white sympathy for the civil rights cause, it was not sympathy they wanted but something much more elusive: full and complete acceptance as people.

For Kenneth Clark, the black psychologist whose research on the ill effects of segregated schools influenced the Supreme Court's *Brown* v. *Board of Education* decision, these echoes of black frustration sounded like firebells in the night. "The Negro youth, as I see them here in my work at Harlem Youth Opportunities Unlimited," he said in June 1963, "seem increasingly alienated from white America. The Black Muslim philosophy of hatred for whites has permeated their thinking to a disturbing extent. In general, Negro youths seem to feel that they cannot hope for justice from white America and that, therefore, they must experiment with techniques of complete isolation—separation from the whites." Sociologist Harold Isaacs, in a 1962 article on the black mood for the Jewish intellectual magazine *Commentary*, worried that "a new kind of despair rises side by side with hope, often in the breast of the same person, bringing with it a new uprush of alienation: if I am really never going to get *in*, a man says to himself, then let me get the hell *out*." This deepening frustration was not lost on the great purveyor of hope, Martin Luther King, who said in 1963: "You must defeat segregation in Chicago because the de facto segregation of Chicago is as bad as the de jure segregation of Birmingham. We're through with tokenism and gradualism and see-how-far-you've-come-ism. We're through with we've-done-more-for-your-people-than-anyone-else-ism. We can't wait any longer. Now is the time."[43]

The frustration reached into every corner of black America. A UCLA study of the 1965 Watts riots found successful blacks steeped in profound frustration and as likely to riot as the poor.[44] In a curious way many blacks took a strange and defensive pride in both the riots and the militants. When King toured the burned-out streets of Watts after the riot, he was astounded to hear young black men tell him, "We won." King asked how they could say that when so many people died and the community was destroyed. "We won," they responded, "because we made them pay attention to us." Anger was an assertion of independence from a white society that didn't want them anyway, a safety valve for the creeping recognition that integration would likely never come about. And it was coupled with another phenomenon of the time, an emerging sense of black identity that was inspired by the anticolonial rumblings in Africa and found expression in new media outlets such as soul music radio and publications like *Ebony*. A new black approach to race relations was beginning to take shape, one no longer defined by accommodation and patience but instead by pride, power, defiance, anger, and an uncompromising insistence on being treated as equals.

For black Americans, anger is and has always been a double-edged sword. It is difficult to navigate society with it, yet it is impossible to be human without it. For much of our nation's history blacks hesitated to express their anger, not only because they feared retribution but also because they saw themselves bound to the society that made them so angry. The fact that overt expressions of anger can be self-destructive and further compound one's alienation is not lost on many blacks. But by the early sixties blacks also began to see it as cathartic in another way: Black anger scared whites. Some blacks took deep pleasure in this insight, believing that it turned the table on years of white dominance over blacks, on years of lynch mobs, shuffling, and overseers' whips. But as appealing as this anger may have been psychologically, it was a disaster for the integration ideal. Not only did it signify a break from white society, but it reinforced the tendency of blacks to distrust whites and ensured that whites would not want to get close enough to blacks to feel the full power of their wrath. Try as King and others might to channel it creatively and maintain the high moral ground, the frustration was real and could barely be contained even during the nonviolent civil rights years. It then fed off of white backlash, which itself fed off of black anger. This combustible combination was yet another factor present in the early 1960s that all but guaranteed the impossibility of real racial integration in America.

The True Prophets

It is deeply wrenching to look back at the sixties and not to see Martin Luther King's dream as a prophecy. But a candid look at the social forces swirling back then suggests that those with a more tragic perspective were indeed the true prophets of the day, people like the brilliant black author James Baldwin, who described the rage blacks feel when whites accept them "in ballparks, and on concert stages, but not in our homes, and not in our neighborhoods, and not in our churches."[45] To Baldwin, who wanted so badly for integration to succeed but knew it was ulti-

mately futile, the best we could expect was a peaceful desegregation, not true integration. Or we think of then-liberal author
Norman Podhoretz, whose shockingly candid 1963 essay "My
Negro Problem—and Ours" challenged the prevailing civil rights
image of racial harmony by describing the palpable but rarely acknowledged reality below the genteel surface, what he saw as an
abiding black hatred for whites and a visceral white fear of blacks.
Podhoretz saved his special contempt for Northern liberals who
spoke the integration game but then fled "in droves to the suburbs" or, if they stayed in the cities, sent their children to private
schools. "And it is because I am convinced that we white Americans are—for whatever reason, it no longer matters—so twisted
and sick in our feelings about Negroes that I despair of the present push toward integration," he wrote.[46]

Even more eerie is how the poisoned vision from the racial
fringes of the sixties seems today to have been almost prescient.
Former Mississippi governor Ross Barnett, a staunch segregationist who gained notoriety for trying to block the desegregation
of the University of Mississippi, reveled in the reports of white
flight in the North. "The Northern people don't really want integration," he said. "They don't want it any more than we do, even
though they say they do."[47] How right he was. Militant black
leaders like Malcolm X and Stokely Carmichael saw that integration was a futile waste of energy because whites would have none
of it. And even if whites were more willing, the whole idea of integration was an insult because it was built on the premise of black
inferiority. "Integration . . ." Carmichael wrote in 1966, "speaks
to the problem of blackness in a despicable way. As a goal, it has
been based on complete acceptance of the fact that *in order to have*
a decent house or education, blacks must move into a white
neighborhood or send their children to a white school. This reinforces, among both black and white, the idea that 'white' is automatically better and 'black' is by definition inferior." Now, it
is said that history, like politics, makes strange bedfellows, so
compare Carmichael's words with a 1995 opinion of Supreme
Court Justice Clarence Thomas, who views racial separation as a
matter of choice and sees nothing inherently wrong with it as a
fact of American life. "It never ceases to amaze me," he wrote,
"that the courts are so willing to assume that anything that is

predominantly black must be inferior. . . . [Their] position appears to rest upon the idea that any school that is black is inferior, and that blacks cannot succeed without the benefits of the company of whites."[48] Thomas may not want to trace his intellectual pedigree back to Carmichael, but their shared doubts about integration are increasingly finding voice throughout a growing and ideologically diverse swath of the black community, from supporters of Afrocentric schools to spurned integrationists resigned to a separate America. We have thus come full circle, from an era in which the skeptics of integration stood outside the mainstream to a present in which the mainstream—like it or not—resembles the prophesies of these skeptics.

Today as a nation we honor Martin Luther King because he speaks to our dreams and our aspirations to be free of the racial demons that have haunted us for nearly four centuries. These other, tragic prophets speak to our realities, to our frustrations and to the seeming hopelessness that we will ever lead anything but racially separated lives. Perhaps this is why so many young blacks today respect King but viscerally relate to Malcolm X. One symbolizes an unlikely ideal, the other a likely future. There is nothing wrong with looking back on the 1960s as an era of possibility. But sadly, it just doesn't apply to racial integration.

HOW
DID WE
GET HERE?

CHAPTER FIVE

What Keeps Us Apart?

A black father is speechless when his ten-year-old son asks him why there are only a handful of white kids left at his school. A white mother gropes for words when her daughter tells her about the laws that used to force black people to use different bathrooms and drink from different water fountains—and then asks why we're still separate if the laws no longer keep us apart. A teacher consoles a black thirteen-year-old girl, the only black student at school, who wants to know if she's really ugly or if there's another reason why the boys don't pay attention to her. We adults may be numb to the racial realities of American life. We may hesitate to move beyond the myths, evasions, and excuses that govern black-white relations. We may not want to plumb the depths of the chasm dividing us. But our children deserve an honest answer.

For most whites, race is an issue they would simply choose to avoid. Look, they might say, the civil rights laws took care of racism three decades ago and there's plenty of evidence that a black person who works hard and gets an education has all the advantages in this country. There are black celebrities, black millionaires, blacks on television, and blacks in high-profile government positions. Don't tell me this society hasn't opened up for blacks. Considering where we were forty years ago, we're doing pretty well. So what's the problem? Why keep bringing it up?

Why keep making it the white person's problem? Isn't it up to blacks to get the rest of their house in order?

Only when pressed further, only when pressed to admit that they avoid blacks whenever possible, will whites finally get to what they see is the heart of the matter. To them, the answer is unpleasant to acknowledge but seems eminently rational: they fear violent crime—specifically, black violent crime. Sure, they concede, not all blacks commit violent crimes, but who wants to take the additional risk. Freedom is meaningless without personal security, and if blacks are more likely than whites to threaten that security, it is appropriate to fear them. If it means unfairly suspecting someone simply because he's black, that's the price we all have to pay until blacks stop the random violence and killing. Life is about calculating risks and making choices, and one of those choices is to steer clear of blacks unless they're in a controlled environment, like work. It may be a bit of a stereo-type, and it risks stigmatizing innocent black people, but you can't take extra chances when life, family, children, home, and livelihood are all at stake.

In one of his more moving speeches on race relations, Presi-dent Clinton lent support to this view. Blacks, he said, need to "understand and acknowledge the roots of white fear in Ameri-ca . . . a legitimate fear of the violence that is too prevalent in our urban areas." Indeed, whites may not like strong-arm police tac-tics against blacks, and most abhorred what they saw in the Rod-ney King case, but deep down they acknowledge and accept the logic behind it. Many whites may feel a tinge of shame and regret when they click their car locks while driving through a predomi-nantly black neighborhood, even a middle-class black neighbor-hood, but click they do because the fear seems so real. Even Jesse Jackson admitted that he would "feel relieved" if the footsteps he heard on the street behind him belonged to "somebody white." Today, blacks make up about 13 percent of our population but commit about half the robberies and murders. Black teens are about eight times as likely to commit homicide as white teens. Prisons are filled with black men all out of proportion to their share of the population. Whites also point out that the sharp rise in violent crime began in the 1960s, not long after blacks began to crowd the cities. Unlike the Irish and Italians, whose crime rates soared during their first years in America but dropped to the national average after a generation, black crime rates have been consistently high over the years. And the difference today is that crime is so much more prevalent, in both fact and perception. In 1996, nearly 1.7 million violent crimes were committed in the United States, approximately one every nineteen seconds. According to one frequently cited estimate from the Department of Justice, five in six Americans will be victims of violent crimes, either completed or attempted, at least once during their lives.[1] Crime is a threat that feels palpable and real.

To many in the civil rights community, however, the white fear of black crime is way overblown and may be a cover for deeper prejudice. They argue correctly that most violent crime, more than 80 percent, occurs among people of the same race, which means a white American is much more likely to be murdered or robbed by another white than by a black. They point out that the upsurge in violence has no color, that according to FBI statistics the number of whites arrested for violent crimes has increased almost threefold in the past three decades, and that the white homicide rate would still surpass that of Europe and Britain. They also note that most blacks never commit a crime, and only a tiny fraction—below one percent—are ever charged with a violent crime.

Certainly these are compelling statistics. In a thoroughly analytic world they would impel whites to reconsider their reflexive association between blacks and crime. But the world is not analytic. Most people don't go through life calculating every action on the basis of a statistical spreadsheet. And it doesn't mean they're irrational. White people receive other information about blacks besides the statistics they might see in a newspaper. It just so happened that the rise in urban crime coincided with the growth of local television news as the primary source of information and images about our civic life. Especially in the 1960s, the only black people most whites saw were porters, domestics, and janitors during the day and criminals beamed into their living rooms at night. As crime became more lethal, and as blacks continued to commit a substantial share of it, the white association between blacks and crime began to harden. We will explore the issue of crime on television in more depth in the next chapter, but suffice it to say that in the early 1990s, during the height of the drug violence, Washington, D.C., residents were exposed to about a murder a night on their television news, almost all committed by blacks. An advertiser couldn't ask for better exposure to persuade the public. Even if whites commit as many or more crimes as blacks, most white Americans have plenty of other personal associations with whites. But they don't with blacks. They don't live near blacks, learn with blacks, socialize with blacks, or pray with blacks. Indeed, whites know very little about black life in America, except for what they see on television. So the black criminal stands out to whites in a way that he might not stand out to blacks. It is the reason why the Willie Horton image of a black man who raped and murdered a white woman resonated so powerfully with whites during the 1988 presidential campaign. It helps explain why aggressive or expressive behavior by young black males is often seen as threatening or intimidating by whites. It might tell us why, as one survey reported, large numbers of white university students say they have a physical fear of their black peers.[2] Add to all this another factor: regardless of their feelings for blacks, most whites suspect that blacks harbor a generalized resentment toward whites and an almost unconscious desire for payback after all these years. So whites add it all up. If blacks commit a lot of crimes, and if blacks don't like whites and at some level may want to get even with them, it may simply be better to avoid blacks altogether except in safe and public settings. The tragic irony here is that we are stuck in an integration endgame: racial separation magnifies white America's fear of blacks, which in turn impedes any progress toward ending that separation.

   White fear of black crime helps to explain a number of white behaviors toward blacks today. It helps explain why white ethnics living in inner-ring suburbs move when lower-income black neighborhoods begin to push up against the suburban borders. It helps explain why whites feel queasy about sending their kids to an inner-city high school with blacks. It helps explain why whites don't see law and order rhetoric as a political code for racism—and resent the implication when it is made. But white fear of black crime cannot explain white America's entire resistance to integration. Certainly it cannot explain the almost visceral reaction of whites to private or intimate contact with blacks. Although the black urban crime rate has exceeded the white rate for much of this century, violent crime was not much of a national issue or personal concern in the 1950s, when the current pattern of racial separation began. It would be hard to argue that fear of crime induced whites in the 1950s to prevent the few black GIs who had the means to buy a home from doing so in Levittown or communities like it or to flee from school districts when a few black first-graders sat down next to their children. Today the Hispanic crime rate is relatively high, but it doesn't seem to stop whites from accepting Hispanic families—even low-income Hispanic families—into their neighborhoods more readily than they accept blacks. Nor is crime very relevant today when it comes to explaining the continuing resistance to intermarriage and social interaction, or the discomfort whites feel when blacks are too closely associated with a consumer product, particularly a personal-care product. In Matteson, Illinois, the town described in chapter 2 that is trying to stem white flight through an advertising campaign, the fear of crime may initially have motivated some white residents to move out, but the fact that the crime rate has not increased for more than a decade and that the incoming black families have equal if not higher incomes than the remaining whites suggests that some other factor must be causing the continuing white evacuation. Black crime also cannot explain why the rare black homeowner living in an otherwise white suburb is advised to hide the family's identity in a box if they want to have even a prayer of selling their home, or why that same home might be appraised at a higher value if a white family happens to own it.

Certainly the other conventional explanation, affirmative action, cannot explain it. Whites moved their families away from blacks and complained about blacks getting better breaks even before the words *affirmative* and *action* were ever linked in a sentence. To suggest, as some do, that affirmative action leads whites to see blacks as inferior or less capable ignores the fact that affirmative action was designed partly as a counterbalance to these same prejudices. Those who say that affirmative action promotes balkanization and separation also have a tautological problem, given that the policy would never have been proposed if we had not been separated in the first place. To treat cancer with an experimental cure and then blame the cure for the cancer may make emotional sense but not logical sense. It is also curious that the critics who see affirmative action as divisive or promoting stereotypes cannot apply the same analysis to those who benefit most from the policy, white women. Clearly white men and white women are not about to live in separate neighborhoods, go to separate schools, or socialize at separate clubs because of affirmative action. Nor are white men about to think that their wives and daughters are less competent, capable, or intelligent because they have a little extra help in the job search. Politicians know that affirmative action is palatable to white audiences when described as a policy to benefit women, but associating it with blacks is a kiss of death. When Senator Jesse Helms ran his notorious 1990 campaign ads against affirmative action, he railed about racial quotas but stayed silent on women. The dispute over affirmative action appears more like a visible symptom than an underlying cause of our racial separation.

This is not to suggest that those who blame affirmative action for dividing us are not on to something. Affirmative action is the most conspicuous and evident manifestation of a larger trend in society, the rise of group rights, demands, grievances and solutions. Much has been written about our culture of victimization, a culture that seems to nourish group identity based on how strongly its members feel aggrieved. From the black perspective, feeling aggrieved as a group is perfectly justified. Indeed, it was almost imposed on them. After all, with the exception of native Americans, blacks are the only ethnic group in America that has been consistently defined as a group by law, and for most of our history it has been to their severe disadvantage. That they now seek recompense as a group seems logical, agree with it or not.

Whites, of course, look at it differently. To most whites, whose ancestors came to this country to escape group identification and persecution, this type of thinking seems eminently grating and atavistic. "Get on with your life and stop making excuses" is the refrain most often heard. As whites see it, they're tired of hearing the same old grievances from blacks. Interactions with blacks involve a moral burden that most whites no longer want to carry or feel they should have to carry. "My family didn't enslave anyone," is the typical white response. Whites see their own lives as tough and can't imagine that blacks—particularly as the most visible beneficiaries of such programs as affirmative action—can have it any tougher. Whites who feel this type of racial fatigue may be much less willing to interact with blacks privately and socially.

Racial fatigue may help explain why whites prefer the proximity of Hispanics and Asians to blacks, because immigrants, while occasionally aggrieved, also seem genuinely grateful to be in this country. It also may explain why whites often say there are two kinds of blacks, the few who act white and won't be a burden to spend time with, and the many who blame society and walk around with a righteous attitude, a chip on their shoulder. Whites simply cannot see how blacks can define themselves as a group— how they can walk around saying "It's a black thing; you wouldn't understand"—and then point the finger of racism at any white who dares to speak critically about blacks. Whites see so many racial double standards that they would prefer not to deal with them at all. Most whites choose their words carefully and always are amiable and polite when around blacks. But self-conscious civility is an effort, and it's just plain easier to avoid blacks altogether.

For their part, blacks may be equally hesitant to spend precious personal time with whites who claim to support integration but have little interest in understanding the black experience or accepting anything black, except for the black role in sports and entertainment. If whites criticize blacks for dwelling too much on race, blacks resent whites for not acknowledging the ubiquity of race. If whites condemn blacks for blaming their problems on racism, blacks see that condemnation as further evidence of racial insensitivity. Blacks see plenty of hypocrisy in the way whites denounce racial remedies for denying individual responsibility, and then use the transgressions of a few black individuals to generalize about the entire race. Perhaps most irritating to blacks is when white acquaintances pay what they see as the best compliment of all, "I don't think of you as black, you're different"—as if there were something about blacks that these whites find offensive, present company excluded, of course. So once the workday is over and there's no need to deal with whites, blacks ask themselves why they should put up with the racial double-talk and bother with people who make them so angry. All of this may explain a common phenomenon among blacks, that they often test a white person for racial sensitivity before opening up as a friend or accepting him into their social group—which whites frequently interpret as a sign of disinterest or hostility. Given these racial dynamics, the first victim is integration.

It is obvious to see how the racial strain over group identity and victimization has contributed to the maintenance of black-white separation, but as an explanation it only goes so far. Certainly it cannot explain why black homeowners must put their belongings in a box, why a black-owned home is appraised for less, why some whites feel mildly uncomfortable trying on clothes that a black customer has just tried on, why many whites balk at being seen by a black doctor, why whites will flee when more than a few blacks—even affluent blacks—move into the neighborhood, or why a white person is many more times likely to have an intimate relationship with an Hispanic or Asian than a black. And so we search for other answers.

Our journey takes us deeper into the chasm, where we are faced with questions that make few of us comfortable. "I have, for most of my adult life," wrote author Anthony Walton, "wondered what, exactly, is the stain we black Americans carry, what it is about our mere presence, our mere existence, that can inflame such passion."[3] Thirty-six years ago *Newsweek* offered an answer, and the question is whether it is still relevant today. In a 1963 analysis of race relations, *Newsweek* concluded that the reason "white Americans draw the line at the prospect of closer association with Negroes" is because of a general "revulsion" toward blacks. As *Newsweek* put it back then, "One conclusion that can be drawn from the patterns of prejudice is that the greater the suggestion of physical contact, the greater the white antipathy—and even revulsion." As evidence, the magazine found that 71 percent of whites in a Harris poll felt that blacks "smell different." Whites described blacks as dirty, oversexed, wild, and threatening. In a poll three years later, *Newsweek* still found a majority of whites saying that blacks "smell different."[4] Thereafter the question disappeared from the polls, no doubt an acknowledgment that whites understood the new social norm against bigotry and would answer accordingly. But the fact that it disappeared from the polls does not mean it disappeared from the people.

In his classic 1954 book *The Nature of Prejudice*, Gordon W. Allport described "sensory aversion," particularly to odor, as a basic indicator of prejudice. That there is no biological or scientific foundation to blacks and whites having different odors does not seem to change or mitigate the prejudice, Allport wrote, because it is the prejudice, not any odor, that drives the aversion. Other writers have attributed prejudice to a general repugnance based on the dominant group's ideal of beauty. According to this view, unpleasant qualities related to intelligence and morality are attributed to those who do not fit a society's visual standards.[5] In other countries with caste or ethnic divides, such as Japan, India, and New Zealand, out-groups are perceived as filthy, ugly and polluting the mainstream. For years Germans complained of a foul odor among Jews and described them overall as morally and physically unappealing. Certainly this is territory we explore with great trepidation today, because most Americans like to think that our society has been cleansed of such deep-down feelings, and most of us would never admit to them even if we held them. But it is at least fair to ask whether this aversion—or "revulsion"—persists in any form today, and whether it can explain, for example, why a white person might not want to live in a house previously owned by a black, or have an intimate relationship with a black.

There is a long history in America of white revulsion toward blacks. Thomas Jefferson, for one, described blacks as a race of inferior beauty and intelligence characterized by "a very strong and disagreeable odour."[6] So powerful was the notion of a black taint that white Americans developed the "one drop of blood" rule to define someone as black. Revulsion was also evident for years in the physical depiction of blacks, who were drawn with exaggerated, simian features that blurred the line between human and animal. For more than a century some whites have adopted pseudoscientific theories to rationalize this revulsion, the earlier theories suggesting that blacks are simply an inferior species, and the more recent ones claiming that blacks are genetically wired with a different sex drive, brain size, temperament, physique, and cognitive ability. The public brouhaha over the controversial 1994 book *The Bell Curve*, which claimed to prove racial distinctions in intelligence and cognitive ability, attests to the continuing power of pseudoscience among some whites.

How deep this revulsion goes among whites—if indeed it continues to exist in any consequential way—may be well nigh impossible to gauge. Many blacks would argue that the standard of beauty prevailing in society is a daily reminder of the way whites view blacks. Black models must have light skin, straight hair, and Caucasian features, especially if they are ever to be included in an ad for personal-care or luxury products marketed to whites. The black critic Stanley Crouch observed during the O. J. Simpson murder trial that Nicole Brown Simpson was constantly described as "beautiful" and "blonde," but O.J. was never referred to as "handsome, brown, woolly-headed O.J."[7] Thick lips, wide noses, kinky hair, brown skin—these characteristics evoke plenty of images among whites, but rarely is beauty among them. The 1960s "black is beautiful" philosophy, which celebrated these features, spoke directly to this prejudice.

Survey research offers another clue to the persistence of this deep-down prejudice. Given the antiracist norm in society and the tendency of whites to self-censor any bigoted expressions, the fact that it shows up even indirectly in polls suggests deeper roots than we might want to acknowledge. Perhaps the most accurate survey data available are from the General Social Survey conducted by the University of Chicago's National Opinion Research Center (NORC). Unlike most other polls, which ask yes or no questions as to whether blacks are less intelligent or more prone to violence than whites and thus send up a red-flag alert to respondents unwilling to be labeled racist, the NORC survey asks people to rate various characteristics of ethnic groups independently and then compares the answers. According to this survey, which has been conducted periodically throughout the 1990s, a comfortable majority of whites see blacks as less intelligent, lazier, and more prone to violence than whites—in other words, less appealing and at a lower level of civilization than whites.[8] The more conventional polls generally reveal a lesser degree of prejudice because of how they word the questions, but even they suggest troubling conclusions. A 1996 *Washington Post* poll found that one in six white Americans agreed that blacks fare worse in society because they lack an "in-born ability to learn."[9] What comes through in these findings is a clear message: they are not the same as I am, and it has to do with something inside them, not something that's been done to them.

Rarely does white aversion to blacks show up overtly anymore in our public culture. When it appears, it is usually when whites have their defenses down or see no risk of being accused of racism. It might rear up in a private communication, as in the notorious case of the Los Angeles police officers who described dealing with blacks as "monkey-slapping time" or "gorillas in the mist," or when people privately compare some high-profile black athletes to monkeys. It can come out during an unguarded moment in a newspaper interview, as when a Kansas business executive told the *Wall Street Journal* that he wouldn't move into a house vacated by blacks without painting the walls and replacing the carpet: "I can tell when the last person in my rental car or hotel was black," he told the paper, adding that people of different races have different, though "not necessarily bad," odors. It also shows up in all-white focus groups that discuss race, like one in which a white college student told his peers, "They're just different. It's kind of bad to say, but I mean they do have an odor that's different from the white people unless they cover it up with a deodorant or cologne or something of that nature. You know, their hair is different. . . . It's just that I don't seek interest in these people and I don't think I'm prejudiced because of that."[10] In the case of Rutgers University president Francis Lawrence, known as a racial progressive and ardent supporter of affirmative action, it came out when the fatigue of speaking got the better of him and he blurted out a connection between low SAT scores among blacks and their "genetic, hereditary background." In the case of a George Washington University student who fabricated a rape story involving two "muscular, young-looking black males . . . wearing dirty, torn clothing" and having "bad body odor," it was a useful stereotype to help her push buttons about the horrors of rape.[11] When a white minister confessed during the October 1997 Promise Keepers rally in Washington, D.C., that he used to wash his hands every time he shook a black man's hand, what struck some black observers as remarkable was not that he felt this way but that he admitted it.

Are these merely isolated instances? Or is there evidence beyond the anecdotal? Like public opinion surveys, traditional social science research faces various limitations when exploring the depths of feelings on race. When dealing with race, people are so well defended and wrapped in so many rationalizations that the research design has to be doubly evasive to avoid triggering the socially accepted response. That said, a number of research studies suggest that this aversion is fairly prevalent, that the mere sight or mention of a black person arouses in whites an assortment of unflattering thoughts and images about blacks. One classic 1970s study by University of Delaware psychologist Samuel Gaertner found that white liberals (members of New York's Liberal party) were six times more likely to hang up prematurely on a caller seeking help if that caller sounded black over the phone. In the experiment, the caller said he was trying to reach a towing company but must have gotten the wrong number. Since he was out of dimes, he asked the person to call the tow truck company for him. Click. As Gaertner and a colleague concluded in a later study, "Even if people genuinely attempt to reject the socially less desirable stereotypes and characterizations of blacks, it may be difficult for even the most well-intentioned white persons to escape the development of negative beliefs concerning blacks." In a more recent experiment, University of Wisconsin psychologist Patricia G. Devine studied hundreds of white students to test the depth and prevalence of racial stereotypes. She found that all the students were familiar with at least some negative stereotypes of blacks—such as aggressive, criminal, low intelligence, lazy, sexually perverse, ostentatious, and dirty or smelly—and automatically associated these stereotypes with blacks. Those who appeared to harbor less prejudice toward blacks also thought of these stereotypes but simply made a conscious effort to repress them. "Thus," she wrote, "even for subjects who honestly report having no negative prejudices against Blacks, activation of stereotypes can have automatic effects that if not consciously monitored produce effects that resemble prejudiced responses."[12]

This revulsion or aversion among whites would certainly be evident in the most personal of all interactions, physical intimacy with blacks. Fortunately we have come a long way from the days when it was not unusual for a white woman dating a black man to be committed by her family to a psychiatric institution. But the fact that this no longer happens does not mean the concern behind it has disappeared. It is just expressed more subtly today. For example, white women who date black men are stereotyped as sex crazed, as if the only thing that could possibly attract a white woman to a black man is his animal, primal side. Dr. Alvin Poussaint, a psychiatrist at Harvard Medical School, told us he receives requests for help "regularly" from white parents whose children—daughters, most often—date blacks. "They're calling me to ask me to do something for them. That something's wrong with their daughter for dating these men," Dr. Poussaint said. "Whites see it on a level that the person is mentally disturbed or emotionally troubled and needs psychotherapy." He knows liberal white families that boast about their racial tolerance until their son or daughter starts dating someone black, when it becomes "a different story." Dr. Poussaint believes that whites don't want blackness in the family, and don't want black grandchildren.[13]

Parents are not the only ones uncomfortable with interracial relationships. Various surveys indicate that as many as one in five white Americans (translating to about 27 million white adults) believe that marriage between blacks and whites should be outlawed, that a large majority of white women would not marry a black man, and that almost two-thirds of whites would object to a close relative marrying a black—and we assume, as we do with most polls on race, that they underestimate the real feelings of whites. Indeed, just look at the personal ads, which almost universally stipulate their potential mate's race.[14] Also worth noting is the fact that children of mixed marriages between whites and Asians tend to be accepted as white whereas children with white and black parents are usually labeled as black. In other words, in the eyes of white society, the child with a black parent is tainted.

Are we to conclude that something deep down—perhaps a fear of the unnatural, of contamination, filth, or impurity—is at work? Could this apparent aversion to personal intimacy be functioning when whites hesitate to buy a house lived in by blacks—as if the house were soiled, unsanitary, and unclean? Do whites draw the final color line because of this? We cannot forget that white Americans, for more than three hundred years, had to create moral and psychological justifications for the existence of slavery and segregation in this land of equality and freedom. How else could whites justify the contradiction except to eliminate the contradiction, to suggest that there was something repugnant, less human, about blacks—something that made black people the reason why slavery and segregation should exist. A justification so central to American culture for so long does not go away just because the institutions it was designed to justify no longer exist. It simply gets filtered down and manifested in more subtle ways—the result is the box that black homeowners must place their identity in. Even the most well-meaning whites are bound to internalize traces of this cultural legacy in much the same way they internalize the great ideals of our nation. We like to think we can divorce ourselves from the history we would prefer to forget, but is that truly possible?

There may be another way to look at this white fear of intimacy with blacks. If there is a constant in American history it is the desire to get ahead, to seize opportunity, to never look back. In the great competitive race to improve one's standing in life, Americans rarely want to be associated with what they've left behind, except when they act out of noblesse oblige. We see it in the children of immigrants who leave behind and often reject the customs and ways of the old country. We see it in the weak appeal of unions and other social justice movements, which remind Americans of where they were rather than where they want to be. We see it in the general rejection of redistributionist economic policies, as Americans identify less with the bottom and more with the top because they see themselves reaching the heights someday. We see it in the frantic search for status symbols—from cars to homes to clothes and designer labels—that will separate us from the hoi polloi.

Perhaps we apply this template to race. Throughout American history, blacks have stood at the very bottom of the social status ladder. Historian Edmund Morgan has observed that racism was not endemic to the American experience, but took root in the seventeenth century when the planter class needed to keep white servants and black slaves from uniting in common cause against them. "The answer to the problem, obvious if unspoken and only gradually recognized," wrote Morgan, "was racism, to separate dangerous free whites from dangerous slave blacks by a screen of racial contempt." Poor whites thus found compensation and satisfaction in their newly acquired status over blacks.[15] It is a pattern that has held ever since. Every new immigrant, as black author Toni Morrison put it, knew that "he would not come at the very bottom. He had to come above at least one group—and that was us."[16] To be associated with blacks is to be associated with someone at the bottom, and that is not the direction most Americans want to take in life.

Now consider the black-owned house that whites might be reluctant to buy: Because black people lived in the house, it might not be valued as much in the community, and thus the potential buyers would be stigmatizing themselves with their neighbors by purchasing it. Taking a job in a black-owned company might be seen among whites as wasting one's talents, a bad career move. Even the tensions aroused by interracial dating can be explained in this context. A white male might see his own reputation tainted if a sister or former girlfriend starts dating someone black. A white son or daughter who marries a black person would likewise be falling in status, not moving up in life. Status anxiety is a powerful force in American life, and it is even more powerful when intertwined with race.

The fact that white Americans have different thresholds of racial discomfort should be no surprise. The mere presence of blacks makes some whites anxious, while to others it is fine to work with blacks but not to live among them, and there are some who live in the same neighborhood with blacks but neither socialize with them nor see them as potential intimates. Though there are indeed some truly color-blind people who have no racial boundaries, rare is the white American who does not draw a color line at some level of intimacy. The difference among most whites is not whether they have a color line, but where they draw it. This shifting color line among whites helps explain why some whites move from a neighborhood as soon as the first black family moves in and others stay until the area is three-quarters black. It might also explain the political phenomenon whereby a larger percentage of whites are willing to vote for black candidates

at the faraway federal level than at the closer-to-home city council level.[17] Because there is no longer one clear, rigid, and legally
defined color line, as existed under segregation, and because
the racial comfort zone is much more elastic than at any other
time in our nation's history, we can maintain the illusion that society is integrating more than it is. But where integration truly
matters—in our lives, homes, neighborhoods, schools, and intimate relationships—white America still draws the line and will
continue to do so in the years ahead. W. E. B. Du Bois said the
problem of the twentieth century was the problem of color line; it
will continue to be the problem in the century ahead.

Perhaps there is no better word than bewildering to describe
the current discontent among blacks with the integration ideal.
At no time in our history has life been better and more promising
for the vast majority of black Americans. Their overall standard
of living is up, they have more plentiful economic opportunities
than ever, their dollars count in the consumer economy, and they
have a highly visible role in our public life and media. For years
blacks labored under the deep desire to be included in society.
They hoped and indeed assumed that increasing contact would
break down white prejudice and lead to a true acceptance, a true
integration that would acknowledge society's debt to them but
transform skin color from a decisive to an incidental factor in in-
terpersonal relationships. But after years of forbearance and for-
titude, after making such significant strides, the mood among
blacks seems to be souring and many are now questioning integration as an article of faith. Why?

Almost a century ago W. E. B. Du Bois wrote of a "double-
consciousness" or a "twoness" almost every black American feels,
the "sense of always looking at one's self through the eyes of others, of measuring one's soul by the tape of a world that looks on
in amused contempt and pity." To Du Bois, the great striving
among every black American is to be free of this double-
consciousness, "to be both a Negro and an American" without being constantly reminded that being a Negro will limit his life as
an American.[18] In many ways Du Bois articulated the integration
ideal that has defined race relations for much of this century. To
see a black person without first seeing his color will liberate

blacks from their twoness and whites from their prejudice, and lead to a society ready for real integration.

The trouble is, we are nowhere close to this ideal, and most blacks know it. Many blacks believe they will never be free from the yoke of twoness and will forever be condemned to live under its weight. So out of anger, fatigue, resignation, or affirmation, they seek to minimize this burden by limiting their contacts with whites and gravitating to what they see as nonracial, predominantly black environments. If their worklife is defined by this twoness, they certainly don't want the rest of their lives determined by it. The fact that whites see this retreat as self-segregation or as a race-conscious rejection of integration is ironic to most blacks, who seek this racial safe haven partly because they do not believe whites are capable of interacting with them in anything but a race-conscious way. As blacks see it, the only way to transcend race is to be with people capable of transcending it, and few whites seem to qualify. To whites, it may sound illogical to hear that predominantly black environments are nonracial rather than race-conscious, but to blacks it makes perfect sense—much the way whites don't think twice about being around all whites, or the way Jews often describe living in Israel. In many ways blacks, within their limited context, are seeking to replicate the carefree interactions of life as a racial majority, for the majority never lives with the burden of twoness. To a white person who claims he is blameless, that blacks are the ones who have pushed race consciousness through policies like affirmative action, blacks just laugh to themselves and wonder what that white person would do if three black families moved onto the block or if a black man started dating his sister.

To almost any black person, every day spent living among whites requires racial coping skills, the ability to navigate the twoness Du Bois described. Blacks are aware that every decision, every action, every gesture and word might be judged by whites in a racial context. Black men know that walking down the street and simply looking at a white woman will elicit fear and suspicion. Blacks who regularly eat lunch together at work wonder how that's interpreted by their white colleagues, who themselves never seem concerned that they might be sitting at an all-white lunch table. Will a memo with a few typos or grammatical mistakes be judged racially? Will whites take offense if I put an Africa or Nelson Mandela poster in my office? If I don't outperform everyone will that bring discredit to my race? Author Melvin Van Peebles summed up these feelings when he wrote, "If I stand, I'm loitering. If I walk, I'm prowling. If I run, I'm escaping." It is a feeling that at times reaches almost absurd levels. *Washington Post* columnist William Raspberry writes that he knows blacks who pretend not to like watermelon simply because they don't want to fit into the stereotype of blacks who eat watermelon.[19]

But whether absurd or sublime, this twoness is deeply felt among blacks. "I'm so highly visible when I go searching for a home," one Long Island black executive said, "that immediately everything I've worked for is shredded, and I become naked again to man and I seem to become a Mississippi sharecropper." Respected journalist Charlayne Hunter-Gault told *Fortune* magazine, "The reason even well-heeled blacks are angry is that even if you live in an ivory tower, work in a glass-enclosed office with Picassos on the wall, carry a briefcase, and dine at '21,' you're still never far from that old line: 'What do you call a black man with a Ph.D.? A nigger.'" Earl Graves, the wealthy publisher of *Black Enterprise*, observed, "You can graduate from Yale and Harvard business school, but you can't graduate from your blackness."[20] Is it possible that blacks read too much into their dynamics with whites? Certainly. Does every comment or reaction from a white derive from racial prejudice or discomfort? Certainly not. But is there enough evidence to suggest that blacks have a legitimate reason to be defensive? It would be hard to deny it.

The degree to which race infiltrates the very mind-set of blacks can be seen in a late-1980s survey that asked Americans whether they believe their lot in life is determined by factors within their personal control. Nearly 70 percent of whites said yes, but fewer than half of all blacks did.[21] Blacks may find ways to cope with racial issues but rarely do they think they can control them. Many blacks who want to believe in the declining significance of race and pursue the integration path often find that they or their children face racial situations or limitations they weren't prepared to deal with, and often they return to their racial roots for refuge. Blacks socializing among themselves will often expend a lot of energy talking about the latest remark, scenario, or incident involving a white colleague, pedestrian, employer, or public figure. Whites who overhear such a conversation might think that mountains are truly being built out of molehills, but such a conversation cannot be separated from the accumulation of indignities large and small to which blacks are subjected in life. Certainly talking about it, even dwelling on it in conversation, is one way to cope. "We laugh at the ignorance of white people," wrote one black author. "But it is a laugh with layers of bitterness and rage. We laugh instead of striking out."[22]

For many blacks these layers of bitterness and rage cannot always remain hidden by laughter. "I think we, the children of the dream, often feel as if we are holding 30-year bonds that have matured and are suddenly worthless," wrote author Anthony Walton in 1989. "There is a feeling, spoken and unspoken, of having been suckered. This distaste is festering into bitterness."[23] Members of the black middle class in particular feel they have done everything white society asked of them, yet whites still move away when more than a few blacks move to the neighborhood. Blacks bristle at the idea that bigotry is a thing of the past because it denies the subjective reality of their daily lives. They resent the notion of equivalence between their own grinding experience in America and that of the white male who believes he was wronged by affirmative action. They get tired of hearing whites tout their own tolerance credentials and proclaim their own racial virtue when in truth these same whites barely acknowledge blacks outside the office and would probably pull their kids out of the local public school if too many blacks enrolled. Especially irritating for blacks is how whites criticize them for dwelling on race but never acknowledge how they themselves make so many judgments based on race. To blacks, white hypocrisy and sanctimony seem to be everywhere. Like compound interest, the resentment builds on itself and pushes blacks further from whites.

Containing this resentment is a greater struggle for blacks than most whites realize. Journalist Sam Fulwood III told us that part of being a middle-class black is learning "to control your rage around white people. You only show it or flash it when you're in a safe environment around other black people. When you go home you can express your outrage, your anger towards 'the man,' 'the system,' or 'whiteness.' "[24] The daily indignities may add up, but middle-class blacks at least have the financial and psychological resources to channel their anger or take the edge off it. A vacation can help, or a night on the town, or an evening at the movies, or the Sunday afternoon gathering to watch the football game. Middle-class blacks also know that in this day and age, no slight or indignity can take away what they have earned in life. For young people and those more vulnerable in life, however, the defenses against venting anger are not always so available. "I sometimes get out of hand and my hate comes through," a black high school student said in a Montgomery County, Maryland, focus group discussion with his peers, "and I talk about hurting them because they talk down to us and think that we're nothing and they don't want us to be anything and they don't realize what we go through and what we put up with every day." Those with the least at stake in society are often the ones most overwhelmed by their frustrations. "They take it out any way they can," said the student in the focus group.[25]

Perhaps the most corrosive effect of black anger is the one it has on blacks themselves. Years ago blacks internalized the anger and turned it to a form of self-loathing that resulted in the desire to bleach their skin and straighten their hair. Today, some young blacks turn their anger on themselves when they transform the words *bad, gangsta* and *nigger* into compliments and scorn peers who succeed in school as "acting white." Even more chilling is the startling rise in suicide rates among young black males. Between 1980 and 1993, the rate for boys 10 to 14 years old increased 73 percent for whites but 358 percent for blacks; for teenage males 15 to 19 years old it increased 23 percent for whites but 157 percent for blacks; and for young men between the ages of 20 and 24, it fell slightly for whites but increased 30 percent for blacks.[26]

In adults, racial stress is often manifested in their outlook and health. One researcher found "an overwhelming sense of hopelessness" among entry-level black corporate employees, while another found high levels of hypertension and other ailments among black workers who experience discrimination.[27] Racial stress also leads to the angry defensiveness of some blacks toward even legitimate criticism by whites, as if pointing out something negative means that the critic is calling the entire race inferior. As part of our own research we interviewed a number of prominent black leaders and citizens, and three of the most accomplished we talked with, in near stream-of-consciousness conversation, spilled out the deep rage contained within. One described how alcohol nearly destroyed him, another said he needed to maintain his optimism "to keep from committing suicide," and the third told us that the only thing keeping him from going "crazy" and coming to work "with an AK-47 [to] shoot people" was the separation he maintains from whites in his private life.[28] None of the three will ever resort to these behaviors, but the fact that such distinguished and brilliant men have these feelings so close to the surface shows how compelling and real the anger must be.

Whites are not blind to black anger and see it on or just below the surface. Part of white fear of black crime is the idea that black-on-white crime is not really random, that black rage toward whites actually leads to violence against whites. Whites describe how they consciously bite their tongues and refrain from obscene gestures when irritated with a black driver, but wouldn't show the same restraint if the other driver were white. Blacks know their anger frightens whites and pushes them even further away. That is why middle-class blacks work so hard to contain it when they are around white colleagues and employers. Other blacks take advantage of white fears by channeling their anger to arouse white guilt and perhaps obtain some short-term political benefit. Still others take silent pleasure in finally having a way to put white people on edge. Some young blacks even have fun with the anger, using it to intimidate whites in a nonverbal mind-game that seems momentarily satisfying when they are walking on the sidewalk or crossing the street—put on an attitude and see how they run.

Anger is exhausting, both to feel and to fear it. Even turning it into a mind-game with whites means you are expending energy on an emotion built on payback and resentment. It is perhaps the primary reason from the black side why integration cannot work. There's little evidence that black anger will disappear or dissipate. Nor should it, under current circumstances, because it is a human reaction to deep frustration and indignity—and to carrying the heavy burden of twoness. But as long as it remains a powerful force in black America, it will push blacks away from whites and whites away from blacks. Many blacks simply ask themselves: Why even try to integrate if whites will not change and if all my efforts will only increase my anger?

In many ways, the black anger we see today is an offspring of the integration ideal itself. To create an unreachable ideal and to hold it up as a measure of progress is to set black America up for resentment and frustration. "The integrationist's assurance that individuals need only an opportunity to prove their worth has led innumerable underachieving ethnics into a blind alley," wrote historian John Higham twenty years ago in a book on ethnic assimilation in America. "They must conclude either that they are indeed unworthy or that the proffered opportunity was fraudulent. The result is either self-hatred or alienation from society. It can frequently be both."[29] For blacks, this blind alley must seem endless, for their challenge has not been one of achievement but of acceptance, and thus they have little ultimate control over the end result. Indeed, most blacks have played by the rules, worked hard, sacrificed, taken their lumps, even earned their own small corner of the American Dream. Yet they have seen other ethnic groups—even those considered the most difficult to melt—gain enough acceptance to enable them to shed their own double-consciousness. So they are left with an integration ideal that inspires but frustrates, that promises but disappoints. And they are tired of feeling angry. They are fatigued by race relations, by chasing the dangling carrot of integration. All this explains why so many blacks are now determined to build up their own communities, businesses, markets, and institutions so that they will, at least for part of their existence, be free from the double-consciousness that continues to rule their lives.

CHAPTER SIX

Virtual Integration: How the Integration of Mass Media Undermines Integration

The *Time* magazine cover called it "a death in the family." The *New York Times* described the outpouring of grief "as if it were a death in the family. In a way it was." Americans black and white, from every region and social standing, grieved with Bill Cosby at the tragic loss of his son, Ennis, who was gunned down on the side of a freeway in January 1997. Few Americans knew much if anything about Ennis Cosby before his death, but we reacted almost as if we knew the family personally. And in a way we did. Seven months later we grieved again when Britain's Princess Diana lost her life in a sad and gruesome car accident. She was Diana to us, someone we felt we knew, a constant presence in our lives, a woman whose wedding we vicariously attended and whose intimacies seemed more familiar to us than those of our closest friends. For many of us the loss was profound and deeply personal. It reminded us of the shared national mourning for a dead president more than three decades earlier, when we felt the pain of a grieving widow and her two small children who were too young to comprehend the enormity of their loss. Since those poignant days in November 1963, the Kennedy family has become our own.

For half a century now people like Princess Diana and Bill Cosby have entered our lives and homes through the remarkable medium of television. Television has brought us national leaders and fictional characters, personalities and eccentrics, Kennedys and Seinfelds, Oprah Winfrey and Dan Rather, Beaver Cleaver and Mr. Whipple, Ronald Reagan and Michael Jordan, Barbara Walters and Bart Simpson—a list so long yet so personal that it is almost dazzling to think of the many names and faces, celebrities and entertainers who have become part of our conversations and lives. What they all have in common is the power of television to project them into our living rooms and turn them into neighbors, friends, extended family, into people we truly believe we have come to know. Television is an intimate medium that creates a bond between actor and viewer, between a character and the public. It offers what two communications scholars call a "synthetic experience," a substitute for reality that feels very real.[1] An actor who plays a doctor on television becomes a doctor, a television lawyer becomes our model for the real thing, and a fictional character—Murphy Brown—engages a real vice president in a national debate. And so we ascribe personality traits to the images on the screen, we track every career move and romance of our favorite actors, and we discuss their lives and futures as if they were connected to our own. The name of the popular show *Friends* describes more than just the fictional friendship among the characters portrayed in the show—it is also a metaphor for the relationship we have with these and so many other actors on television, people who visit us weekly in our homes and whose lives are finely detailed in the mass media that wallpapers our lives.

Ours is an unsettled nation of people constantly on the move. The westward spirit of the nineteenth century remains alive today in a restlessness that constantly seeks new frontiers and challenges. These very dynamics of American society have weakened ties both to family and to the geographically defined communities of old. We reach out and touch someone not over a table breaking bread but over fiber-optic phone lines and in cyberspace. In the modern American era, we yearn for a sense of community that in reality has become more and more elusive. And so television has stepped in to fill the void. It has become our virtual community, a stable presence in the living room that packs our lives with characters that in an earlier age we might have met in the union hall or town square. Americans today spend more time watching television than doing any other activity besides sleeping. By the time the average American teenager graduates from high school, he or she will have logged more hours in front of the television than in front of the teacher. Television viewing has become a surrogate for civic activity, a chance to participate in the lives of others in what has become our electronic village.

Now think of the average American, whose daily life usually consists of clicking the garage door open in the morning, driving to work, putting in the eight hours, getting back in the car, stopping at the store, and driving back home for what will likely be a comfortable evening in front of the television set. On a typical evening in the late 1990s, close to half of all American households are watching TV, and one network alone—NBC—holds the attention of more than one in five households every Thursday night. Now think more specifically of the average white American family. They may not watch the same prime-time series as most blacks, as we discussed in chapter 3. But even on the shows they do watch they see more blacks beamed into their living room on a typical evening than they have seen at any other time or place during the day. It could be Michael Jordan or James Earl Jones pitching a product, Bill Cosby or Della Reese starring in a show, Whoopi Goldberg or Denzel Washington doing the celebrity interview, Ed Bradley or Bryant Gumbel describing a news story, or any combination of black newscasters, reporters, athletes, entertainers, or actors who populate the airwaves hour after hour, day after day. Some of them we think we know, like Bill Cosby or Bryant Gumbel, while others simply pass through our lives, like the blacks featured in advertisements, but they are all there in our living room, joining us in the intimacy of our own homes, creating the impression that the world is more integrated than it truly is.

For whites generally unaccustomed to interacting with blacks, who walk out their front doors and see few black faces in the neighborhood, the mere presence of black images in their homes blurs the line between what is imagined and what is real about race relations in America. It also helps, as author Benjamin De-Mott points out in his book *The Trouble with Friendship: Why Americans Can't Think Straight About Race*, that most of the blacks whom whites see on television either work with whites, have white friends, or operate in a predominantly white context. They have been tested, they are safe, and they fit in.[2] So what television has done is to give white Americans the sensation of having meaningful, repeated contact with blacks without actually having it. Black people have become part of white people's lives, virtually. We call this phenomenon *virtual integration,* and it is a primary reason why the integration illusion—the belief that we are moving toward a color-blind nation—has such a powerful influence over race relations in America today.[3]

So powerful is this virtual integration that it seems to promote a color-blindness toward black celebrities almost unattainable for blacks in the real world. Columnist Clarence Page, a former television reporter in Chicago, describes how he used to be greeted warmly in the same white ethnic neighborhoods that once pelted Martin Luther King with rocks and bottles. "You're not black anymore, Clarence," a white producer explained. "You're on television now."[4] The rise of black media images over the last three decades has come at precisely the same time that celebrity has become the measure of individual success in America. And being on television automatically confers celebrity, whether to a Frank Perdue who hawks his own brand of chickens, or to a low-paid weathercaster stuck in a small-market television station who nonetheless becomes a local personality. So whites have made room in their lives for black celebrities, indeed for almost any black they see on television, and have embraced them as evidence of their own open-mindedness and as proof that the nation isn't so hard on blacks after all. Blacks like O. J. Simpson, before his fall, are welcomed not only into the virtual neighborhood but into the actual neighborhood as well, as if their celebrity erases any negatives that whites otherwise would associate with their color. "I'm not black, I'm famous," the black lead singer of the rock group Fine Young Cannibals once said. Or, as the redneck rapist tells the black sheriff in the film of John Grisham's book *A Time to Kill,* "I seen you play for the Rams. The way I figured a nigger sheriff's okay, been on TV and all. No offense."[5]

Television has certainly come a long way since the days when stations in the South were deluged with complaints because white singer Petula Clark innocently put her hand on Harry Belafonte's arm during a music special, and NBC couldn't find a sponsor for *The Nat "King" Cole Show* and had to cancel it after one year. Until Bill Cosby broke the color line in 1965 as costar of the secret agent show *I Spy*, there had never been a black star of a dramatic series. Until Lever Brothers featured black and white children playing together in a 1963 commercial for the detergent *Wisk*, no black had ever been on a nationwide television ad in a nonstereotypical role. At that time the only blacks who appeared regularly on television came via live sports telecasts. As recently as the early 1980s, advertisers approached by Michael Jordan's agent responded by saying "What on earth are we going to do with a black basketball player?"[6] So it would be difficult to argue that the change in television has been anything but deep and profound.

Yet there are some who claim that the medium has a much longer way to go than most of the viewing public might believe. They say there are no dramas on television built around a black family or protagonist, that most comedies are segregated, that too many black-oriented comedies reinforce clownish or sexual stereotypes, that the networks have few black programming executives with the power to green-light projects, and that there should be more ads featuring blacks other than athletes or entertainers. During the 1996–97 season, they point out, only three comedies on the top three networks featured more than one regular black character, and some high-profile shows—*Seinfeld*, *Friends*, *Ellen* and *Cybill*—had none at all. Of the 245 made-for-TV movies on the four major networks in 1995 and 1996, only about 20 had blacks in leading roles.[7] These are serious, valid criticisms and must be addressed. But from the white perspective they may seem irrelevant or off base because the cumulative presence of blacks on television already provides such a contrast to their predominantly white lives that their virtual world seems thoroughly integrated as is. A black regular on *Seinfeld* or *Friends* probably wouldn't make much of a difference to whites, who believe, courtesy of television, that the world already is fully integrated.

Nothing better illustrates our virtually integrated world than the two prime-time specials aired by ABC on Sunday, November 2, 1997. More than one out of every four TV sets in use at the time was tuned into these shows. In the first, a Walt Disney update of Rodgers & Hammerstein's *Cinderella*, the future princess looks very different from the blond, blue-eyed Cinderella of the Disney animated version and the many storybooks that have followed. This Cinderella is played by the black actress Brandy, and the entire production is a bold and striking example of a new highbrow trend in the arts called color-blind casting. Cinderella's stepmother is white, one stepsister is white and the other black, the fairy godmother is black, the prince is of Filipino descent, his valet is white, the king is white, the queen is black, and the multiethnic cast of extras interact seamlessly in a fairy-tale kingdom of harmonious diversity broadcast right there in our own living room. Immediately following *Cinderella* that night was a well-publicized made-for-TV movie starring Oprah Winfrey, *Before Women Had Wings*. Again, the audience welcomed a black into their homes as Winfrey, who also produced the film, played the role of friend and savior to two white children abused and neglected by their mother. Also note that these two shows aired after a full afternoon of televised football with its many black sportscasters and players. In short, much of white America spent the afternoon and evening in a virtually integrated environment. Although Monday morning at school or work might not come close to resembling the living room integration the night before, that might not matter in a virtually integrated America in which the image becomes the norm and the reality is made to feel like the exception. For whites whose lives are virtually integrated, the power of the image makes the racial reality all the more difficult to believe.

With the possible exception of the military, the television screen may be the most integrated part of American life. We tracked three days of television programming in the fall of 1997 and found that black faces, personalities, newscasters, athletes, actors, and entertainers were intricately woven throughout the shows that most whites watch. To illustrate, we offer a snapshot of one evening, at this writing the highest rated on television, Thursday night on NBC.[8]

First up on October 2, 1997, was the local news at six, which featured one black anchor and four black reporters. We both live in the Washington metropolitan area, home to a large black population, so here one might expect a well-integrated local news team. In fact, though, throughout the country a racial mix on the news is fairly common. There are black men and women anchoring, reporting, forecasting the weather, and discussing sports on stations in every other market we checked: New York, Houston, Boston, Cincinnati, Kansas City, Omaha, Raleigh, and San Francisco. One scholar who viewed news programs on twenty-eight stations nationwide found that blacks made up 11 percent of the journalists he saw, a number almost equal to the percentage of blacks in America. As public opinion pollster Geoffrey Garin put it, there are so many black anchors and reporters on television that even Southern whites "never think twice about it" anymore.[9] In this respect, then, our Washington sample seems no different from the rest of the nation. Nor are the network news broadcasts any different. The *NBC Nightly News with Tom Brokaw*, the top-rated network news show during our viewing period, featured two black reporters doing major stories on the night we watched. A check of the other network news programs found a similar black presence.

The NBC prime-time schedule that Thursday night featured four sitcoms—*Friends, Union Square, Seinfeld,* and *Veronica's Closet*—and one dramatic series, *ER*. Although *Seinfeld* and *Friends* attract few black viewers, they have for a number of years been among the most highly rated comedies on television, which means their audience is almost exclusively white. *Friends* began the evening at eight o'clock. Although set in ethnically diverse New York City, the show has no black regulars. In a previous season one of the characters on *Friends* had a pet chimpanzee, which led a critic to quip that monkeys had a better shot at getting on the show than blacks. But *Friends* may simply be more honest than many shows about the way we lead racially isolated lives, even in the big city. The token black cast member on the periphery of some other sitcoms can seem very contrived at times, leading one stand-up comedian to imagine network executives in a story meeting insisting that "three of the Klansmen in that sketch need to be black."[10] On the evening we watched, *Friends* was true to form, the only blacks being two extras sitting in a restaurant. But that doesn't mean the half hour was devoid of visible blacks. Commercials consume about 25 percent of all television time, and blacks played key roles in four ads during the show, including one for McDonald's showing a black male airline passenger and a black female car rental agent, and another for an NBC show that included a black female attorney. In other words, even during a show like *Friends*, the white audience welcomed a number of virtual blacks into their living rooms.

After *Friends* came a show called *Union Square*, whose six regulars include a black West Indian man who runs a diner that has a racially mixed staff and clientele. Again, blacks played prominent roles in the commercials, this time in five of them. Next up was *Seinfeld*, like *Friends* a show set in New York with an exclusive cast of white regulars, although this particular episode included a scene with a black female university dean. Four commercials included blacks, most of them professionals. On the following show, *Veronica's Closet*, a black male plays a regular though somewhat marginal part, and that night a few other blacks were visible as supporting cast and extras. Only one ad included blacks. Finally came the crown jewel of the evening, the number one show in America, *ER*. The show features two prominent black members of the ensemble cast, a doctor and a physician's assistant, as well as seven blacks in recurring roles. That evening, as with most episodes of *ER*, there were a number of black extras serving as hospital employees, patients, and visitors. Of the twenty-four commercials interspersed throughout the hour-long show, ten featured blacks, including a number that portrayed black executives.

Think about the cumulative number of blacks on television that Thursday evening. The black characters on *ER* alone exceeded the number of blacks with whom many white Americans interact meaningfully each week. The other blacks on the commercials, the news or the other shows further embroidered the integrated image they saw. Rarely did the typical viewer go for more than a few minutes without seeing a black face on the screen, even if one or two shows didn't include blacks. Over three or four hours of television that night, whites saw blacks on news shows, entertainment shows, promos, and commercials—as anchors, reporters, stars, supporting cast, walk-ons, extras, and product endorsers. Nor was there anything unusual about it. The presence of blacks in the living room has become a normal part of our virtual lives. Television represents reality, even if it doesn't represent mine, right?

Channel-surf through the rest of television and you'll find much the same thing. Whether in prime time or daytime, children's hour or late at night, the typical white American will have an integrated viewing experience. According to the Center for Media and Public Affairs, a research organization, blacks played 17 percent of all characters in prime-time entertainment shows in 1992, up from half a percent in the early 1960s.[11] Today you see blacks on the morning shows doing the news and the weather, blacks reporting stories for the newsmagazines, blacks playing and announcing sports, blacks interviewing or being interviewed, blacks on the cop shows investigating homicides, and blacks offering up opinions on the political talk-show circuit. Black TV surgeons treat white TV patients and black TV lawyers represent white TV clients in far greater proportion than they do in real life. Blacks are likewise well represented in commercials, constituting more than 12 percent of on-camera actors and more than 17 percent of all the extras in ads produced in 1995, according to the Screen Actors Guild. A 1989 study found that blacks appeared in 26 percent of all prime-time ads, though they were less likely than whites to be the main focus of an ad and more likely to be part of a group, a sequence, or the background cast.[12] Ads feature high-profile black celebrities, entertainers, and athletes as well as black professionals, families, and blue-collar workers. The advertising images of blacks are so common they cascade one on top of another: clips of Will Smith and Tommy Lee Jones promoting their movie *Men in Black*, a black construction worker waiting for his white colleague in a spot for Tylenol Extra Strength, athletes Shaquille O'Neil and Deion Sanders drinking Pepsi while hanging out in a white kid's bedroom, a group of white guys and their one black buddy ogling women in a bar on behalf of Bud Lite, a black man playing one of the Three Musketeers in an ad for the candy bar, a group of black and white kids warming up the image of the Chevy Astro van, a FedEx spot featuring a black business owner interacting with black and white employees. The list could consume this book.

On children's shows like *Wishbone*, *Barney*, and *Magic School*

Bus, almost every group of cartoon characters or kids looks like the United Nations. A few teen and twenty-something shows are pushing the color line even further: MTV's dating game, *Singled Out,* is fully interracial, and Fox's *Party of Five* featured an ongoing interracial romantic relationship. Then there are the daytime soaps, faithfully watched by millions of college students and stay-at-home moms. Almost every soap opera features at least two regular black characters, including doctors, cops, musicians, lawyers, nurses, nannies, reporters, executives, models, photographers, and just plain people. Behind them are plenty of black extras who stroll the beach, shop at the malls, attend social events, and work at hospitals. Interracial friendships are common and a few soaps have shown interracial relationships and marriages. As with most (though not all) television shows targeted to a predominantly white audience, soaps take color-blindness to the absurd point that the black and white characters, even those in interracial relationships, rarely discuss race. The audience may want realistic portrayals, but not when it comes to black and white. In the virtually integrated world of our living rooms, the last thing we want is the discomfort of reality intruding on the illusion.

Let us not be mistaken: the rise of black images on television and throughout the visual media is an extraordinarily positive development. Television may not be truly color-blind, but if it can help increase interracial familiarity, shatter some stereotypes, fortify the comfort zone and multiply the number of black role models for everyone in America, then it has served an important goal that most other institutions in society have not been willing or able to accomplish. To suggest, as we do, that television undermines real integration—that it enables whites to lead virtually integrated lives without having much real contact with blacks—is not meant to condemn the visibility of blacks on TV but rather to explain its impact. Indeed, the only academic study to look at the phenomenon we call "virtual integration" tested black viewers and found that they, like whites, "more frequently perceived that racial integration is more prevalent, that blacks and whites were more similar, and that blacks were middle-class."[13]

By its very nature television creates imaginary or virtual relationships among people. What makes its impact on race unique is that for most whites their television contact with blacks is the closest they will ever come to crossing the color line. More than half of all whites in one survey say that what they know about blacks they get from the media.[14] "You sure gotta hand it to 'em," the Edith Bunker character said about blacks on the show *All in the Family*, "I mean, two years ago they was nothing but servants and janitors. Nowadays they're teachers and doctors and lawyers. They've come a long way on TV." Certainly it is ironic that one of the few visible institutions where black participation has advanced so far may also provide whites with an excuse not to move much beyond the status quo. If the world is so integrated, then my all-white neighborhood or social club just happens to be an exception, so it's not that big a deal. If the world is so integrated, if a black person can become famous, make so much money and appear on television, then it is they who push us away through all their whining and self-righteous anger. How can I be part of the problem if my kids idolize Michael Jordan and Barry Sanders and if I watch Bill Cosby and Della Reese every week on TV?

In New York City there had never been a black female news director at a local television station until 1996, when Vassar College graduate Paula Walker took the job at the NBC affiliate. Almost immediately she grasped how local news perpetuates the fear of black crime. Typically, a reporter describing a crime will dutifully draw on the police report, which might list the suspect as a black male, five-eight, 160 pounds. On the surface there seems nothing wrong with this description. But, as Walker told us, there are thousands upon thousands of people in the viewing area who fit it. Given that the purpose of putting out a description is to help the public finger the criminal, Walker sees no point in broadcasting such useless information when the only tangible impact will be to increase suspicion of blacks. "What you're doing is making all those women who are walking down the street clutch their pocketbooks closer to them," she said. To her, there would be nothing wrong with including race if the description also mentioned specific clothing, hair style, identifying characteristics such as a scar or a limp, and the neighborhood in which the suspect was last seen. Skin color then becomes relevant and serves a purpose.[15]

If the televised image of black actors, athletes, and entertainers leads whites to think the world is integrated, the portrayal of black crime on television news helps keep real integration from ever happening. There is no irony in this aspect of television. Whether by accident or unconscious design, the face of crime on TV, especially on local news, tends to be black. It is true that blacks commit a disproportionate share of violent crimes, especially in urban areas, but it is also true that blacks are identified with criminal acts on television all out of proportion to the number they commit. Advertisers have long known that repetition, not to mention saturation, sells on television. The relentless association between blacks and crime on the news has colored white perceptions of blacks and has seriously undermined any hope for racial integration in America.

Years ago in the segregated South it was not uncommon for local newspapers to run all sex-crime accusations against blacks on page one, even if the incident took place on the other side of the country.[16] Today there are few if any in television news with such an intent to malign—yet in many ways the result is the same: crime in general is associated with blacks. Findings from a number of research studies clearly document the distortion.[17] Even though most violent crimes are committed by people the same race as their victims, one 1994 study of local TV newscasts in Chicago found that the majority of perpetrators portrayed in the news were black or persons of color, while the majority of victims shown were white. A study of Philadelphia newscasts found that nonwhites were almost twice as likely to be shown as perpetrators than as victims of crime, almost the reverse of the portrayal of whites. Another study found that the percentage of blacks shown as suspects on one Los Angeles station far exceeded the percentage of violent crimes committed by blacks in Los Angeles County. This distortion is also evident in reality-based television programs, such as *COPS* and *America's Most Wanted*. According to one study, half of all the blacks who appear in these shows are criminals, versus 10 percent of all whites, while another found that stories about white victims lasted 74 percent longer than stories about black victims. Furthermore, research shows that blacks accused of the same crime as whites tend to be portrayed as more threatening and intimidating on television news. Whites arrested for crimes might be shown next to their attorneys, if they are shown at all, whereas blacks tend to be shown in handcuffs, on police walks, or being physically restrained by the police. News reports also provide the names of black suspects less often than they do for white suspects, leading one scholar to conclude that the individual identity of black suspects is less important than their race.

Put all these studies together and the composite is clear: whites are vulnerable to crime, blacks are responsible for it. So powerful is this image that when Charles Stuart, a white, killed his wife in Boston and Susan Smith, white, killed her children in South Carolina, both were able to point a finger at an imaginary though vaguely described black killer, knowing full well that the public would almost reflexively believe them. According to research by two University of California–Los Angeles professors, Shanto Iyengar and Franklin Gilliam, Jr., even when news reports of a crime made no reference to a suspect, 42 percent of viewers later remembered seeing a perpetrator, and two thirds of these viewers recalled this phantom criminal as black. When the news report did show a perpetrator, viewers disproportionately recalled him as black. Nor were white viewers the only ones making this mistake. Black viewers did as well, though to a lesser extent, further attesting to the power of racial images in televised reports of crime.[18]

The black criminal image on the news is also part of a larger problem with the news media. Television news feeds on a dramatic structure in which every report must have a plot, an emotional story line, and a moral. Crime fits the mold perfectly: there's a villain, a victim, fear, and human interest. As the entertainment programmers have learned, it's simply good and gripping television. Although the emphasis on crime distorts the portrayal of daily life, this is incidental to the imperative of holding the audience and getting a good story—so much so that coverage of murders on network evening news increased 721 percent since 1993, even though the nationwide homicide rate declined by 20 percent.[19] Blacks are simply caught in this media vise, their image held hostage to the very nature of TV news and its focus on the seamy side of reality. When the *New Orleans Times-Picayune* surveyed local evening news broadcasts for one week in 1993, it found that more than 42.1 percent of the total black images were crime-related and only 18.5 percent involved political or community issues—this in a heavily black city with blacks in charge of city hall.[20] In part this may be due to television's overemphasis on black crime; it is also likely due to television's overall fixation on crime. Because television news plays up crime regardless of color, and because the white majority has little or no contact with blacks except for what they see on television, even an accurate portrayal of crime—one showing how whites victimize mostly whites and blacks victimize mostly blacks—will still likely magnify the role of the black criminal among whites. The fact that the information is frequently reported by a black reporter or anchor validates it further.

Compounding the problem is that people take what they see on the news personally, as if the reality they see is the reality of their lives. By its very dependence on graphic images and compelling visuals, television news evokes emotions and creates impressions. People don't just think about the news—they feel it. That may be why surveys show that the public has more trust in the local TV news than the local newspaper. Surveys also show that up to two-thirds of Americans say their attitudes about crime are stirred by the media rather than their own experiences or those of friends.[21] Now add up all of these factors: the disproportionate portrayal of black crime, the emphasis on crime in the local news, the emotive power of the medium, the accumulation of images, the proximate reality of what's reported, the lack of real contact with blacks among the white audience, and the implicit validation provided by black journalists reporting the news. The result is a generalized fear of crime that translates to a generalized fear of blacks. It is a sad commentary to suggest that the only way to eliminate white fright is to eliminate the reporting of black crime altogether, not merely to make the reporting more accurate. But there may be no other way to change the defining image of crime that so profoundly shapes white Americans' view of their fellow black citizens.

For most white Americans, the only kind of integration they know is the virtual kind, and it may be the only kind they want.

Virtual integration enables whites to live in a world with blacks without having to do so in fact. It provides a form of safe intimacy without any of the risks. It offers a clean and easy way for whites to establish and nourish what they see as their bona fide commitment to fairness, tolerance, and color-blindness. White Americans may genuinely feel they are open to blacks, as long as blacks—with their criminal tendencies—don't move into the neighborhood. So television giveth, in the form of the virtual community that transcends race, and it taketh away, by reinforcing an association between blacks and crime that makes real community building all but impossible. This curious television dynamic explains how, as Harvard Medical School psychiatrist Dr. Alvin Poussaint told us, "white kids who worship Michael Jordan will beat up black kids who come into their neighborhoods." It is another sad and tragic irony of race relations in America, brought to you in living color.

CHAPTER SEVEN

Noble Negro, Angry Black, Urban Outlaw: The Iconography of Our Racial Separation

Frenetic may be an appropriate word to describe the typical Monday morning in downtown Washington, D.C. This is a city with neither time to waste nor patience to waste it. Deals must be cut, legislation crafted, bureaucracies moved, and strategies developed. Washingtonians wear their long hours at work as a badge of honor, a sign that they are indeed important and are in the legislative or political loop. There is one predominant lifestyle choice among the political class in the nation's capital, and that is work.

That is why one particular Monday morning in October 1995 seemed so unusual and even eerie. Although it was not a federal holiday, the downtown corridor and the lobbyists' conference rooms were all but deserted. The streets seemed silent and the sidewalks were almost free of the usual pedestrian bustle. It was the day of the Million Man March, a mass gathering on the Mall organized by Nation of Islam leader Louis Farrakhan. Nearly one million black men from around the country were expected to converge on Washington for what was billed as a day of unity and atonement.

But why was the downtown empty that day? Even if all the black men working downtown had gone to the march, it wouldn't have hollowed out the offices. In political and official Washington, there are not enough black men to make such a difference. No, the people who did not show up for work tended to be whites, apparently tens of thousands of them who stayed home in large part because they feared the march might get violent. There are stories of frantic phone calls the night before from out-of-town relatives, urging sons and daughters to stay away from the city the next day. No other march on Washington in recent years has been met with such whispers of trepidation and fear— neither pro-choice nor anti-abortion marches, nor the gathering of nearly a million men, mostly white Christians, for the October 1997 Promise Keepers event. Part of the fear can be attributed to white unease over the mercurial Farrakhan, whose compelling exhortations on black empowerment are sadly punctuated by bilious statements about whites and Jews. But Farrakhan had spoken at plenty of Washington rallies before, and the only resulting violence was confined to a war of words between his supporters and critics. And there was no hint from him or any other organizers that the day would be dedicated to anything but peaceful and sober reflection. So why was white Washington nervous? There is really only one explanation: Whites believed that a gathering of so many black men was bound to get out of hand, and the potential for violence seemed palpable and real. Peel away from most whites their color-blind pretense and you will find a deep and abiding fear of black men, of almost all black men. The thinking goes like this: these black men are angry, undisciplined, prone to violence, and you never know what will happen with that buried rage when more than a few of them get together, especially under the leadership of a man like Farrakhan.

The march went off as planned that October day, and there were no incidents and no reports of violence. Although Farrakhan railed about a Masonic conspiracy and the mystical power of the number 19, the march was much bigger than his involvement and already holds a near mythic status in black America's living memory, much the way Woodstock captured the imagination of white Baby Boomers. But as much as the march tells us about the aspirations of black men, about their desire to be affirmed as fathers and taxpayers, not deadbeats and muggers, it also tells us about the deep-seated feelings that whites have for blacks. As *Newsweek* put it, "When it turned out [that whites] had nothing to be afraid of—the day passed with no violence and only one arrest—many whites were left to ponder their own preconceptions."[1]

Economists like to see human behavior as a process built on empirical choices and rational self-interest. But it is difficult to look at society without seeing the role of images, parables, and preconceptions in determining how we live and act toward each other. History is strewn with examples of people acting out these preconceptions even if, from a purely rational perspective, the behavior is hurtful, misguided, or self-defeating. And nowhere is this more evident than in the context of race. The power of parables and images to shape our choices, identities, and expectations is finely interwoven into the history of American race relations, and the particular ones that characterize blacks go a long way toward explaining why integration has not succeeded in the past and why it won't succeed in the foreseeable future.

Consider the overriding narrative in American politics today. It is the story of the virtuous middle class, the people "who do the work and pay taxes, raise the kids, and play by the rules," as Bill Clinton described them upon accepting the Democratic nomination for president in 1992. These are the people, according to the story, who built America, on whose backs and brains we have prospered, who stand for the very American values of loyalty, neighborhood, patriotism and decency. Many of them take pride in their immigrant heritage, their ancestral devotion to the American Dream. They are good people who ask no favors and seek nothing more than a fair and equal shot at getting ahead in life. You'll find them at the bowling alley, the barbecue, the barber shop and the hairdresser. Patrician George Bush ate pork rinds to show he was one of them. Since the late 1960s almost every politician with national ambitions has curried favor with and flattered the middle class. First they were called the Silent Majority, then the Reagan Democrats, and now they are simply described as the average American family. Whether this portrait is based on caricature or reality is less important than the fact that it has assumed mythic proportions in our public culture. It is how middle America sees itself.

There's something else worth noting about this story of the middle class: it rarely includes blacks. At least seven in ten American blacks can be labeled as working-class, middle-class, or affluent, an accomplishment, given the obstacles, as breathtaking as the immigrant story in America. But the virtual absence of these blacks from middle-class iconography has led a number of writers and scholars to view them as the "invisible men" of the 1990s.[2] Politicians who wrap themselves in the middle-class image, as Clinton has done in his campaigns and as Richard Nixon, Ronald Reagan, and George Bush did before him, are effectively aiming their appeal at whites. Clinton's pollster Stanley Greenberg admitted as much when he reported that for whites in focus groups, "not being black was what constituted being middle class; not living with blacks was what made a neighborhood a decent place to live."[3] When California's governor, Pete Wilson, announced his bid for the White House in 1995, he said he had a "duty" to seek the presidency in the name of "fairness" for people who "work hard, pay their taxes, and obey the law"—and then he based his campaign message on a proposal to end affirmative action. It appears that fairness from a black middle-class perspective is not the same as fairness from a white middle-class perspective, so the easiest way for politicians to resolve the conflict is simply to hand the middle-class franchise to whites.

We have become so accustomed to the association between whites and the middle-class image that news reports will routinely distinguish between middle-class voters and minorities. "Once in the White House," wrote a respected *New York Times* reporter, "Mr. Clinton forgot for a time that he had won . . . as a New Democrat, the self-anointed champion of the middle class, less obligated than most of his recent predecessors to labor unions, minorities, and other interest groups."[4] A 1996 *New York Times Magazine* article on the "lunch-pail vote" included three photographs with nineteen people, none of whom were black.[5] So pervasive is this image that it has even seeped into sports, America's consummate metaphor for life, with white athletes often portrayed as hard-working, dedicated, blue-collar types, a description rarely applied to blacks. "He's . . . blood and guts. He's more than blue collar," was the description, typical of the genre, of one white Baltimore Oriole outfielder. In some cases there is an implied comparison to blacks, as in this description of a white basketball player who bears little resemblance to a well-known black player: "One could no more imagine John Stockton dying his hair green, for example, or throwing a tantrum at a coach's decision, or beating his chest and howling after committing a good play than seeing him do something dumb on the court."[6]

If blacks are not part of the great American middle-class narrative, then how do we make sense of their lives? How do we define their American experience? Blacks see their story as one of struggle, of rising up from slavery, of encountering obstacles with determination, faith, and forbearance. Other images have encroached upon but have never replaced this central narrative of deliverance. But the white majority's version of the black narrative is and has been very different. This version is like a prism through which whites understand blacks, a prism that has had an enormous influence on relations between the races. To borrow a biblical phrase, whites see blacks through a glass, darkly.

For far too long—indeed well into this century—the white image of blacks was based on the most demeaning of stereotypes, first to justify slavery and then to rationalize segregation. With little shame or self-consciousness, whites openly described blacks as lazy, foolish, unintelligent, and undisciplined, not worthy of white civilization but desperately in need of white tutelage and guidance. Cartoons, postcards, children's games, and ornaments routinely depicted Sambo, Mammy, or Uncle Tom images, reducing blacks to frivolous and childish caricatures who required the supervision of whites if they were ever to make anything of their lives. Remarkable as it may seem, the most influential and authoritative history of slavery through the first half of the twentieth century and up to the mid-1950s described black children as "pickaninnies" and slavery as "benevolent in intent and on the whole beneficial in effect." Blacks, wrote Ulrich B. Phillips, the author of *American Negro Slavery*, "for the most part were by racial quality submissive rather than defiant, light-hearted instead of gloomy, amiable and ingratiating instead of sullen, and [their] very defects invited paternalism rather than repression."[7] In 1963 it was still possible to read in *Time* magazine this description of blacks: "Birmingham's Negroes had always seemed a docile lot. Downtown at night, they slouched in gloomy huddles beneath street lamps, talking softly or not at all."[8]

Of course, not all imagery made blacks appear innocuous and

benign. In the white imagination, the same primitive nature that made blacks seem simple also made them appear dangerous; the resulting fear was exhibited most vividly in white torment over the apparent black male desire for white women. Thus if white benevolence was not enough to control blacks, lynchings would have to do. Between 1882 and 1964, according to records kept by Tuskegee Institute, whites lynched 3,445 blacks. But for obvious reasons the image of the uncontrollable black and ruthless white had little appeal among whites. The social order—not to mention the white self-image—were better served by a narrative of docile or primitive blacks dependent on the goodwill and paternalism of whites.

As blacks sought civil rights and integration in the 1950s and 1960s, the national image of blacks began to change in important ways. With television showing almost daily the sacrifice and nobility of the civil rights movement in the face of unrelenting segregationist brutality, it was no longer possible to see blacks as simple and carefree, grateful for the doting beneficence of whites. In its stead arose a new image, that of the noble Negro. In many ways this new image was the deliberate product of Martin Luther King's brilliant nonviolent civil rights strategy. King understood better than anyone else that the way to move white America was to appeal to its conscience. He knew that most white Americans at least privately felt uncomfortable with how the racial reality of segregation contradicted the national ideal of equality. He also knew that the Puritan metaphor of suffering and redemption continued to hold sway in modern America. So he and his colleagues transformed the righteousness of their cause into an image of dignity and forbearance—of religious witness to injustice that white Americans could not but recognize. "We marched in suits and ties, carrying Bibles with our books," recalled Jesse Jackson. "We knew we were creating a contrast with the white police with billy clubs."[9] To be beaten, hosed, and viciously attacked without fighting back or losing cool offered America an image of self-restraint, determination, and virtue that was diametrically opposed not only to the twisted segregationists but to the primitive, carefree image of old.

The noble Negro image did more than simply reshape white views of blacks. It flattered white America as well. For it was the perfect image for whites living in an age of relative prosperity and missionary liberalism. A nation primed to see good versus evil outside its borders could now rectify its essential injustice at home. It gave white liberals in particular someone to rescue, someone to save, and it provided them with the ideal martyr who has suffered for America's sins but will now show us the way to absolution and redemption without bitterness or recrimination. Americans, never very comfortable with the angry mob, might be willing to accept the quiet, dignified victim. "It seems to be indispensable to the national self-esteem," novelist James Baldwin said in 1963, "that the Negro be considered either as a kind of ward, or as a victim."[10] Although this image has little in common with the prior image of the docile black, in an important way the two are similar: in both, blacks depend on the goodwill of whites.

The power of this image could be seen almost a decade before the 1956 Montgomery bus boycott began to crystallize it in the popular imagination. In 1947, Jackie Robinson withstood hatred and taunts to break the color line in our national pastime. His demeanor in the face of hostility, his patience and self-restraint, became the prototype for the image of civil rights activists who would stare down and defeat legal segregation in America. But Robinson's story was true to the noble Negro image in another way: it involved the paternalistic white man—Brooklyn Dodgers president Branch Rickey, or Mr. Rickey, as Robinson called him— who supported and protected Robinson and guaranteed the success of what he called their "noble experiment."

It wasn't long before popular culture seized on this image and began presenting stories of selfless and noble Negroes and accepting or principled whites. In the classic 1962 film *To Kill a Mockingbird*, for example, a black man named Tom Robinson tries to help a white woman who then accuses him of rape. Throughout his trial he sits with quiet dignity, never indignant, ably defended by the good white lawyer Atticus Finch. Actor Sidney Poitier played variations on this theme throughout the 1960s in such films as *A Raisin in the Sun*, *A Patch of Blue*, and *Guess Who's Coming to Dinner*. Society was wrong, blacks were virtuous, and all but the most malevolent whites were decent at heart. Today, it is almost impossible to produce a mainstream film about the civil rights era that in some way does not follow this basic script, though in almost every case it is the whites who are given the heroic roles against the backdrop of noble black victimhood. The most notorious of the genre, the 1988 film *Mississippi Burning*, was billed as a story about the 1964 murder of three civil rights workers but instead turned out as a drama about white goodness on behalf of powerless, even faceless, black victims. "At this point in time," the film's director said, "it could not have been made any other way." Since then there have been a number of such films, including *The Long Walk Home*, about the Montgomery bus boycott featuring a courageous, compassionate white Southern woman and her noble maid; *Ghosts of Mississippi*, about a white prosecutor's search for justice in the murder case of civil rights leader Medgar Evers; and *A Passion for Justice*, a made-for-TV movie about the fight against segregation in Mississippi told from the perspective of an intrepid white female newspaper publisher. Film portrayals of black South Africa's fight against apartheid were even put in this framework—blacks as virtuous victims, the good whites as moral heroes.[11]

In its early 1960s heyday the noble Negro image served the political needs of blacks and the psychological needs of many whites. Its continuing power today attests to its heroic imagery, its nostalgic appeal and the need for positive black images that are unthreatening to whites. In many ways the noble Negro is the quintessential image of the integration illusion, for it gives whites the impression of making common cause with blacks when in truth there is little common ground in our lives and neighborhoods. A noble Negro with few human flaws makes integration appear agreeable and easy, especially when the terms of integration are determined by whites and most of the integrating takes place hypothetically or on TV.

From the perspective of real integration, however, from the standpoint of whites and blacks seeing each other simply as people with virtues and flaws, the noble Negro image was a setup for failure. Not only did it prime whites to expect blacks to swallow their very human anger, but it also implied that blacks were victims who could be rescued only by the goodwill of whites. The minute black frustration bubbled over and Black Power forcefully emerged in the mid-1960s, the image of the noble Negro martyr could not be reconciled with the new reality. Unlike the quietly

dignified noble Negro, blacks were expressing anger and re-
nouncing patience, and a number of more militant leaders declared that there was no room for whites in their organizations
and that blacks must take full control of their own cause. "You
cannot have real integration when you have a patronizing relationship," a black New York activist told *U.S. News & World Report* in 1968.[12] As a result, many whites felt vindicated in their
deep-seated though socially indecorous suspicion that most
blacks were not so noble after all. Whites played the clever psychological game of "good Negro, bad black": since some blacks
gratefully participate in the system, whites could conclude that
there must be something wrong with those that don't. Whites who
told pollsters they would welcome a few Negroes into the neighborhood now felt fully justified in wanting nothing to do with
blacks who seemed to have a chip on their shoulder. All they
needed to do was cite the angry and separatist rhetoric of some
black militants.

Liberal whites felt especially betrayed, for their own savior image no longer looked so noble after being tarnished by vocal
black leaders who spurned white largess and accused liberals of
joining the cause more for their own moral gratification than for
the needs of blacks. Indeed, many of the same liberals whose very
identity and moral stature were built on helping blacks began to
see blacks as ungrateful and even racist. In part this accounts for
the rise of neo-conservativism in America, the political movement fueled by former liberals that began to gain popularity in
the late 1960s. The noble Negro image that had been so central
to the liberal imagination suddenly became a millstone in black-
white relations.

The image had one other unintended effect: by creating such
a dominant portrait of blacks as victims, it helped create the impression among blacks that they were beyond criticism from
whites. Legitimate white attempts to scrutinize black crime rates
or family problems were met with cries of racism. Blacks weren't
at fault, society was, the argument went—and society had better do something about it beyond criticizing blacks. The most
notorious case of this occurred in 1965, when Daniel Patrick
Moynihan, then an assistant secretary of labor in the Johnson administration, wrote a report in which he contended that slavery

and discrimination had undermined the black family structure and consequently created a new problem, a ghetto "tangle of pathology," that rivaled anything whites could do to harm blacks. Because he suggested that part of the problem lay in the black community, he was almost immediately scorned as a racist and his report was excoriated for blaming the victim, an attack that chilled open discussion of the black family for two decades. Victimhood thus became a defensive shield used by blacks ranging from the wayward kids on the street who blame whitey for their troubles to a Supreme Court nominee who fended off sexual harassment allegations as "a high-tech lynching of a black man." Little wonder that northern white ethnics, many of them second- or third-generation Americans whose own lives seemed full of hardship, found it offensive to be told that they were the oppressors and that blacks, even black criminals, were the victims. "We will never come to grips with the problems of our cities—the factories closing, the housing filled with rats, the hospitals losing doctors, the schools pockmarked with bullet holes, the middle class in flight," wrote Senator Bill Bradley in 1991, "until a white person can talk about the epidemic of minority illegitimacy, drug addiction, and homicides without being called a racist."[13]

Sad to say, the noble Negro image that helped make the black image more human ironically resulted in yet another caricature of blacks. It reinforced among whites the belief that the only good blacks were those without anger or faults, and for blacks it turned the righteous-victim image into a defensive posture that could stifle criticism and turn away even friendly whites. Such an image was no framework for productive interaction or real integration.

By the mid-1960s, the noble Negro image began to give way to another image that pulled us apart even further. "When I make a speech about cooperation between whites and Negroes, I'm given about four or five inches of space [in the newspaper]," complained Urban League president Whitney Young in 1968. "When Stokely [Carmichael] talks about 'killing whitey,' his whole speech is reprinted and gets television coverage."[14] Whether angry at whites or not, most black Americans simply spend their lives working hard and playing by the rules. But the media-driven image that began to emerge in the mid-sixties emphasized the anger and the grievances almost to the exclusion of all else in black American life. A product of black radicalism, white resentment and the media's need for conflict, a new image began to shape the white view of blacks, and it continues to influence us today. Welcome to the image of the angry, entitled black.

For many blacks in the 1960s, there were sides to this image that were curiously though deeply liberating. Race riots and radicalism may be thoroughly self-defeating in a consensus democracy, but they also offered a sense of control, catharsis, and self-assertion that most blacks had never before felt in America. Although few blacks actually participated in the riots or joined the militant groups, sympathy for them ran deep in the black community. For the first time in American history, the power of racial fear had turned against whites, who no longer had the law or the lynch mob to put blacks down. Many blacks relished this role reversal. They became masters of the moment, even if through methods and means that most blacks feared would further alienate them from the mainstream. By the late sixties, particularly on college campuses but throughout the political system, blacks were making demands, not requests. To be owed something, to be entitled to something, was quite different from asking or begging for something. After three centuries of sacrifice it was high time for white America to recognize that its black citizens deserved something back without their having to get on their knees to ask for it. To be entitled seemed not only justified but fair.

Whites of course saw it very differently. To them, the image of anger and entitlement became the template for all blacks, not just the militant leaders given a platform on TV. Perhaps most jarring for whites was that blacks no longer seemed deferential or grateful for incremental gains. As the *National Advisory Commission on Civil Disorders*, commonly known as the Kerner Commission, noted in its 1968 report on racial unrest, many blacks felt a strong undercurrent of hatred for whites. "Watts blew up," a Johnson administration official observed in 1966, "and there were the Negroes—the very people we had loved because they were oppressed—in the role of the aggressor. The mental adjustment was just too much for some white people and we lost them after that."[15] To whites, in the place of the noble Negro was now a "special-interest," a black who put a claim on everyone else's American Dream and cried racism when things didn't go his way. Pick up the newspaper or turn on the news and it was hard to avoid the image of the angry black with brows furrowed, fingers pointed, mouth opened and teeth bared in self-righteous rage, making one demand or another on whites. Just picture Angela Davis or Stokely Carmichael in the late 1960s, Jesse Jackson in the 1970s, and New York's Al Sharpton in the 1980s—to whites, these were the images that personified black America. Rare was the moderate or middle-class alternative.

Whites saw blacks demanding and themselves giving—it was a one-way relationship. Many whites felt this way even before a single affirmative-action program was in place. Indeed, it was not unusual for whites to see themselves "giving" civil rights to blacks. "What do they want now?" was a common question whites asked throughout the sixties. The whole idea of racial preferences, welfare or any other proposal that seemed to reward blacks just for being black provided the perfect rationalization for this growing white resentment. Soon whites began to see *themselves* as victims, as people of goodwill who had worked so hard and given so much that now they were losing out to people who didn't even bother to lift a finger or say thank you anymore. "It's not like it was in the old days, when you gave a black man a job and he appreciated it and didn't try to stir things up," a small business owner told *Business Week* in 1991.[16]

So the image of entitled, angry blacks appeared regularly in a white America that itself felt aggrieved. The image was central to Ronald Reagan's apocryphal "welfare queen" story of the Chicago woman who allegedly accumulated eighty names, thirty addresses, and twelve Social Security cards and whose "tax-free income alone is $150,000," and in his story about the food stamp recipient buying T-bone steak as you waited at the checkout counter with a pound of hamburger. It was evident in the notorious Jesse Helms ad during his victorious 1990 Senate reelection bid against a black candidate, in which a white worker crumpled a job-rejection letter while a narrator says, "They had to give it to a minority because of a racial quota." Whites who responded favorably to these messages saw themselves as justified, not angry. From their perspective, they'd already accepted integration—they just didn't like special privilege for anyone. If anyone was angry, it was the black person who used anger as a cover for his ill-gotten gains. According to a 1994 survey by the University of Chicago's National Opinion Research Center, 78 percent of whites thought blacks more likely to prefer being on welfare than being self-supporting. "Half of them over there," a white teenager from Chicago told *Time* magazine in 1997, "they got better cars than we do. And they don't even have jobs. They got free rent, and their grocery bills paid. You know something? I don't have no pity in my pinkie toe for those people."[17] It never seemed to matter that blacks constitute a minority of all welfare recipients, that the courts have found a high proportion of reverse-discrimination claims to be without merit, or that most blacks work hard every day and just want a fair shake in life.[18] The image trumps the reality.

In many ways this image of the angry black victim has helped to create the racial endgame we are in today. Blacks who see government programs righting or at least mitigating historical wrongs are met by whites who see blacks as political hustlers, gaming the system to get something for nothing at white America's expense. Blacks who assert their concerns in the public forum are met by whites who view it as whining and special-interest complaining. "Sometimes I wonder if they really want what they say they want," Ronald Reagan told *60 Minutes* in a 1989 interview before leaving office, "because some of those leaders are doing very well leading organizations based on keeping alive the feeling that they are victims of prejudice." Whites then point to selected immigrant groups and ask why blacks by comparison are so ungrateful. Look, whites argue, we've given you civil rights and bent over backward to accommodate you, so why are you complaining so much? Blacks of course resent the notion that they are complaining and the implication that anything has ever been "given" to them. What they want is what they've earned through more than three centuries of forbearance.

This isn't the first time in American history that whites objected to footing the bill for what they saw as whining and undeserving blacks. During Reconstruction after the Civil War, whites

resented programs such as the Freedman's Bureau, which provided aid to former slaves, and it was fairly common to see
posters and cartoons that caricatured blacks for wanting government benefits without having to work. "Whar is de use for me to
work as long as day make dese appropriations," one disparaging
cartoon asked.[19] The difference today is that we pretend to be
color-blind and maintain integration as an ideal. No matter how
much sweat has poured from black brows in building this country,
the entitlement narrative tells whites that too many blacks are
prospering through ill-gotten gains. Much like the noble Negro
image, it is a caricature that undermines real integration.

The anger-entitlement image tells whites that blacks can make
it in America only through illegitimate means. So too does the
other image that took hold during the 1960s, an image that remains an insidious influence today: the black man as a violent or
criminal outlaw. What makes this image so strong and resilient
are its many sources in culture and society. It is part romance,
part fear. It is part exploitation, part self-destruction. It is part
pose, part reality. It gathers momentum in the news media, in the
entertainment media, in urban street culture, and in more than
three hundred years of black-white dynamics. It is driven by the
imagination of white conservatives, white liberals, black and
white academics, and Hollywood moguls. Law-and-order politicians have built careers exploiting this image much the way radical intellectuals have gained fame celebrating it. It is also an
image in which whites see themselves as victims. The fact that
most black Americans are sickened by crime in their neighborhoods and want the criminals locked away does not seem to
soften this image. Nor does the fact that only a tiny proportion of
blacks actually commit violent crimes—only about a tenth of one
percent of blacks fifteen to thirty-four years old are charged with
homicide each year.[20] Nor the fact that white Americans themselves have high rates of violent crimes: the U.S. murder rate
without counting black homicides would still far surpass that of
Europe and Britain.[21] The image of blacks as primitive that made
antebellum whites in the South fear for their daughters has
ripened into the one of threatening, uncontrollable, alienated
blacks who have robbed our lives and neighborhoods of their
pristine innocence.

Whatever the mitigating facts or factors, no one should deny the troubling reality of crime, particularly black-on-black crime, in parts of urban America. Because of this reality we are able to wrap the image of the black as an outlaw in the clinical language of crime statistics and law enforcement jargon. But underneath the numbers is a caricature that taints almost every black man. By a subliminal logic, white fear of the underclass becomes fear of the violent criminal, fear of urban America, and, finally, fear of all black men. Civil rights groups rightly criticized the *Los Angeles Times* for a 1981 article headlined MARAUDERS FROM INNER CITY PREY ON L.A.'S SUBURBS, but the headline was merely a manifestation of a deep and abiding dread. White fear of black violence is almost a reflexive response, regardless of contrary evidence or experience. A 1989 *Nightline* broadcast showed this graphically when white pedestrians recoiled with visceral fear and uncertainty when black high school students asked them for change for a dollar, even though the black teens were neatly dressed and the street was full of people.[22] In Oak Park, Illinois, long considered a model integrated community, all the years of living together and building trust did not diminish the reflex among whites after a couple of 1994 incidents involving black and white teens. "When my kids are beaten up and bloody, and it's black kids causing the problem, what am I supposed to think?" one white mother asked.[23]

The image is so ingrained, so pervasive that individual illustrations barely do it justice. It is woven so finely into daily life that most white Americans barely blink when hearing that jewelry store owners bar young black men from their stores, that black college students are questioned about a crime near campus, or that whites steer clear of large black gatherings, as they do in Atlanta, when whites avoid downtown during the annual Freaknik party for black college students, or as they did in Washington, D.C., the day of the Million Man March. It is an image so powerful that some advertising executives say there's no point in featuring a black man in an ad about a luxury car because whites will end up associating the car with drug dealers or crime.[25]

The outlaw image has become a filter through which whites imagine, see, and think about black men. When a promising black Bay Area basketball player didn't score the minimum on his college entrance exams, he was written off in the media as yet another inner-city kid lost to a culture of crack, alienation, and crime—until a black *Oakland Tribune* columnist probed further and found the youngster studying hard, improving his grades, and serving as the sole supporter of his mother and sister.[25] When Donald Cherry, a white man, told Nashville police that his toddler had been shot to death by some black teens after a traffic dispute, everyone believed him—just as they did Charles Stuart and Susan Smith—until his story began to unravel and Cherry finally admitted that he was trying to buy drugs when his child was killed.[26] When black students at an elite private high school near Washington, D.C., wanted to hold a go-go dance, school administrators balked, certain it would lead to violence, until one of the black teachers reassured them and the dance took place without incident.[27] "The image is that young black men are like dry tinder waiting for an idle spark to set them off," observed Harvard professor Henry Louis Gates, Jr.[28] To most whites a white teenager in sweatpants is a jock, but a black teen in sweats is trouble. When a 1989 ABC/*Washington Post* poll asked whether it was "common sense" or "prejudice" for whites to avoid black neighborhoods because of crime, three-quarters answered common sense.[29] "My appearance is not menacing, but I am perceived to be a menace," wrote a Harvard-educated black man in a letter to the *New York Times*. "It is unfortunate but true that every black male is Willie Horton and Willie Horton is every black male."[30]

Perhaps most distressing about this image is how it has been internalized in law enforcement culture, among the very people who must make snap decisions about life or death, trust or fear. Given that police officers deal with crime and violence every day, it is certainly understandable that they might look at any person and suspect the worst. But far too often with blacks, especially black men, the presumption is criminal until proven otherwise. The Rodney King case was only the most blatant manifestation of this presumption. Rare is the black man who hasn't been pulled over or questioned, or who can't tell such a story about a friend. Wearing a suit or driving an expensive car is no inoculation from this presumption. According to criminologist Jerome G. Miller in his book *Search and Destroy: African-American Males in the Criminal Justice System*, a 1993 study on the criminal justice system in California found that "92 percent of the black men arrested by police on drug charges were subsequently released for lack of evidence or inadmissible evidence."[31] These men thus have arrest records they don't deserve, black men yanked into the criminal justice system because of the color of their skin. In an equally disturbing development, black police officers are increasingly mistaken for criminals and shot by their white colleagues at crime scenes, a phenomenon documented by Amnesty International in a 1996 report on the New York City Police Department. After one such incident in New Jersey, an executive of the National Black Police Association observed, "Black police officers live and work in fear. How does one of our officers get shot in uniform [while] doing his job?"[32]

But what about the criminal culture of our inner cities? Doesn't that vindicate the image? Aren't whites justified in their fear? Don't police have cause for their suspicions? Certainly there is little that is healthy about the underclass environment. This is a culture isolated from the mainstream, surrounded by ghetto walls built of despair, hopelessness, joblessness, and random violence. The only money many central city residents see in the neighborhood comes from drugs and guns. There are no Microsoft campuses nearby, no computer chip plants, not even factories anymore, and barely any banks or fast-food restaurants. Only the outlaw seems to be making it, driving the most expensive cars, wearing the most expensive jewelry. The more hard-core a gangsta rapper or drug dealer becomes, the more he flouts white society and swaggers before the authorities, the more he seems to fulfill the very American fantasy of wealth and fame. His is a tangible, not an abstract, status. It is more immediate than the vague promise that hard work in school will mean success in life. It seems more rewarding than a low-wage, back-breaking job that involves long hours and pays barely enough to put food on the table. The outlaw culture says that if you're going to die young you might as well die proud and rich rather than scared and poor. That's the lesson too many inner-city kids take from the life of rap artist Tupac Shakur, gunned down like so many others at a young age, who gained his fame precisely because he was an outlaw. Deep down these kids may be vulnerable and scared, but the mask they must wear is of cold-blooded intimidation, and they make no apologies. That is the culture in which they must try to survive, even though many may not survive it.

This portrait is chilling. Urban outlaws want to instill fear. And they do, in both middle-class America and in the vast majority of inner-city residents. But that's the point. Most Americans—black and white—are afraid of these outlaws. In fact, the urban outlaw culture represents only a tiny fraction of black America. These outlaws are isolated from most other Americans, including most black Americans, and as crime statistics bear out, the threat they pose is primarily to themselves and their immediate neighbors. Just how isolated they are can be seen in a revealing *Los Angeles Times* survey taken days after the 1992 Los Angeles riots: nearly 80 percent of city residents said the devastation and unrest of the riots would have little or no impact on their daily lives.[33] Furthermore, most urban blacks reject the idolatry of crime and never fall into the outlaw trap. Many central-city teens simply want to get ahead and make something of their lives—they want to take responsibility for their choices and their future. A 1996 study by the National Crime Prevention Council and the National Institute for Citizen Education in the Law found that about half of young people living in at-risk neighborhoods volunteer at school, one in three volunteer at church, one in eight volunteer with a local community group, and a majority say they would participate in volunteer programs to help reduce crime—numbers not too different from what suburban youth reported.[34] Unfortunately, their determination to make it out of the inner city is not matched by the opportunities available to them and by their ability as mere teens to navigate the social and psychological land mines along the way. Just ask any central-city teacher, who sees the flame of hope struggle against the inner-city winds every day. Or ask employers in central cities, who report long lines of teens for the few available jobs. These kids may live in the inner city but they do not want to be imprisoned by the inner city. They deserve much better than to be eyed with cold suspicion, to be presumed a hoodlum because of how they dress or talk. More than anything they need our support, because the obstacles are so great. What is truly criminal about the black-as-criminal image, is that every inner-city kid trying to make it out must labor not only under the weight of an underclass culture but under the additional weight of a mainstream view of blacks that does not distinguish between the black kids who carry guns and those who carry books.

It is difficult to underestimate the immense damage wrought by this image—particularly on the psychology of blacks, on black-white relations, and yes, on integration. A white society conditioned to equate blacks with violence or crime may pause before integrating with people who just might turn on them. Yet in what can only be called a perverse form of racial romanticism, there are many whites and blacks who actually glorify the urban outlaw as the authentic image of blacks. The true black American lives in the "hood," according to this view, and defiance is the only way to survive with dignity in a white-dominated, racist society. Bad becomes good, intimidation becomes an attitude, and the cross hair of a gun becomes a symbol of survival. Unfortunately, romanticizing the outlaw is like adding pain to misery. Try as they might to portray themselves as compatriots of blacks, those who celebrate this outlaw image are merely applying the flip side of a caricature that they detest when conservatives exploit it for political gain.

Among whites, the phenomenon is manifested most prominently today in teenagers who identify themselves as "wannabes" or "wiggers," a word that melds white and nigger. These white kids, often from the suburbs, dress, talk, and act in a style that has all the trappings of inner-city life. "Yo, whassup?" is their typical greeting. They strut rather than walk, with baggy pants loosely hanging below the waist. Urban slang punctuates their sentences. With boom box in hand they are a prime market for the gangsta rap music performed by groups like Scarface and Niggaz With Attitude, on such labels as Death Row Records. In fact, most know little about ghetto blacks except for what they see on MTV and in the movies. Theirs is a virtual integration different only in style and intensity from what the rest of white America feels after a few hours of television. *New York Times* critic Michiko Kakutani trenchantly describes them as "cultural tourists [who] romanticize the very ghetto life that so many black kids want to escape.

Instead of the terrible mortality rate for young black males, they see the glamour of violence. Instead of the frustration of people denied jobs and hope and respect, they see the verbal defiance of that frustration."[35] As one black high school girl asked, "Why is it cool to be in the ghetto? My family worked hard to not be there."[36]

Today's wiggers may see themselves as unique, but they are actually the latest in a long line of rebellious white youths who throughout much of this century have romanticized a stereotypical "authentic" image of blacks. It is a classic case of defiance through association. In the 1920s members of the white New York avant-garde saw themselves as living on the edge when they traveled uptown in suits and furs to experience the exotic thrill of Harlem culture. In the 1950s the goateed Beatniks saw themselves as white Negroes, "dragging themselves through the negro streets at dawn looking for an angry fix," as Allen Ginsberg put in his poem "Howl," living what Norman Mailer called a Negro life of "ever-threatening danger" and "primitive" pleasure diametrically opposed to the stiff and conventional society against which they were rebelling. "At lilac evening," wrote Jack Kerouac in the Beat manifesto *On the Road*, "I walked with every muscle aching among the lights of 27th and Welton in the Denver colored section, wishing I were a Negro, feeling that the best the white world had offered was not enough ecstasy for me, not enough life, joy, kicks, darkness, music, not enough night." A decade later the white student radicals of the sixties assumed a more militant black mantle, took up the ghetto cause, and elevated blacks on the streets as the true voice of black American life. To white youth, prison writing became authentic black writing. With copies of Eldridge Cleaver's *Soul on Ice* in hand, they took over administration buildings on campus in solidarity with black student groups or the Black Panthers. It was an honor to be associated with black militants in any way possible. "To the cops, we're all niggers," a sixties student organizer said with pride. Yippie leader Abbie Hoffman used to call his youthful rebels just a bunch of "white niggers."

Most of these past and present wiggers have little interest in identifying with, being like, or learning about most blacks—hard-working folks who aspire to the middle-class American

Dream. The black they choose to see is a metaphor for rebellion. It is a way to act out an image of defiance. It is a badge of authenticity. One white rapper named Vanilla Ice went so far as to create a fictional past about growing up in a rough neighborhood and attending a predominantly black school. He sold millions of records. To some extent wiggers are simply the most visible examples of a very American brand of teenage rebellion. Marketers know this better than anyone. They know that suburban white kids want their comfortable lives to feel authentic, to appear close to the edge, which is why some fast-food, soft-drink, entertainment, athletic-shoe and clothing companies target white teens with ads featuring rap music or romanticized inner-city images. White kids get the mainstream goods wrapped in a defiant package. As author John Hoberman writes, "The barren emotional landscape of the ghetto is converted into pure style, so that a white male audience can take a vicarious walk on the wild side."[37]

Some might see this white youth culture as evidence of racial crossover. But crossover should not be based on caricature. There may be some white kids who truly transcend race and appreciate the many varieties of black culture, but most wiggers ultimately grow out of their rebellion and return to their white middle-class roots. In the sixties white student radical Kathy Boudin's association with the black underground had cachet that resonated with her generation, but when she was arrested in 1981 with a number of black bank robbers she was pitied for never having grown up. In the early 1990s Marky Mark was a popular white rap artist. In 1997 he began to resurrect an acting career as Mark Wahlberg. "Why did you stop being Marky Mark?" an interviewer asked him. "I grew up," he answered. The outlaw culture might be cool for whites when they are young, but it is black America that gets left with the residue, and integration that ultimately suffers. Perhaps that is why some black teens are less than enthusiastic about their wigger compatriots, whom they see as identifying not with real people but with a media-driven stereotype. "They're black to be cool," one told the *Washington Post*. "Then they're 'nigger this, nigger that' when they're home with their parents."[38]

To be sure, wiggers are not the only ones who playact the black outlaw caricature. There are plenty of middle-class blacks who themselves collude in the creation and perpetuation of this cliché, particularly black youths and young adults who see their authentic black credentials jeopardized by the scent of upward mobility, suburban comfort, middle-class status or anything else that could make them a candidate for the oreo label—black on the outside, white on the inside. So they overcompensate, stylize their anger, and identify with the most visibly alienated part of the black population. True blackness thus becomes an outlaw pose, expressed a generation ago by the beret, the sunglasses, the bullet belts, and the Black Panther chic, and today by a "down" or urban street style designed to "keep it real." These middle-class "outlaws" dress the part, speak the slang, and assume a posture of hip-hop alienation from the white mainstream. They might resent it when whites cross the street or clutch their purses, but they also relish the idea of intimidating whites. Given that whites want blacks to muzzle their anger altogether, perhaps this outlaw pose is an understandable accommodation and is in fact preferable to more overt expressions of rage. But those who get so caught up in the act that they carry it over into reality need not commit a crime to become an outlaw because the image itself becomes a prison. "Bad" becomes a compliment, success in school means "acting white," intimidation becomes sport, and whitey is to blame when anything goes wrong. By acting out the same caricature that white America uses to rebuff them, these middle-class "outlaws" not only harm themselves but they undermine integration.

It is a very human quality to look at life through the filter of images and caricatures. But it is a sad commentary that most white Americans seem to see blacks *only* that way. Perhaps this filter wouldn't be so harmful had the black experience been incorporated into the middle-class image that dominates our public culture. That unfortunately has not happened. Of the three recent images that shape the white view of black life in America, the noble Negro is certainly more appealing than the entitled black or urban outlaw images. But to be typecast as a virtuous victim is no solace to blacks who simply want to be seen as people with talents and quirks, beauty and blemishes. Yes, there may be a kernel of truth in all three images. Yes, blacks have contributed to the creation and perpetuation of all three. And yes, blacks who support the notion of group identity leave themselves open to being viewed as a group. But as long as whites either pity blacks or resent them for prospering through illegitimate or criminal means, as long as whites look at blacks not as participants in the American Dream but as impostors wanting in, there can never be a true and honest integration of equals in this great and diverse American nation.

CHAPTER EIGHT

The Perception Gap

To Robert Shoenberg, his remark was nothing more than an innocent spur-of-the moment quip that would break the ice at what was certain to be a candid and tense meeting. Shoenberg, a white Maryland educator, was the chairman of a four-member court-appointed panel that was looking into school desegregation in majority-black Prince George's County. The March 1997 meeting with representatives of the NAACP and the county school board was about to begin when school superintendent Jerome Clark, a tall black man weighing more than 250 pounds, walked in. That was when Shoenberg made his remark. Using a familiar metaphor meant to describe a powerful institution or person who throws his weight around—in this case Clark and his influential role in the desegregation debate—Shoenberg greeted the superintendent by saying, "Here's my eight-hundred-pound gorilla." To Shoenberg's chagrin, no one laughed. Within days the local NAACP would be asking a U. S. District court for Shoenberg's removal. His comment was unacceptable, a black school board member wrote to the presiding judge, loaded with one of the most racially offensive stereotypes used against blacks. "We understand what gorilla means," an NAACP attorney told the *Washington Post*. "African Americans have always been referred to as animals, especially gorillas and monkeys." When a white school board member defended Shoenberg, saying it was a misunderstanding, there were calls for her resignation too. "You have certainly indicated to the staff how you feel about African Americans," a retired school administrator told her at a public meeting. Shoenberg soon apologized, explaining that he meant "nothing racial" by the offending comment—he had made it purely "with the intention of being light, referring to the superintendent's stature and position in the school system." The judge, also white, rejected the NAACP's motion to dismiss Shoenberg, calling his record on racial matters "unimpeachable," but agreed "that the remark was inappropriate." The local NAACP president responded that the judge's decision to keep Shoenberg "puts a cloud over" the panel's work.[1]

Four words and one career-threatening controversy later, Shoenberg and everyone else involved in the incident stood at the precipice of a vast and deep divide in American race relations, one that represents the profoundly different ways that black and white Americans—even those who consider themselves friends—interpret their lives and the world around them. It is what we call the racial perception gap, and it is a chasm so wide and at times unbridgeable that one must wonder whether blacks and whites will ever be able to reconcile their respective worldviews.[2]

Shoenberg wasn't the first to stand at the precipice, nor will he be the last. In his case a remark that would be considered benign in a nonracial context took on a completely different meaning in the world of black and white. Although Shoenberg apologized and the white judge called the remark inappropriate, many white observers were left mystified, wondering how a common phrase could raise such fury and resentment among blacks. Had Shoenberg used the expression in a clearly bigoted or racial sense, he would deserve complete condemnation, many whites thought. But Americans use the 800-pound-gorilla phrase all the time to describe politicians, corporations, organizations, and almost anything large and influential. It once showed up on the cover of the *New York Times Magazine* in an article about Microsoft, complete with a photo of a gorilla holding a computer monitor. A college board chairman once said, "The eight-hundred-pound gorilla in all this is the cost factor." A database search of newspapers shows countless uses of the phrase in countless settings. Clearly, as

Shoenberg's supporter on the school board tried to say, he meant nothing by it. Why be so sensitive? Lighten up.

But to blacks, there's nothing light or funny about a comment like this. Though less common in public today than in years past, describing a black person as a monkey, gorilla, or some other species has long been typical racist fare, whether uttered by crude racists who depict blacks with simian features, by genteel racists who discreetly regard blacks as more physically but less intellectually endowed, or by pseudoscientific racists who, earlier this century, used charts and figures to classify blacks as a lower form of hominid. Nor is it just the simian depiction that reeks of racism—it's the implication that blacks are unintelligent, brutish, uncivilized, and ugly, and are capable only of physical, not mental, exertion. As one writer who grew up near Washington, D.C., in the 1960s recalled, it was not unusual for his all-white high school class to debate whether blacks were human beings and deserved civil rights or a lower species that could be denied civil rights.[3]

Today this image is rarely used so openly. It will crop up in the literature of hate groups like David Duke's National Association for the Advancement of White People, or occasionally a fringe talk-radio host will let loose, as when New York talk-radio host Bob Grant rants on about the "millions of subhumanoids, savages" in this country, uncivilized people who would "feel more at home careening along the sands of the Kalahari" in Africa. More often than not, though, deliberate references these days are hidden, are made in private with a wink and nod, or are scrawled anonymously in public places, an acknowledgment that the social norm has made overt expressions of racism unacceptable. Los Angeles police officer Laurence Powell's computer message describing blacks as "right out of *Gorillas in the Mist*" probably would have remained private had he not been tried for beating Rodney King. A picture of former mayor David Dinkins defaced with gorilla lips was circulated quietly among whites around the New York City police department. High-profile blacks regularly receive anonymous hate mail, such as the letter sent to *Boston Globe* columnist Derrick Jackson in which he and his family were described as "foul-smelling monkeys." How many whites can honestly say they have never once heard a black referred to in conversation as a jungle bunny, monkey, gorilla or ape?

This is the backdrop to Shoenberg's remark. No one in the controversy disputes Shoenberg's basic decency and overall good intentions, but given the history, blacks can never be too sure what lurks beneath the surface of any white. After all, Francis Lawrence, the president of Rutgers University, was a noted racial progressive and affirmative action supporter; his comment attributing the low test scores of blacks to their "genetic, hereditary background" just seemed to slip out. Look at Bush administration official Frederick Goodwin, a respected scientist and a former head of the federal Alcohol, Drug Abuse, and Mental Health Administration, who thought it scientifically valid to investigate the link between "hyperaggressive monkeys who kill each other" and inner-city youth violence. Look at Senator Ernest Hollings of South Carolina, a racial moderate and segregation opponent when he was governor in the 1960s, who truly thought his 1993 joke about Africans "eating each other" was funny. Or look at the public relations staff at AT&T, a company that touts its commitment to diversity, which failed to notice anything wrong with a newsletter that showed people on every continent talking by phone, except in Africa it wasn't a person but a gorilla. There are plenty of other examples. A Reagan administration official said that blacks have not yet overcome the effects of "ten thousand years of jungle freedom"; a well-regarded basketball announcer called a black player a "tough monkey"; a football commentator attributed black athletic ability to "breeding from the time of slavery." Are these people color-blind, innocent, and misunderstood, as they claim, or do they harbor a very deep, subliminal, and insidious prejudice? Can they be taken at their word, that they act out of a fundamental sense of equality, or are their actions colored by an unconscious belief in black inferiority? How many times can a black person see or hear the monkey connection and be told it means nothing or is just a joke?

A classic example took place at our own institution, American University, in the spring of 1997. It was election time on campus, and the president of the Black Student Alliance was running for student government vice president. But she failed to win the endorsement of the student newspaper because, the white editors explained, she might be too beholden to a particular segment of the campus community, blacks. The student then submitted an op-ed article criticizing the paper for its "top-down racism," which the paper printed. But it wasn't the newspaper's editorial or her response that caused the campus to ignite. What did it was a cartoon placed right beneath the black student's column that featured three baboons complaining about animal testing and one saying, "It's payback time." Within hours black students lodged a protest. To them the cartoon placement—in the context of the earlier editorial—was a transparent expression of racism. They met with the university president, a white man, who responded by writing a letter to the campus community calling the decision to run the baboon cartoon "morally repugnant." The newspaper editors couldn't believe it. The cartoon to them was a space filler. They say it was chosen for no particular reason other than its availability. But they dutifully apologized, made a public display of contrition, acknowledged that they acted improperly—and then privately expressed disbelief and denied what they did was racist. Was it?

It is a mistake to think of the perception gap as merely a disagreement over political issues like affirmative action, for it goes much deeper than that. Built into almost every interaction between blacks and whites is the entire history of race relations in America. The past is truly prologue here; it shapes who we are and how we understand the world. Although blacks, by virtue of their minority status, are reminded of it daily, no American is free of this cultural and historical dowry. In most black-white interactions the history remains buried and rarely springs forth, but when it does, as in the Shoenberg and American University examples, it releases a coiled-up tension almost four centuries in the making. Whites, so often oblivious to the history, are taken aback and even offended when blacks react with such deep anger over a remark that might on the surface seem innocent. They're overreacting again, whites often say, attributing something racial when it doesn't belong. What whites don't understand is that blacks often see more than an isolated incident, that to blacks an entire history is rolled up into it. Blacks can never be sure whether the incident is indeed isolated or is another manifestation of the same old prejudice. Just as Winston Churchill once called Russia a riddle wrapped in a mystery inside an enigma, so too can we say that race relations in America is a riddle wrapped in a quandary hidden inside a history.

Perhaps the reason we seem shocked when controversy erupts is because we tread so lightly and gingerly over our differences today. It is said today that black and white interactions, when they happen, often suffer from a contrived politeness, a forced earnestness, an avoidance of honest dialogue, an unwillingness to delve below the surface, from what one scholar called a "politeness conspiracy."[4] We prefer to back off from conflict rather than confront it. Is it because no one wants to offend or say something hurtful? Or because we fear stepping inadvertently into the perception gap and releasing the bottled-up genie of our collective history?

But as much as we try to avoid the tension, we cannot evade the perception gap, which inheres even in our most polite and casual encounters. It can be seen in a simple cash-register interaction when a white cashier puts the change on the counter rather than in the black customer's hand. "So the cashier doesn't want to touch me," the black person says to himself. It can be seen when a white teacher asks the only black student to explain an issue involving race to the rest of the class, a well-intentioned request that quietly infuriates most blacks because they don't see their role in school to be educating whites about race. It was evident when a Maryland school district wanted to portray an image of diversity and chose a candid shot of six kids in an ethnically mixed group for its 1996–97 school calendar cover, only to face a protest by blacks because the three kids in the foreground were white and the three minorities were partially obscured behind them. "That picture sends a very clear message," said a local black leader. "If you're white, it's all right, but if you're black, get back"—to which a white school board member responded that it was "absurd" if every row in a candid photo had to have a certain number of minorities. The calendars, already printed, were scrapped.[5]

But of all possible examples of the perception gap, none shows its magnitude and depth more vividly than the notorious O. J. Simpson criminal trial. Speaking for many Americans after the verdict came in, President Clinton said he was "surprised" by the tensions the trial had unleashed—but the only surprise should be that these tensions are not manifested more often. As much as we want the surface comity of everyday life to be the racial norm in America, it is more like a membrane that covers over our roiling differences. The Simpson case simply tore that membrane off. It did not worsen racial divisions in America, it merely illuminated them. Blacks and whites disagreed on almost every detail of the trial, as if each point represented a larger and vehement truth about race relations in the United States. What was a persuasive defense strategy to blacks was racial dema-goguery to whites. What was a suspicious investigation to blacks was an airtight case to whites. What was reasonable doubt to blacks was a racially driven verdict to whites. Which side is right depends on which perspective you take—but that's the point. The very essence of the perception gap is that whites and blacks look at the same phenomenon from different angles and reach opposite but still valid conclusions. Whites looking at the scien-tific evidence could easily conclude that Simpson committed the murders. Blacks looking at police motives could just as easily rea-son that he did not.

That is why history is so relevant in understanding what hap-pened. For the Simpson trial was as much about the evidence as about the basic assumptions we use to evaluate it. Simply to say that blacks and whites chose their sides according to race is to ig-nore the role of history and experience in shaping our percep-tions. We don't quibble with this notion when explaining that Japanese and Americans have different views of age, hierarchy, and authority. We understand it as a cross-cultural difference tempered by our respective histories. That is the content that must apply here and to every other example of the black-white perception gap.

History can certainly help us understand why blacks and whites reached different conclusions about the prosecution's sci-entific evidence. Generally, Americans place a great deal of faith in science. Science is the linchpin of our American belief in progress. As a society we have created a cult of expertise, a faith in data, and a trust in numbers. The reason why advertisers throw phrases like "seven out of ten dentists" at us is because they know it sounds authoritative and they know we buy it. Social science is built on a foundation of statistics that are often contradictory but nonetheless sound convincing and irrefutable. In a fundamentally insecure and frenetic culture, scientific certitude offers us stability and security. It is our civil religion.

If we share such a faith in science, why did blacks and whites disagree on the Simpson evidence? There is one important difference in the black and white perspectives on science. Whites see themselves to have generally benefited from science, whereas blacks have seen science used against them. They have seen racism wrapped in the scientific method and the trappings of science used to classify blacks as a lower species or less intelligent— the latter claim made just as recently as 1994 in Charles Murray and Richard Herrnstein's book *The Bell Curve*. They have also seen blacks as unknowing guinea pigs in medicine, as in the infamous Tuskegee experiment, which wasn't halted until 1972, in which blacks with syphilis were left untreated so that researchers could track the full impact of the disease. It is a history that leaves blacks with a whiff of skepticism about any scientific claim that directly or indirectly involves race—so much so that many blacks question the scientific claim that AIDS can be traced to a monkey virus that was first transmitted to people in Africa. So what might appear to whites as minor flaws in the prosecution's case—such as contaminated and missing evidence—raise red flags to blacks, leading to doubt, reasonable doubt—which is all our legal system requires. In fact, one juror stated afterward that the forensic witness for the defense who concluded "there is something wrong here" had more impact on the jury than all the other witnesses during the trial.[6] To black America, whose world view is forged by this history, the jury acted rationally. But to white Americans, who had little reason to doubt scientific claims, the mostly black jury was unreasonable.[7]

Further compounding the Simpson perception gap is our very different views of law enforcement and the police, the very same people who built the evidentiary case against Simpson. Most whites have full faith in the police. A cop is just a regular guy in the neighborhood who visits schoolchildren, answers our 911 calls, and puts his life on the line to protect us. According to every survey we have seen on the issue, most whites see police misconduct as an aberration and believe they would receive fair and just treatment from police. Whites feel that police deserve the benefit of the doubt.

This experience and expectation make it hard for whites to understand why blacks don't feel the same way. But they don't. It's not that blacks are anti-police. Blacks want the police to protect them as much as whites do, and research shows that the typical black interaction with police does not involve conflict but rather a black request for help. So the black view of police is more gray than the stereotype suggests. That said, the black experience with law enforcement has enough of a history to turn even a Pollyanna into a skeptic. To blacks, the only thing truly exceptional about the Rodney King case was that someone videotaped it.

Indeed, surveys taken even before the Rodney King incident showed a widespread distrust of law enforcement among blacks. Today blacks see a large percentage of their own children processed through a criminal justice system run predominantly by whites. They know that the vast majority of drug users are white but the majority of drug arrests are black. They know from personal experience that they may well be pulled over and interrogated for no other reason than the color of their skin. They suspect that police fabricate charges against them, and in at least one instance found those suspicions confirmed when six Philadelphia police officers pleaded guilty to framing blacks in 1995. They also see a disproportionate number of black elected officials under investigation for corruption and read about studies showing that black officials are far more likely to be probed for corruption than whites.[8] From there they turn to history and remember how white sheriffs in the segregated South often worked hand in glove with the Ku Klux Klan, as happened in the Philadelphia, Mississippi, murder of three civil rights activists in 1964. They know how police used to treat "uppity" blacks. And they know that whites were rarely tried and never convicted for committing violence against blacks, but blacks were almost always convicted by all-white juries for even imagined violence against

whites. These experiences may not represent the entire law enforcement system to blacks, but they certainly frame the picture.

Enter Detective Mark Fuhrman. What are blacks to think when
one of the key police officers in the Simpson case, a detective who
handled critical evidence, perjures himself over his use of the
word "nigger" and is heard on tape saying he has considered
planting evidence in order to charge blacks with crimes. To
whites, Fuhrman's comments might have no relevance to the
facts of the Simpson trial, but to blacks his attitude fits an all too
familiar law enforcement pattern. Again it raises doubt, reasonable doubt.

In the trial blacks also learned that Detective Fuhrman report-
edly hated interracial couples. That raised yet another aspect of
the case with visceral historical resonance for both races—the fact
that Nicole Brown Simpson was white, and O. J. Simpson was
black. Many blacks believe there would have been significantly
less interest in the trial had the victim been O. J.'s first wife, a
black woman. Blacks know that most whites are uncomfortable
with interracial intimacy, and they also know that some of the
most brutal injustices in American history arose from
this interracial dynamic. Very alive in black America's collective
memory are the cases of Emmett Till, who was savagely beaten
and murdered in 1955 for talking with a white woman, and the
Scottsboro Boys, the nine Alabama teens sentenced to death in
the 1930s after two white women falsely accused them of rape.
Blacks also know that the Ku Klux Klan portrayed itself as the de-
fender of white womanhood, and that white leaders of the antebellum South whipped up fears of black men raping wives and
daughters. For blacks to hear that the lead detective in the Simpson case shared this discomfort could not but heighten their
doubts about his credibility.

Whites generally dismiss these arguments as yet another racial mirage used by blacks to project blame back on whites. To
them, Simpson was a celebrity who killed two people, plain and
simple. What turned this trial into a racial referendum, most
whites believe, was the racial imagination of blacks and the cynical manipulations of Simpson's defense team. It should have
been a straightforward murder trial determined by the scientific
evidence. So what if the evidence wasn't handled perfectly, it still

led to only one conclusion. And so we come to a standstill, at the edge of America's perception gap. The process that took us there in the Simpson trial was no different from what happened in the Shoenberg eight-hundred-pound gorilla case. It is sure to be repeated many times over.

We turn to another example of the perception gap, but this one is not about how we react to an incident but how we perceive one of the most significant figures in American life today, Nation of Islam leader Louis Farrakhan. How we respond to Farrakhan has become an ongoing Rorschach test for American race relations, and in many ways our opposing views of him cut to the very heart of where we come from and what divides us.

To whites, it is hard to believe that Farrakhan has so much credibility in black America, for what they see is a dangerous demagogue whose hatred overshadows all else. Whites ask how black leaders can stand against racism everywhere but refuse to condemn a racist in their midst. After all, Farrakhan's bigoted, separatist rhetoric clearly violates both the antiracist norm and the integration ideal that blacks fought so hard to establish during the civil rights years. If a white leader used the exact same words to vilify blacks that Farrakhan uses against whites and Jews, that person would be roundly condemned as a racist. A white America that believes it has integrated sees Farrakhan as the culprit trying to pull us apart. Whites feel that blacks who defend Farrakhan or fail to condemn him collude in reinforcing his divisive message.

Blacks see it differently. Many acknowledge Farrakhan's anti-Semitism and don't like it, but they also see a leader who preaches clean living, keeps peace in housing projects, fights drug abuse, promotes marriage, promises redemption, and makes no apologies for the black struggle to survive in the United States. Blacks see an America far from integrated and don't mind when Farrakhan derides the pretense. At bottom is a message of empowerment that speaks to people who are tired of feeling powerless and lied to. Many blacks feel that no matter how much they've earned or achieved in life, they are subject to the whims of a white society that either patronizes or tolerates but rarely respects them. This feeling is widespread, from hip-hop youth to affluent professionals. Indeed, part of Farrakhan's appeal is based less on what he

says than on the fact that he says it and is not afraid of the consequences. When he makes whites squirm, when he commands the
attention of politicians and the media, and when he questions
white motives, even blacks who are offended by his rhetoric feel a
vicarious sense of power and control. And the more whites denounce him, the more they try to suppress him, the more they
lean on black leaders to isolate him, the more he becomes a symbol of black defiance and self-respect. During the 1995 Million
Man March it was fairly common to hear blacks say that they participated not because of the messenger, Farrakhan, but because
of the message. To many whites that sounded strange—you can't
separate the two. But blacks will argue that they have been separating messenger from message throughout our nation's history.
How else could black soldiers fight for freedom in a segregated
army representing a Jim Crow culture? How else could black domestics care for and love the children of slaveholders and segregationists? To function and survive in America, blacks have
learned to look beyond the bigotry of whites, to find virtue in a
tainted package. That is precisely what they do with Farrakhan
today.

To illustrate, imagine the following scene. It is the summer of
1984 and Farrakhan, in the national spotlight because of his
odious statements about Jews and his association with the Jesse
Jackson presidential campaign, was about to speak before the
prestigious National Press Club in Washington, D.C. The room
was sold out, about two-thirds white and one-third black. Seated
next to each other at one table were a white Jewish man from the
public policy world and a black woman who worked in radio. Farrakhan hadn't started yet, so the man—who identified himself as
Jewish—asked the woman what she thought about Farrakhan.
Farrakhan "fascinated" her, she told him, though she found
many of his views repellent, particularly his anti-Semitism. He
then asked why she thought so many blacks refused to denounce
Farrakhan. Because, she responded, "he is his own man" and "he
stands up to whites and takes orders from no one." To the Jewish
man this explanation made sense. This woman was clearly not an
anti-Semite.

Then came Farrakhan's speech. It was laced with remarks
about Jewish power and Jews as a type of fifth column in Ameri-

can society. At precisely the most anti-Semitic and anti-white words, many blacks in the audience spontaneously stood, cheered, and applauded, including the same black woman who had said she loathed Farrakhan's anti-Semitism. Saddened and in a mild state of disbelief, the Jewish man resisted the temptation to get angry and was left to conclude only one thing: that though he and his black table companion listened to the same speech, they heard two different things. He heard hatred, she heard self-determination. Though seated next to each other, they were standing on different sides of the perception gap. The Jewish man, in case you were wondering, is the co-author of this book.[9]

The Farrakhan and Simpson examples are meaningful not only because of the headlines they generate, but because they clarify in a public arena the real but often private role the perception gap plays in our daily lives. Beyond the headlines and the sound bites, beyond the controversy and the passion, the perception gap quietly shapes how blacks and whites interpret the world, their experiences, and each other. It shows up in our assumptions and rationalizations, in our decisions and politics, in our neighborhoods and schools. To be sure, not all whites think alike about race, nor do all blacks. But the consensus within each race is striking. Given that blacks and whites live apart, pray apart, socialize apart, dine apart, and share intimacies apart, it should be no surprise that we think apart. In our divided America not only do we live separately, but we perceive our separate lives separately.[10]

To be sure, let us not overlook an important area of consensus: blacks and whites share a nearly unanimous distaste for overt expressions of bigotry and blatant acts of discrimination. Considering the state of our nation just four decades ago, we should not underrate this accomplishment. We should be proud of establishing the norm and knowing it will not change. Beyond this, however, there is little consensus.

Most compelling are the different ways whites and blacks view the problem of discrimination. According to surveys on race conducted over the years, a substantial proportion of whites say that the civil rights gains of the 1960s largely ended the problem of discrimination in America. Whites see themselves as well meaning and concerned about racial equality. They believe themselves to be fair, if not color-blind, and they cannot imagine themselves as blatantly discriminating. With Jim Crow gone and outright bigotry diminishing, most whites just don't see discrimination as a major barrier for blacks any longer. They think Dr. King's integration dream is within reach. "Large majorities think blacks now have the same opportunities as whites in their communities in terms of obtaining jobs, housing and education," the Gallup Poll News Service reported in 1989. "Many whites are unable to name even one type of discrimination that affects blacks in their area."[11] As columnist William Raspberry observed in 1995, "Younger whites know the cruder facts: that America once had slavery and Jim Crow and now has Colin Powell. Their sense . . . is of a problem confronted and mostly resolved."[12] The problem is so resolved, most whites believe, that society has gone too far to accommodate blacks. Significant majorities of whites tell pollsters that prejudice harms blacks much less than affirmative action harms whites. Whites are not oblivious to the problems discrimination can cause blacks, but if anyone is to blame for black problems today, whites point the finger at blacks. They simply don't have the willpower or motivation to improve their lot, whites believe. All of these views are not of recent mint— as we discussed earlier in the book, they actually began to form during the early civil rights days in the 1960s, before affirmative action and welfare became national issues. So it is safe to say that whites have a fairly static and consistent view of black life, which has developed over the past three decades: discrimination no longer unduly hobbles blacks, government has helped blacks at the expense of whites, and blacks have only themselves to blame for their problems. Given these assumptions, white opposition to affirmative action and other government programs seems logical.

Needless to say, blacks don't view discrimination the same way. Most blacks see or experience at least some type of discrimination whenever they come in contact with whites. Whereas whites see racism as a rare exception today, to blacks the exception is when race *doesn't* enter into their daily lives. Although our nation has made remarkable progress in the past four decades, blacks today feel almost as strongly about the prevalence of discrimination as they did before the major civil rights bills were passed in the mid-1960s. When the Gallup organization asked blacks whether they had as good a chance as whites "to get any kind of job for which they were qualified," 74 percent said no in 1963, and 66 percent said no in 1993.[13]

The discrimination may be more subtle today, but blacks feel it just as deeply. It is expressed not in the blatant fifties style—"blacks need not apply"—but in the subtle cues and decisions that are made on a daily basis. Blacks also see how whites hear about jobs and opportunities—through their church, union, sports club, community group or fraternity network—and they know they will never be part of that. So as blacks see it, they have made progress in spite of these obstacles, with little help from whites. Their dream of the integration of truly color-blind equals remains precisely that, a dream. Blacks don't deny they are partly at fault for their problems, but they see society changing much less than whites think it has changed, and they see whites growing indifferent to racial problems altogether. As scholars Lee Sigelman and Susan Welch write in their 1991 book on racial attitudes, *Black Americans' Views of Racial Inequality: The Dream Defamed*, "According to the world view of the typical black, significant racial discrimination persists and largely accounts for where blacks as a group stand today. As a remedy, government action is necessary, even though blacks themselves are seen . . . as having gone a long way in helping their own cause."[14]

These different views of discrimination spill over into the larger perception gap about life and politics in America. Generally speaking, whites believe that our nation's problems with racism and civil rights were solved three decades ago, while blacks see racial discrimination as an ongoing and daily obstacle to opportunity and equality. When blacks see discrimination, whites see equal opportunity. When blacks say civil rights, whites say special interests. When blacks support affirmative action, whites label it quotas, preferential treatment, and reverse discrimination. And where blacks see racism, whites respond that they are being overly sensitive.

What emerges is a cycle of misunderstanding that begins with a gap in perceptions and escalates as whites and blacks deal with the consequences. The chain reaction begins when whites deny the extent of racial discrimination in America. The more whites minimize discrimination and elevate "reverse discrimination" as the moral equivalent of the black experience in America, the more blacks feel compelled to validate, defend, and amplify their grievances. To the white ear that makes black demands seem strident and aggressive, which then reinforces the white view that blacks are complaining. If whites do not see discrimination as a serious problem, attempts to remedy it will indeed seem outrageous to them, which then "justifies" the view in the white community that those special-interest blacks are getting "special treatment" or an undeserved advantage at the expense of whites. To whites, "special treatment" when they see no visible evidence of discrimination conveys a message of injustice and runs contrary to the long-held American belief that people should be treated as individuals, not as members of a group. To blacks, the white inability to acknowledge the prevalence of discrimination is reason enough why affirmative action must continue. If whites can't recognize discrimination, how can they say it is negligible? Or are white people really insinuating that we black folk imagine these things? The finger-pointing intensifies on each side, not unlike the story line in Spike Lee's 1989 film, *Do the Right Thing*, in which a dispute over white celebrity photos in a pizzeria in a black neighborhood ultimately leads to a race riot.

Misunderstanding, bitterness, and polarization are all by-products of the perception gap. Integration is its primary victim. A product of history, experience, culture, and the ongoing peculiar role of race in American society, the perception gap serves as an invisible boundary between black and white America. It may not be as obvious as a border between nations, but it is every bit as effective in separating us.

CHAPTER NINE

Rhetorical Integration: The Political Exploitation of a Dream

"Not since Congress passed the Fair Housing Act of 1968, six days after the killing of the Rev. Dr. Martin Luther King Jr.," read the lead sentence in a *New York Times* story, "has the capital seen such a flurry of official civil rights activity." The article detailed a number of administration initiatives, including a school desegregation suit, amendments to the fair-housing law, an executive order encouraging minority business contracts, and a Justice Department effort to enforce the Voting Rights Act in two Mississippi counties. In its coverage of the same story, *Time* magazine described a visit to the Mississippi Delta by the assistant attorney general for civil rights. "With Jesse Jackson as his guide," *Time* wrote, "the [assistant attorney general] dined on catfish sandwiches and grits, listened to horror stories and, holding Jackson's hand, sang 'We Shall Overcome.' Then he returned to Washington and dispatched federal registrars to five Mississippi counties to register voters."[1]

If you think these stories are about the Clinton administration, think again. They're not about the Carter, Bush, Ford, or Nixon administrations, either. The dateline was July 1983, the assistant attorney general was William Bradford Reynolds, and the president was Ronald Wilson Reagan. To describe "a flurry of civil rights activities" not seen since 1968 may sound completely at odds with the conventional wisdom about Reagan's civil rights record, but it is not. That's because Reagan's political operatives understood America's racial dynamics better than most, and took full advantage of them. They knew that most white Americans do not want real integration, that they do not want blacks living in their neighborhoods or going to school with their children. But they also knew that these same white Americans do not want to be seen as racist or as supporting a president who could be so labeled. So what the Reagan administration did that week was gift-wrap a number of warmed-over proposals and unexceptionable civil rights activities, one of which was court-ordered anyway, and package them in a well-orchestrated show of racial goodwill that was aimed not at the supposed beneficiaries, blacks, but at the real Reagan audience, middle-class whites. It was a script the Reagan team would follow throughout his administration: counter a civil rights agenda seen as inimical to blacks with racially inclusive symbols reassuring to whites. And they so much as admitted it. "It's less important to win over black voters than it is to maintain an open door with the black community and to convince many whites who care about these issues that this remains the party of Lincoln," said White House communications director David Gergen in 1982. Or as another senior official candidly explained with respect to the July 1983 civil rights week, "Even a conservative administration has to have real concern when it comes to blacks because the most conservative opinionmakers, like thoughtful Americans of every stripe, do not consider themselves racists. . . . And in moderate Republican circles, we feel the race issue is beginning to hurt us more than any other part of the fairness issue."[2]

So the same president who tried to gut the United States Civil Rights Commission and supported a tax exemption for racially segregated schools also signed the Martin Luther King holiday into law, met with King's widow at the White House, and embraced the rhetoric of King's "I Have a Dream" speech. The same president who initially resisted and then attempted to weaken an extension of the Voting Rights Act also spoke before both the Tuskegee Institute and the NAACP, and was photographed embracing the NAACP's chairwoman, Margaret Bush Wilson. The same president who made opposition to affirmative action a litmus test for his administration also visited a predominantly black elementary school and went to the home of a Maryland black family that had been victimized by a cross burning. Instead of policies that might ease the integration of blacks, the Reagan administration offered symbols of integration that salved the conscience of whites. Reagan was willing to say what most whites believed all along, that when it comes to integration we've done a pretty darn good job as a country, and blacks, not whites, bear responsibility for whatever problems remain. "[I was] under the impression," Reagan said, echoing what many whites think, "that the problem of segregated schools had been settled."[3] To the majority of white Americans it was the best of both worlds: a president who wouldn't kowtow to the black "special interest" but would, with avuncular reassurance, affirm their self-image as basically good, tolerant, and decent people committed to the color-blind ideal and incapable of bigotry or hate. The message resonated well with whites: despite constant and conspicuous black criticism of the Reagan racial record, a 1989 Harris poll found that half of all whites said Reagan had been helpful rather than hurtful to blacks.[4] The Reagan team understood the power of the integration illusion, and they played it like virtuosos during his two terms.

Much has been written about the way some politicians cynically use code words and racially charged appeals to solidify their support among angry whites. To stoke racial fires and fears simply to win votes is unconscionable and inexcusable. But perhaps more significant—and in the long run as racially debilitating—is a phenomenon we call *rhetorical integration*, which is the substitution of benign and uplifting pieties of integration for any real effort to address the racial ills of our nation. Politicians may not be too popular these days, but let us give them their due: they know how to tap in to the national mood. And when it comes to race, they know that most white Americans don't want to be integrated with blacks but also don't want to be seen as unwilling to integrate with blacks. They know that whites don't want too much proximity with blacks but want very much to be seen as broadminded and friendly to blacks. They also know that whites have little interest in civil rights but don't want to be associated with a politician perceived as openly hostile to civil rights.

The solution, as is so often the case in politics today, is to offer the trappings without the substance, the rhetoric without the risk, the image without the intent. So politicians pay homage to the integration ideal but avoid anything more than a surface look at the integration reality. They righteously condemn the outright bigotry of the few but never ask why the rest of us pull up stakes when a few black families move in nearby. And they reassure the nation that we are indeed on the right path to the promised land without ever risking political capital to get us anywhere close to there. Symbolism becomes truth, image becomes reality, language becomes action. The integration illusion has found its priesthood in our politicians. Wearing the cloth of the civil rights era, they bless us with their rhetoric, proclaim their own moral purity, and absolve us of the nation's original sin. And so the majority of Americans—heartened by the image of racial progress and comity—walk away confirmed in their goodness, believing even more fervently that as a nation we have done our racial duty, wondering why blacks seem so incapable of fulfilling the promise of American life.

To be sure, there's nothing inherently wrong with elected officials quoting King or using the soaring language of brotherhood. The problem begins when the mere act of speaking the words or embracing the symbols becomes a self-congratulatory or even a courageous end in itself. Though disguised as racial solicitude, rhetorical integration is yet another form of racial denial, and insofar as it sustains the integration illusion, it is as powerful as any code word in keeping real integration a distant and unreachable dream.

For a textbook case of rhetorical integration, consider the 1996 Republican Party convention. Think what you may about the Republican approach to race relations and civil rights, but the bare facts are these: it is nearly an all-white party; only about nine percent of America's blacks identify themselves as Republicans; it is the party to which Southern whites fled after blacks got the vote and began supporting Democrats; it is the party that courted urban ethnic whites worried about black political power; Senator Jesse Helms and commentator Patrick Buchanan are among its most influential figures; and finally, the party's primary civil rights issue is the complete elimination of affirmative action. By 1996 even the Republican hierarchy had come to understand that this image is not what the public associates with tolerance today. So the party, knowing it had to soften its image and reassure the moderate majority that they were after all fair-minded people about race, used the trick bag of rhetoric and symbolism to create the integration illusion.

Before our very eyes, on television, the Republican party transformed itself into a middle-class incarnation of Jesse Jackson's Rainbow Coalition. Although Patrick Buchanan entered the convention with the most delegates after nominee Robert Dole, his image of intolerance meant there was no high-profile speaking slot for him. Instead, the party scheduled black speakers like General Colin Powell and Representatives Gary Franks and J. C. Watts for the prime-time spotlight. It also loaded convention speeches with references to Martin Luther King, showed black and white children in its convention videos, featured a little black girl with the AIDS virus, and leaned on the network control booths to focus their cameras on the few black delegates in the convention hall. Although only 2.7 percent of the Republican delegates were black, about 20 percent of the network reaction shots during Senator Dole's acceptance speech were of blacks.[5] When the white woman who served as convention secretary learned that the biggest perk of her job, announcing the roll call vote, had been given to a black woman, she told the Associated Press, "Well, all you have to do is look at her. She's black and I'm white." Then, realizing she had punctured the illusion, she quickly added, "This isn't about race."[6] Of course not.

One of the most typical and effective rhetorical-integration techniques is to use—some would say abuse—the words and image of Dr. King. King has become a prop used by many politicians today to illustrate their own moral purity and devotion to integration, and it is rare to find an elected official who does not incorporate King's stirring words into a speech whenever a racial issue comes up. To cite King is to reaffirm a feeling, a vision, a desire for integration that overlays an illusion of unity on top of our racially separated daily lives. Ronald Reagan quoted King even though he opposed every civil rights bill King worked so hard to pass in the 1960s. "I am wholeheartedly in support of integration and was long before we had the term 'civil rights,' " he told a class of schoolchildren in 1983. His attorney general, Edwin Meese III, described the Reagan administration's opposition to affirmative action as "very consistent with what Dr. King had in mind." To-day, almost every prominent affirmative action opponent, from House Speaker Newt Gingrich to California governor Pete Wilson, claims that color-conscious remedies violate Dr. King's vision of a color-blind society. Backers of the 1996 anti–affirmative action referendum in California, the brilliantly named California Civil Rights Initiative, even tried to use King's "I Have a Dream" speech in its television ads, until King's widow protested. Associating themselves with King provides these largely white opponents of affirmative action protective cover and enables them to claim the moral high ground as the true defenders of racial fairness and integration. To them, it is the affirmative action proponents and the civil rights leadership who veered from King—who are balkanizing our nation, dwelling on race, and pulling us apart.

The only problem is that most politicians, especially most affirmative-action opponents, are unable to cite anything of King's other than his famous line in the "I Have a Dream" speech, that his four little children "one day will live in a nation where they will not be judged by the color of their skin but by the content of their character." In their zeal to use these words for their own purposes, our politicians have reduced King's message to one line taken completely out of context. They have turned his vision of an ideal future into a prescription for color-blindness that should apply to the present. "I think the best means to achieve the ends of a color-blind society," conservative politician William Bennett said in 1986, "is to proceed as if we are indeed a color-blind society."[7] The King who called for "discrimination in reverse . . . a sort of national atonement for the sins of the past" is nowhere to be found. Nor is the King who called for "radical changes in the structure of society," or for "a Bill of Rights for the Disadvantaged," or for "a policy of preferential treatment to rehabilitate the traditionally disadvantaged Negro."[8] King wrote in his 1964 book *Why We Can't Wait*, "It is obvious that if a man is entered at the starting line in a race three hundred years after another man, the first would have to perform some impossible feat in order to catch up with his fellow runner." He realized that preferential treatment might make "some of our friends recoil in horror," but he also knew that "equal opportunity" without "the practical, realistic aid" to balance the equation was little more than a charade. "Giving a pair of shoes to a man who has not learned to walk is a cruel jest," he wrote.[9] These were the very color-conscious ideas and policies that King thought might lead us to his promised, color-blind land. But they are too threatening to the integration illusion, too incompatible with what the largely white audience wants to hear, and too inconsistent with what the politicians want to say. So white politicians feed a denatured, neutralized King to their constituents, who want to see themselves—and their opposition to affirmative action—as truly color-blind and fair. It is rhetorical integration at its very best.

The first mainstream politician to use King for personal advantage was neither Ronald Reagan nor Newt Gingrich, but John Kennedy. In the fall of 1960, the presidential race was a dead heat, and King was sitting in a Georgia jail on a trumped-up charge. On the advice of campaign aides, Kennedy briefly called Coretta Scott King to express his concern about her husband. To many observers that single call was a decisive moment in the election campaign—arguably as important as the Kennedy-Nixon debate. Nixon could have made such a call but refused. Because of it Kennedy gained enough black votes to shift the razor-thin election his way. To Kennedy it was a lesson in the politics of race. Civil rights was a problem to be managed rather than a cause to be embraced. It was more advantageous to engage it at the level of symbols and words rather than policies and actions. And that is precisely what he did. When *U.S. News & World Report* asked NAACP executive secretary Roy Wilkins in April 1963 for his views on President Kennedy, almost all Wilkins could think of was that Kennedy had called the Coast Guard the morning after the inauguration to ask why there were no blacks in its parade contingent. "Now this was just a gesture . . ." Wilkins acknowledged, "and the fact that not much has been done about real, solid problems is glossed over." But at least Kennedy "has a good attitude," Wilkins added.[10]

Although the Kennedy myth portrays him as a profile in courage on civil rights, almost every historian of the Kennedy years describes him as disengaged from civil rights and racial issues. Observed Taylor Branch in *Parting the Waters*, his benchmark history of the early civil rights years, "the best spirit of

Kennedy was largely absent from the racial deliberations of his presidency."[11] Kennedy showed little interest in civil rights when he served in the Senate, and some say that the most passionate he ever got about blacks was on his inaugural night, when he danced with some black women to the music of Chubby Checker. Robert Kennedy once recalled that his brother rarely thought about blacks or discussed their plight.[12] Nor did the President mention civil rights in his inaugural address. If contact with King became inconvenient, Kennedy would keep his distance—he did not even invite King to the inauguration. It took him almost two years to fulfill his "stroke of a presidential pen" campaign promise to sign an executive order banning segregation in federally assisted housing, and even then he exempted existing housing. When civil rights leaders approached Kennedy in 1963 about a possible march on Washington, Kennedy was cold to the idea, accepting it only when the march became inevitable. "If there is an incident, it will hurt," a Kennedy staffer coolly assessed the forthcoming march. "If not, it may have a faint positive impact."[13] Not until his third year as president, with segregationist bigotry and the blood of civil rights marchers embarrassing America internationally, did Kennedy finally submit civil rights legislation to Congress and give a nationally televised address describing racial justice "primarily as a moral issue." But to many observers, this "moral issue" of Kennedy's rested on a foundation of political necessity and calculation.

It is not our intent—and it may be unfair—to judge a man who, according to his supporters, was about to find his civil rights compass had his life not so suddenly ended. Our purpose is simply to show how the Kennedy approach to race has become the archetype for almost every subsequent mainstream politician in America. Kennedy was the first to show us how to use the symbols that mollify blacks and flatter whites, to let words speak louder than actions, and to condemn racial bigotry everywhere but never become too entangled with racial justice anywhere. Without ever fully committing himself to the cause of civil rights, Kennedy led the majority of Americans to believe that both he and they were good, moral agents in the war against bigotry and segregation. Not even Ronald Reagan and Richard Nixon violated this lesson. Kennedy may have briefly flirted with civil rights legislation toward the end of his presidency, but his lasting racial legacy was to show his successors how the appearance of moral action was politically safer and more rewarding than pushing policies that would satisfy the few but anger the many. The one president who went beyond appearances, Lyndon Johnson, paid a very steep political price. Rarely do you see politicians today model their racial agendas on Johnson's.

Richard Nixon immediately understood that Kennedy's phone call to King's wife may have cost him the 1960 election. His civil rights platform plank was not significantly different from Kennedy's, and he saw no reason why he couldn't hold the 40 percent of the black vote that Eisenhower had reached in 1956. But he didn't, receiving only 30 percent. And it was the phone call that did it. Nixon would never let inattention to racial symbolism undercut him again.

Given the timing of his presidency and the racial significance of his political strategy, Nixon may have been the most influential president on race in the latter half of the twentieth century. He also may have been the most bigoted president of our times, as the White House tapes and the diary of his former aide H. R. Haldeman show, not only in his regular use of words like "jigs," "niggers," and "Uncle Toms" but in his contemptuous view of black abilities and aspirations. A calculating, brooding, hateful man, Nixon also was a brilliant political strategist, and throughout his administration he played a cynical high-wire act on race that showed a ruthless disregard for its long-term impact on our social fabric.

Nixon's first and most paramount goal was to capture the George Wallace vote and to harness white racial anger for the Republican party. In pursuit of this "southern strategy," he actually cultivated white resentments not only in the South but all over the nation, and eventually his strategy succeeded in realigning the electoral map by peeling away white urban ethnic voters from the Democratic column and creating a Republican majority among whites. But Nixon also knew that his strategy would not work if the public thought he was deliberately trying to polarize the nation. He and his advisers believed that whites basically hated blacks, but also that most whites didn't want to see themselves as bigots. Nixon also feared the black reaction to openly divisive policies. So he adopted the Kennedy lesson on racial politics and twisted it for his own political needs. He manipulated racial symbols, described himself as a unifier, indignantly denied that his white supporters were racists, and used high-profile policies to further his deception. It was rhetorical integration at its most cynical.

As explained in Joe McGinniss's *The Selling of the President*, the classic account of Nixon's 1968 campaign, the Nixon racial strategy was evident from the beginning. In this campaign, unlike the 1960 contest, Nixon had no illusions about winning a large chunk of the black vote, not only because Republicans had opposed most of the landmark civil rights legislation of the 1960s but also because his opponent was civil rights champion Hubert Humphrey. And Nixon had his sights aimed on the white vote anyway. But as McGinniss tells it, the Nixon public relations team used every opportunity to portray their man as a tolerant, open-minded leader. That meant including token blacks whenever possible. Typical was the campaign's effort to produce a nationally televised show in which Nixon would answer questions from a panel. For them, a "balanced" panel was crucial. McGinniss captures their thinking: "First, this meant a Negro. One Negro. Not two. Two would be offensive to whites, perhaps to Negroes as well. Two would be trying too hard. One was necessary and safe." In another example, McGinniss quotes a top Nixon aide discussing the need for a black participant in a Philadelphia forum: "And goddammit, we're locked into this thing, anyway. Once you start it's hard as hell to stop, because the press will pick it up and make a big deal out of why no Negro all of a sudden."

The message they wanted to portray was clear: Nixon is not a bigot. And then the campaign went a critical step further. It reassured white Americans that they were not bigots either. One television ad that pictured the very black-associated images of riots, welfare, and urban crime had a voice-over of Nixon describing the "good" and "decent" people of his Silent Majority: "They work, they save, they pay their taxes, they care," Nixon said. And one other thing: "They are not racists or sick." They might even include a few blacks.[14] Nixon's racial strategy was clear even before he was elected. Prey on white fears about blacks, use tokenism to inoculate him (and his supporters) from charges of racism, and flatter whites that the unease they feel about blacks has nothing to do with them and everything to do with blacks.

Nixon's pursuit of this strategy only intensified once he became president. He timed one of his first symbolic acts for the first anniversary of King's assassination, when he dispatched Secretary of Health, Education and Welfare Robert Finch to visit King's widow in Atlanta with a note from Nixon invoking her husband's dream of a day when people would not be "judged by the color of their skin but by the content of their character." Not long after that began the periodic and well-publicized parade of high-profile black visitors to the Nixon White House: singer Pearl Bailey, basketball star Wilt Chamberlain, jazz great Lionel Hampton. There was also the occasional meeting with black journalists, a White House seventieth birthday party for big-band legend Duke Ellington, and Nixon's much-remembered embrace of entertainer Sammy Davis, Jr., the first black American to spend the night at the White House—a fact the Nixon team wouldn't let the press forget. Nixon also appointed civil rights leader James Farmer as an assistant secretary of Health, Education and Welfare, another brilliant public relations stroke. Because Farmer had gained fame as a victim of vicious beatings during the 1961 Freedom Rides to desegregate interstate travel in the South, Nixon could associate himself with an icon against bigotry. After a year, Farmer resigned out of frustration and disgust.

During this time Nixon played his other hand well, whipping up white anger over school busing, focusing on law-and-order fears, denouncing black militants, and reassuring his Silent Majority that while they might not agree with blacks on civil rights issues, they were good and tolerant people after all. His administration pursued only one unequivocal civil rights policy that could have alienated whites, and that was its enforcement of Southern school desegregation. But given the totemic status of the Supreme Court's *Brown* v. *Board of Education* decision on school desegregation, not to do so might have proved politically riskier, and anyway, Nixon was adroit enough to shift the blame to the courts. "It was the Supreme Court, not Nixon, that drew most of the fire" on school desegregation, wrote *Time* magazine in 1969.[15]

Of all Nixon's calculated moves, none captures his wickedly brilliant racial cynicism better than what was known as the Philadelphia Plan, his executive order that imposed racial hiring quotas on construction trade unions working on federally funded projects. As the diaries and notes of his former aides make clear, Nixon knew exactly what he would accomplish with this single act: not only would he emerge as an opponent of bigotry and discrimination, but he would split apart two key Democratic constituencies, blacks and labor, thereby forcing the Democrats to choose between them. Nixon had few friends in organized labor, so that didn't matter to him. Nor did he expect much of a gain among blacks. But he knew the Democrats would embrace the quotas and side with blacks, which would anger labor and further push the white blue-collar worker into Republican ranks.

That was only the beginning. To complete the circle and ensure the success of his strategy, he then renounced these same quotas during the 1972 campaign and made them out to be a Democratic scheme, which further solidified his support among the blue-collar rank and file. "When young people apply for jobs . . . and find the door closed because they don't fit into some numerical quota, despite their ability, and they object," he asserted, "I do not think it is right to condemn those young people as insensitive or even racist."[16] Here was Nixon's racial strategy all rolled into one. He inoculated himself against bigotry, fueled racial resentment among his white constituents, and exonerated these same constituents of any racially hostile feelings they might harbor. It may be true, as *Newsweek* wrote in 1969, when Nixon sent his note to Coretta Scott King, "that the nation that elected him president" was no more ready for Martin Luther King's dream than Nixon was prepared to pursue it.[17] But pouring fuel on the fire was the last thing we needed. To this day we are living with the consequences of Nixon's embittered genius.

Our current president, Bill Clinton, says he is different, very different: "The whole issue of reconciling races in America has been a passion of my life, even before I was an elected official."[18] Perhaps no other president in history has felt so personally comfortable around blacks, especially when compared to Kennedy's indifference, Nixon's unease, and Reagan's near obliviousness to most blacks. Clinton keeps time in the black church, speaks like a preacher before black audiences, enjoys soul food and jazz, maintains close friendships with blacks, and may be one of the only white Americans to know every verse of *Lift Every Voice and Sing*, the song known as the black national anthem. He has acted on his mantra "Diversity is our strength," by appointing a higher percentage of blacks to government positions than any previous president. Nor is he afraid to poke at the integration illusion by occasionally pointing out the reality of racial separation in American life. "Segregation is no longer the law, but too often, separation is still the rule," he lamented in 1997 while commemorating the fortieth anniversary of school desegregation in Little Rock. "And we cannot forget one stubborn fact that has not yet been said as clearly as it should: there is still discrimination in America." Clinton's national conversation on race, the "One America" initiative he began early in his second term, is also unique: no other president has asked our nation to discuss race relations absent a national crisis or civil unrest. If America wants evidence of its own color-blind potential, Clinton would have us believe, they need not look further than the president himself.

And so it is all the more dispiriting that Bill Clinton has played his own variation of the rhetorical-integration game and has largely reinforced the same old national thinking about race. Yes, he's had some good lines in speeches; yes, he occasionally challenges us to cross the racial divide; and yes, he has employed all the redemptive racial symbols we have come to expect from presidents—but the racial message of his presidency bears much more resemblance to his predecessors' than he would like to admit. Bill Clinton may care a great deal, personally, about racial issues, but he is above all a politician. As a politician he has spent his life calculating what it takes to win, which constituencies to please, what symbols to put forth. By the early 1990s almost every Democratic strategist cautioned that white voters perceived the party as too closely tied to blacks, and that the only way to neutralize this view was by telling whites that racism was no longer a compelling problem in America, but that crime and welfare—and by implication, blacks—were. Clinton knew that to get elected in 1992, he needed not only to cater to middle-class whites but also to show them that he was willing to stand up to blacks. One of the leading advocates of this analysis was Clinton's pollster, Stanley Greenberg. Clinton clearly listened.[19]

In his 1992 campaign, the man who called racial reconcilia-tion "a passion of my life" barely mentioned the issue, except for some feel-good lines about racial inclusion—most often said to black audiences—and his campaign promise to have an adminis-tration that "looks like America." The 1992 campaign book he coauthored with Al Gore, *Putting People First*, listed thirty-one "crucial issues" facing America, from agriculture to women, but race relations was not one of them—and that book was written not long after the Los Angeles riots. The book did include a sec-tion on civil rights, but except for the statement "Oppose racial quotas," not a single recommendation relates specifically to blacks, though there were detailed proposals for women, Native Americans, and gays and lesbians.[20] The 1992 Democratic plat-form was similarly silent on race relations, though it too included a renunciation of racial quotas. Crime, personal responsibility, and welfare reform also became major campaign themes, again tacitly pointing the finger at blacks and implicitly vindicating whites. Clinton's response to the Los Angeles riots and the Rod-ney King verdict was to excuse white flight to all-white neighbor-hoods as a rational response to the fear of black crime: "White people have been scared for so long that they have fled to the suburbs of America to places like Simi Valley and Macomb County in Michigan. I understand those fears."[21] Clinton also scored big when he stood up to Jesse Jackson, the archetypal "uppity black." Clinton may not have won over the majority of white voters, but he was following the new Democratic victory script: middle America is virtuous, and we are a good and decent people op-posed to bigotry and willing to integrate once black Americans get their house in order. As for his black constituents, Clinton turned himself into a symbol of goodwill and said, effectively, "Trust me, I talk your talk, I'm on your side." In comparison to his predecessors, it certainly seemed that way. It was rhetorical in-tegration at its most subtle.

With an eye on his 1996 reelection campaign, Clinton veered little from these themes during his first term as president. The sole exception was his politically necessary plea to mend affirma-tive action, not to end it. But this policy decision was less courageous than it seems for two reasons: first, most blacks see support for affirmative action as a litmus test, so he could not have aban-. doned it without seriously damaging the Democratic party; second, despite all the political fireworks over the issue, affirmative action touches the daily lives of relatively few whites, making it politically safe to support as long as he inoculated himself on other racial issues and did not appear too beholden to blacks.

And inoculation is precisely what he did. His two major first-term addresses on race proved a continuation of his implied campaign message that it was black America—not white America—that needed to change before Dr. King's dream ever could be achieved. In the first, a 1993 speech to black ministers that he gave at the same Memphis pulpit where King had delivered his final sermon, Clinton spoke about black crime as an abuse of the freedom that King sacrificed his life to achieve. "The freedom to die before you're a teenager is not what Martin Luther King lived and died for," Clinton said. It was a compelling and heartfelt speech, making clever use of King, but to some blacks it seemed curious that his first major address on race would dwell on black crime and use Martin Luther King as its rhetorical prop. Many felt that his real audience was whites. In the second speech, delivered in Texas on the same day as the Million Man March on Washington, he took a firm but easy stand against blatant bigotry by condemning "racist rhetoric," police misconduct and other racially "destructive ideas." But then, using a rhetorical device by which he repeated the phrase "it isn't racist" four times, he absolved white America of its responsibility by saying that it isn't racist for whites to fear crime, avoid certain neighborhoods, dislike gangs, and criticize welfare. "It isn't racist," he said in one of his refrains, "for whites to assert that the culture of welfare dependency, out-of-wedlock pregnancy, and absent fatherhood cannot be broken by social programs unless there is first more personal responsibility."[22] He never asked if it was racist for whites to leave a community when some black families move in.

Clinton's final inoculation came with his capstone act during his first term: his decision to sign a controversial welfare overhaul on the eve of the fall 1996 campaign, a bill even he found troubling because it could send more than a million children into poverty, but a bill his political advisers, especially strategist Dick Morris, said he must sign to shore up his support among whites. But merely signing the bill wasn't enough. In front of all the cameras at the White House signing ceremony, Clinton surrounded himself with black women who had worked their way out of welfare. And so he encoded a clear message to white America: this bill is good for blacks even though the black politicians don't like it—it's tough love, just what they need—and as you can see by who's around me, I'm really doing it for them. Being firm with blacks and surrounding yourself with blacks—Clinton took a page right out of Nixon's racial playbook.

As of this writing, it is too early to tell whether President Clinton's national conversation on race will amount to anything more than another feel-good exercise that confirms the integration illusion and leaves most white Americans thinking they have done everything possible to integrate with blacks. What is striking so far is that Clinton has chosen to play the role of national moderator, the Oprah Winfrey of our racial conversation, which has largely taken him out of the conversation. But leadership on race requires much more than the chatty skills of an afternoon talk-show host. It requires the "passion" that he claims to feel on racial issues. For him truly to lead on race, he must ask some hard questions. He must candidly discuss why whites move from their neighborhoods when middle-class blacks move in, and why so many successful blacks feel so angry and bitter today. He must also come clean about his own political use of race, for he cannot ask the rest of us to be honest without doing some confessional soul searching himself. He must then be willing to call some of us defensive, more of us prejudiced, and many of us wrong. He must be willing not only to say that discrimination exists but to specify precisely what constitutes discrimination today. He must be willing to dig way down into our basic assumptions and make us very uncomfortable, a role to which few politicians are accustomed. He must even be willing to do what no president has done since Lyndon Johnson: give a nationally televised speech on race. Addressing nearly four centuries of frustration and separation cannot be accomplished through a couple of polite town meetings televised on C-SPAN. It may be that no president will ever be able to lead us to the promised land, but at least an honest and gut-wrenching dialogue might challenge our state of denial, force us to acknowledge the racial realities before us, and help us approach them realistically.

How likely is this scenario? Not very, given white America's comfort with the integration illusion and the lack of any politically safe means for an elected official to challenge it. Although Clinton waited until his second term to begin this conversation, he would like us to believe that it is an act of presidential courage simply to take on race as an issue. Perhaps he is right, since most whites would rather avoid the issue. Perhaps, given the permanence and depth of the racial divide, we should simply be thankful if any politician is willing to put his toe in the choppy waters. But as long as the national conversation leaves our assumptions in place, as long as it salves our racial conscience through the illusion of action, and as long it does little more than place a veneer of reconciliation over the irreconcilable, then Clinton's race initiative will fall squarely in line with the rhetorical integration of his predecessors and offer no greater legacy than the catfish sandwich that Ronald Reagan's assistant attorney general ate before singing "We Shall Overcome" deep down in rural Mississippi.

PART THREE

WHERE DO WE GO FROM HERE?

CHAPTER TEN

Can Integration Work?

Singing the virtues of Shaker Heights, Ohio, comes naturally to Mayor Patricia Mearns.[1] Effusive and brimming with civic pride, she probably sounds no different from countless other mayors around the country. But Mayor Mearns has a special reason to fly the Shaker Heights flag. This small suburban city of 32,000 just outside Cleveland, a city of Tudor homes and Georgian architecture, is probably the single best example of a racially integrated community in America. There aren't many such communities in the United States. Barely five percent of American communities have enough of a racial mix to qualify, according to one estimate,[2] and it would be more accurate to describe many that appear integrated as simply undergoing a slower than normal transition from white to black. Indeed, what makes Shaker Heights stand above the others is the enduring stability of its integration. There is an ongoing comfort level with interracial proximity not seen in many other ostensibly integrated communities, and there is a civic commitment to keep it that way. For nearly three decades, the city has maintained a fairly steady ratio of about one black for every two or three whites, and its well-regarded and thoroughly integrated school system has seen relatively little white flight over the years.

This is not to suggest that Shaker Heights is immune from the process of racial separation that infects the rest of American life. Even the best American communities cannot escape that. Of the nine Shaker neighborhoods, one has turned almost exclusively black, another doubled its black population in the 1980s and is now about four-fifths black, and two neighborhoods—the most affluent ones—are more than 90 percent white. There are reports of less interracial mingling than community leaders would like us to believe. At the public high school, lunchroom separation is common, intramural sports and extracurricular activities often divide along racial lines, and the advanced placement courses tend to be predominantly white, while blacks are clustered in the regular college-prep classrooms. But while Shaker Heights may not be the racial promised land, it is about as close as any American community gets. People who grew up in Shaker Heights but later leave often report that they never fully realized how special it was until they left. Despite the social separation at school, no one stares when white and black kids cross over into each other's groups. White teens don't feel they must adopt the caricature "wigger" pose to have black friends, and black teens need not fear the "oreo" or "sellout" label if they spend time with whites. In three of the city's neighborhoods, blacks and whites live together in almost exact proportion to their overall numbers in the community. And in light of the fact that most white American homeowners get the itch to sell when one or more black families move onto the block, we rub our eyes in near disbelief to learn that in one of Shaker's majority-black neighborhoods, white families are moving in as often as blacks, and doing it enthusiastically.

If there is a secret to Shaker Heights' success, it lies in a phrase that sends a chill up the spine of most Americans: social engineering. Integration in Shaker Heights did not just come about. It is the result of a conscious and intentional policy to integrate— a policy that costs money, provides incentives, and asks some to sacrifice a little personal choice for the greater good of the community. Day after day the mayor and other top administrators dwell on the smallest of racial details, leave little to chance, and always look at the racial consequences of their decisions. Called affirmative marketing or integration maintenance, Shaker Heights runs a sophisticated operation that promotes racial balance in housing, in the schools, and in civic activities. Shaker Heights officials make clear to its white residents that if they try to run they won't be able to hide without leaving the community altogether.

Most innovative is the way Shaker Heights manages its neighborhood housing patterns. The city runs a housing office, the Center for Housing and Community Life, which aggressively promotes integrated housing, and monitors the racial mix of the city's neighborhoods. Whites who go to the housing office seeking real estate information are discouraged from buying in mostly white neighborhoods; blacks are likewise discouraged from settling in neighborhoods that are disproportionately black. Those willing to buy in neighborhoods where their race is underrepresented are eligible for mortgage assistance and special loans from the city. That means whites can receive financial aid by moving into disproportionately black areas, and blacks can gain by moving where there are few blacks. At one time real estate agents even received a bonus for encouraging blacks and whites to settle in these neighborhoods. But Shaker Heights doesn't stop there. If blacks want to move to Shaker Heights but cannot afford a house in a mostly white area, the community offers financial incentives and loans to buy in a more affordable white suburb outside Shaker—with or without that suburb's cooperation—so as not to further the racial imbalance in Shaker's predominantly black neighborhoods. About twenty-five of these loans are issued each year. As Shaker Heights officials explain, blacks seek out Shaker Heights because it is tested, tolerant, and integrated. Nevertheless, if blacks take all the available spots in Shaker's majority-black neighborhoods, integration declines and the city may end up on the slippery slope of racial separation. Besides, these officials add, it's time the other suburbs become friendly to blacks. That would open more choices to blacks and relieve the pressure on Shaker Heights as the one truly integrated haven in the area. Shaker's integration mission transcends its city limits.

Shaker Heights also uses its public school system to ensure that affluent whites who have few black neighbors cannot evade the dynamics of integration. Currently all the elementary schools are racially mixed, and the city has only one middle school and high school. When one neighborhood turned mostly black, its youngsters were paired in an elementary school with children from a predominantly white part of town, and when the system showed other signs of racial divergence, the city closed some schools and consolidated others. In other racially mixed communities, above-average test scores have not kept white parents from sending their kids to private schools. But parents rarely do in Shaker Heights, which means the children of white bankers and lawyers walk the same fluorescent corridors as the children of black secretaries, steamfitters, and surgeons.

Although city government programs are integral to Shaker Heights' brand of social engineering, there's more to the community's integration effort than programs, incentives, and school boundary lines. Shaker Heights has engineered a veritable culture of integration and has deliberately made integration a core part of the city's identity. There are task forces, oversight committees, community associations, planned events, block parties, regattas, student groups, and many other consciously integrated activities that are woven into the Shaker Heights civic life. To fine-tune their efforts, city officials constantly inquire into the racial makeup of sports teams and social functions. Talk about race is encouraged, not avoided. Interracial events are accorded status, not passed off as obligations. High school courses on race attract both blacks and whites, not just blacks and a trickle of whites. People moving into Shaker Heights may like its nice houses and convenient location, but it is also made clear to them that they are buying in to a racially integrated way of life that is emphatically different from what other communities offer.

Other like-minded communities find this total commitment to integration hard to replicate, try as they might. A large part of Shaker's advantage is that it started early, in the late 1950s, which enabled it to ward off the surging white flight that characterized those years and to create and develop an alternative culture of integration. As happened in almost every other all-white area back then, whites in Shaker Heights immediately panicked when the first blacks moved there in 1955. For Sale signs dotted the lawns, and real estate buzzards preyed on white fears to spur panic sales to blacks. Real estate agents saw in Shaker Heights simply another example of what they had seen and profited from elsewhere: a wholesale neighborhood evacuation by thousands of whites, and thousands of blacks moving in to replace them. But unlike most other areas, the black and white residents didn't just give in; they bonded together and formed neighborhood associations to fight back and confront banks for their lending practices and real estate offices for their blockbusting practices. These neighborhood associations also sweetened the pot for whites, providing them with financial incentives to move onto these racially changing blocks.

It is unclear why Shaker Heights took this path when most other communities didn't. Perhaps it is because the city started out as a planned community in the 1920s, a city built on communitarian values that mandated architectural styles and even limited the outdoor paints people could use, and so it might have attracted a core of white people predisposed to an aggressive form of social engineering. It also might be that these same white residents, when given the opportunity to manage integration and slow the black migration into town, were willing to take the risk because there weren't many other places around Cleveland that at the time offered the same benefits of living in Shaker Heights: the good schools, easy commute, and rising property values. And it is certainly possible that Shaker at the time was home to a critical mass of white people who were unwilling to live with the hypocrisy of selling their homes simply because a black dentist moved in. Whatever the reason, the result, four decades later, is the rarest of American communities, one singularly committed to making integration work.

The mayor and others closely involved in Shaker's integration all say the same thing: to become color-blind you first need to become color-conscious. People don't start out color-blind, they say, but you will never get them there without sustained interaction, and the only way to create that is through color-conscious planning. To them it is a lesson based not on ideology but on day-to-day experience. "People want it to happen naturally, but naturally in America is segregation," said Dr. Winston Richie, one of the first blacks to move into Shaker Heights in the 1950s and an early pioneer in the city's integration efforts.[3] Mayor Mearns says with a sigh that "integration is a constant challenge," that Shaker can never rest on its laurels.[4] Would racial separation overtake Shaker Heights without a planned and ongoing effort to maintain integration? "No question," answered Donald DeMarco, an architect of Shaker's integration programs during the 1980s and currently a national advocate for integrated housing. If the housing office were closed, DeMarco added, "You'd see panic."[5]

Currently the city spends more than $600,000 yearly on programs to bring blacks and whites together, and most residents support Shaker's affirmative marketing activities. But whites must accept a government that makes race an issue, intervenes in the real estate marketplace, enforces what amounts to racial quotas in the schools, and monitors almost every activity for evidence of white flight in any form. Many whites would prefer never to ponder their own racial assumptions, but they have no such option if they choose to live in Shaker Heights. Blacks in Shaker Heights also must weigh the sacrifice of maintaining an integrated community. They must swallow the idea that their community, to ensure that some neighborhoods stay racially balanced, pays potential black residents not to move in—as if whites even in Shaker Heights would never accept an integration based on a black majority. They have seen their tax dollars going to marketing materials that all but deny their existence in order to attract whites to certain neighborhoods. Some Shaker Heights blacks argue that the housing choices for blacks are limited enough, that blacks rarely feel welcome in other suburbs, and that the last thing black people need is for an integrated community to accommodate white prejudice and turn them away. They didn't win civil rights three decades ago only to face discrimination on behalf of integration. In fact, so far the only lawsuit against Shaker's affirmative marketing program was filed by a black woman who objected when the housing office refused to provide her with information on a predominantly black neighborhood. It's worth noting that the arguments some blacks use against Shaker Heights' program are the mirror image of arguments most whites use against policies such as affirmative action and busing: that we should not discriminate to end discrimination. In Shaker Heights, though, the vast majority of residents believe the end justifies the means. That can't be said for the rest of America.

What is true in Shaker Heights is also true in the other rare instances of integration in America: real integration depends on social engineering, constant vigilance, government authority, official attention to racial behavior, and a willingness by citizens to relinquish at least some personal choice for the greater good. And so we arrive at a fundamental dilemma of racial integration in America. The same factors that appear essential to successful integration run directly counter to some of our deepest beliefs about self-determination, authority, and individual rights. More than two centuries ago our nation was founded on a suspicion of vested power and an affirmation of individual liberty. The Declaration of Independence is as much about a king who abused his sovereignty as about the inalienable rights of humankind. This legacy remains as powerful today as ever. Most of us distrust authority, reject even a scent of social engineering, and must be dragged kicking and screaming to accept any limit on our personal freedoms. The reason better be good, very good, and it must produce unimpeachable results. Even then most Americans resist. Therefore, we cannot but conclude that what it takes even to break the integration ice in our country is largely unpalatable to most of our citizens.

Blacks may be more willing to accept these conditions because to them integration remains a net gain. But because most whites don't want integration or believe they gain little from it beyond their self-congratulatory acceptance of the ideal, they have little interest in accepting the sacrifice. Even if we grant the dubious assumption that a majority of whites truly want to live among more than a token number of blacks, the process to get us there would still involve a price most whites would not be willing to pay. In short, even an apparent commitment to integration will generally be trumped by our devotion to free will and choice. Policies such as busing, affirmative action, and the merging of urban and suburban schools at least in theory seemed like credible means to counter racial separation. But if prejudice didn't undermine them, our resistance to social engineering did. As long as real integration requires real social engineering and real sacrifice, it is unlikely we will ever see it in the United States beyond the rare and atypical community or institution.

Other examples bear this conclusion out. Corning Incorporated, the famous glassmaking company located in the south-central part of New York state, is widely known in business circles as a leader not only in recruiting blacks but in creating an integrated corporate environment in which they can work.[6] Though there are a select few other companies that have also made strides toward workplace integration—among them DuPont, Xerox, and Kellogg's—Corning's efforts put it at the cutting edge.

Like Shaker Heights, Corning started early, especially when compared to other corporations, and by the late 1960s Corning had already engaged local community leaders in a dialogue on integration. Not long afterward, the company initiated an aggressive program to hire black employees, and by the early 1980s it could claim a slow but steady rise in the number of blacks on the payroll. The program seemed to be working, and most companies would congratulate themselves on a job well done. But not Corning, and especially not its chairman, Jamie Houghton, who made workplace integration a top corporate priority when he assumed the job in 1983. For when company executives took a closer look at the numbers in the mid-1980s, a different story began to unfold. They found that Corning was having a difficult time keeping the blacks it had worked so hard to recruit. As many as one in five black employees was leaving the company each year, almost three times the attrition rate for white men. Actually, Corning's black employee attrition rate was similar to that seen in other comparable companies. Many such companies simply hire new black employees to replace those who leave. *Business Week* calls this the "revolving door" phenomenon, "where a fixed percentage of black employees come and go, simply filling the same slots."[7] Some companies might even prefer it this way, because it relieves them of the burden of truly integrating blacks while still giving them good enough minority hiring statistics to satisfy their public relations needs and maintain their eligibility for federal contracts under affirmative-action laws. Given that the tiny town of Corning is home to fewer than 250 blacks, and the nearby city of Elmira has just over 4,000 blacks, the company easily could have gone this route, or walked away from the recruitment challenge altogether. Besides, it costs a lot of money— up to $50,000—to recruit, relocate, and train a new salaried employee. From a rational economic perspective, Corning had no reason to stake its reputation on integration. But it did.

Corning's first act was to listen. During exit interviews with departing black employees, Corning managers heard them de-

scribe over and over how they felt isolated and largely discon-
nected from the company and the community. Every road to advancement seemed uphill, and they were tired of trying to get
there with little encouragement or support from colleagues and
supervisors, especially when their white peers seemed to fit in so
easily. So they left instead. Some whites might interpret this as
whining or making excuses for not getting ahead, but Corning
took the comments at face value and decided to hold up a mirror
to its own corporate culture. As a result of its findings, Corning
initiated a near cascade of programs and policies aimed at integrating not only the corporate culture but the local community as
well. Recognizing that integration required more than grand gestures and token actions, the company acted in ways large and
small to create a climate in which black employees would truly
feel welcome. White barbers in town did not cut black hair, so
Corning brought in black hair stylists and provided money for a
local black resident to learn the trade. There were few local cultural offerings attuned to black tastes, so Corning used its leverage with the cable company to pipe in a black radio station from
Rochester and to include Black Entertainment Television in its
local listings. Corning also pushed the local school system to hire
more black teachers and administrators, and has provided diversity training to the Corning police force and to local business
owners.

Inside the company, Corning has gone far beyond standard
diversity sessions for its employees. Now, whenever a prospective
black employee interviews for a job, typically a current black employee is involved in the process to help keep unconscious bias
from creeping into the evaluation and to send a message that the
new employee will have a built-in support network. To ensure
that blacks have coaches and mentors in the company, many of
Corning's divisions have instituted formal programs available to
all employees, black or white. To make sure that job opportunities are not wired for friends of supervisors, the company uses
training and education programs to ensure diversity in its career
pipeline. To keep black issues from seeming to be grafted onto an
otherwise white company, Corning now weaves them subtly into
the training curriculum as part of the normal course of doing
business. Unlike many companies, Corning also keeps an eye on

the types of jobs its black employees have. Unwilling to settle for large numbers of blacks in human resource or administrative jobs, Corning actively recruits black scientists, engineers, and marketing professionals, and seeks out black undergraduates in the sciences for internship opportunities. Knowing how easy it is to let things slip, the company convenes diversity councils consisting of division managers and chaired by the two chief operating officers.

Perhaps the most significant change of all is the one that makes whites most nervous: to get ahead in the company, every manager and executive must demonstrate that he or she has gone beyond lip service in hiring, retaining, and promoting black employees. Performance appraisals and bonuses are tied to diversity efforts. Results, not rhetoric, count. The purpose is not to be heavy-handed, but to use color-conscious leverage to create an integrated company—to create a culture in which, for example, recruiting at historically black colleges and universities is as natural as recruiting at nearby Cornell. "We want to integrate diversity into the mainstream so it isn't considered an appendage," said Gail Baity, the manager of human resources for one of Corning's divisions. "We want it integrated into the thought process."[8]

Although Corning may well be the corporate version of Shaker Heights, it too is still a fair distance from the promised land. As of this writing, black attrition continues to exceed that of whites, though by less of a margin than when Corning first noticed the problem. During one phase of corporate restructuring in the mid-1990s, blacks began to leave at levels not seen since the decade before, perhaps because they feared that the company's commitment to integration would be among the first things to go in an economic downturn, and so they might as well leave on their own terms. Blacks also continue to be significantly underrepresented in higher-level executive management positions. Nor are whites uniformly happy with the new corporate culture. What used to be a friction-free rise up the corporate ladder—one eased by friends, neighbors, and business school classmates—now has to accommodate diversity standards that to many whites seems unfamiliar and superfluous to getting the job done. Tying their bonuses and promotions to black opportunity is, to many whites, the functional equivalent of quotas.

Somehow, though, amidst all the noise, Corning's brand of social engineering appears to be working. By March 1997, blacks constituted nine percent of Corning's employees and six percent of its managers and supervisors—far better than in other companies similarly situated. Diversity training has largely given way to a more subtle infusion of racial issues into the regular training courses. Employees seem more comfortable dealing with race than ever before. Blacks, according to Gail Baity, find talking with whites more engaging than the perfunctory basketball, pop culture, and hair-style conversations that used to pass for black-white interaction. There are actually some discussions of cultural differences and history. "The mere fact that we acknowledge there may be a race factor between employees is a breath of fresh air for blacks," Baity told us. But she also reiterated that any letdown in the commitment could undo all that has been accomplished.[9] As in Shaker Heights, integration at Corning depends on how well they maintain and support a very fragile racial ecosystem.

As much as we'd like to say that other companies can easily follow the Corning model, there are reasons why Corning will remain an exception rather than become the rule. One is that it takes time and resources to build the institutional culture, a luxury Corning had because it started early, before the era of downsizing, leveraged buyouts, and biennial restructuring turned many companies into the sum of their quarterly reports and public relations strategies. Another reason is that true integration requires a determined chief executive willing to breathe down the collective neck of the organization and take the heat from employees who feel they have been shortchanged in the process. That could be replicated elsewhere, though it rarely has been. The third reason is Corning's relative isolation. Most of Corning's employees either come from the area or have made a conscious decision to move there to pursue long-term employment at the company. Unlike those in more populated areas, most Corning workers would have to relocate to change jobs. In many ways Corning employees are a captive audience, unlike typically more mobile American workers. And so they must reconcile themselves with what the company wants, or they uproot and leave, not always an attractive option. Corning also has one other advantage:

it has the leverage to overlay the integration culture onto the local community and does not have to contend with a sprawling metropolitan area where black and white employees live in separate neighborhoods and carry the heavy baggage of preexisting racial divisions. To avoid the racial mistakes of most other American communities, Corning the company seems willing to put its corporate weight behind shaping Corning the town.

When all these factors are combined, a pattern very similar to that in Shaker Heights emerges: integration requires social engineering, time and patience, a committed central authority, color-conscious policies, and a population that is either obliged or willing to trim some of its privileges for the greater racial good. This is not a recipe most Americans readily follow.

Corning and Shaker Heights use a modest amount of social engineering to produce modest integration outcomes. To see how much integration results from large-scale social engineering, one need look no further than the United States military, especially the army. Blacks make up more than a fifth of the military overall, and nearly a third of the army. Armed-services personnel eat together, live together, shower together, maneuver together and mourn together. "It is the only place in American life where whites are routinely bossed around by blacks," write the military sociologists Charles Moskos and John Sibley Butler in their perceptive and informative book on integration in the Army, *All That We Can Be*.[10] No other American institution comes closer to achieving the integration promised land, and no other institution bears less resemblance to the type of society in which we live. If it takes military-style social engineering to accomplish full integration in America, we must question whether the ideal ever will be realized in our country.

The reach and depth of the military's integration can be seen in two bellwether findings from the work of University of Michigan demographer Reynolds Farley. One shows the military's influence on intermarriage. White women who have served in the military are seven times more likely to marry black men than white women who have never served, and white men who have served are three times more likely to marry black women than white men who have never served.[11] The other finding shows the military's influence on residential integration: Communities with large military installations dominate the list of the least-segregated metropolitan areas in the United States. To walk around Fayetteville, North Carolina, home to the army's Fort Bragg and nearby Pope Air Force Base, or Killeen, Texas, home to the army's Fort Hood, is to see a level of residential integration rarely matched in most parts of the United States.[12] These findings suggest that integration in the military goes far beyond spending time together in a foxhole or tank, that at least for many military men and women it affects the most intimate aspects of their lives. That is as close to the promised land as we get.

What distinguishes the military from most other institutions is how it does not tolerate—indeed punishes—the corrosive assumptions that in civilian life tend to pull us apart. The military culture roots out prejudice and has no room for the insidious presumption many whites hold that blacks are incompetent. The reason is very simple: nothing can get in the way of combat readiness. Because soldiers and sailors depend on each other for their very survival, the military demands that they judge each other not by the color of their skin but by the content of their character. The military command makes clear that everyone who makes it through basic training has the competence, ability, character, and potential to reach a certain level, handle sophisticated weaponry, and get the job done. "Only a failure to try counts against you," wrote a former air force captain, a black woman, in *U.S. News & World Report*.[13] Those unable to accomplish a goal at first are provided training and remedial programs to succeed. No one carps that standards have been lowered because everyone knows the military cannot afford to have a single person in its ranks who cannot rise to those standards and perform in combat. In civilian life we use test scores and other measurements to determine whether someone is more qualified than another; the military uses this information to see if someone can improve to the level of everyone else. It is perhaps the difference between a civilian culture based on free will, self-interest, and competition, and a military culture that enforces teamwork, sacrifice, and the greater good.

Just how dogged the military is in trying to eliminate even traces of prejudice can be seen in the way promotions are evaluated.

Military leaders hope their officers are color-blind, but they also recognize that few of us are free of the subterranean prejudices that might color our judgment. They know that one prejudiced commander can stifle a subordinate's career and rob the service of a talented officer. And so promotion boards are directed to look at a minority candidate's record for possible evidence of prior discrimination. A poor evaluation might be just that, a poor evaluation—or it might be evidence of racial prejudice by the commanding officer. The promotion board is responsible for figuring that out. If fewer blacks are recommended for promotion than their percentage in the candidate pool, the board must justify it. Nor does it end there. Officers are evaluated on how well they create a bias-free climate. There is no room for even the perception of unfair treatment, regardless of whether the unfair treatment actually took place. Every officer evaluation report has an equal-opportunity checkbox. That single mark can make or break an officer's career. Commanders have been removed over it.

Near Cocoa Beach, Florida, at the Patrick Air Force Base, the military runs a unique institute, the Defense Equal Opportunity Management Institute (DEOMI), dedicated almost exclusively to eradicating prejudice and ensuring that equal opportunity makes it into the very marrow of each armed service. DEOMI is the formal training site for equal opportunity officers in the military, and, unlike the occasional diversity seminar we see in corporations and universities, it requires a near total commitment: almost four months of intensive soul searching and education that ranges from emotional role-playing sessions about prejudice to discussions about power and discrimination to formal courses on equal-opportunity rules. Called the Defense Race Relations Institute when it was created in 1971 but later broadened to include gender issues as well, DEOMI has trained more than 15,000 service members for their two-year stints as equal opportunity officers. More than half the officers it graduates today are white, compared to earlier years when most were black. Successful completion of the program can help a military career, while resistance to the curriculum certainly will hurt.

Upon graduation from DEOMI an equal opportunity officer is responsible for processing and evaluating discrimination complaints. In many ways these complaints illustrate both the virtues and blemishes of the military's integration effort. In 1994 the army received 686 formal complaints charging racial bias, of which about 20 percent were sustained. In a service more than half a million strong, the low absolute number of complaints indicates that the culture of integration is truly working, that most of its soldiers are indeed overcoming racial bias, and that presumably most racial problems in the service are resolved before they get to the formal complaint stage.[14] That same year, however, the navy reported that nearly three-quarters of its bias complaints, 72 percent, were found to have cause. But even that high number suggests the positive conclusion that the navy hierarchy does not condone entrenched prejudice, will not look the other way, and will confront it aggressively.[15]

As long as people are people, not even the most racially enlightened institutions will ever be problem-free. As Moskos and Butler observe in their book, integration of the military is a "success story—with caveats."[16] Blacks make up about a fifth of the military, but only 7 percent of its officers. In all four service branches, blacks are proportionately represented in the sergeant category, but the numbers drop off precipitously upon reaching the commissioned officer level—lieutenant and above. It is unclear how much of this is due to qualifications and education, and how much is due to ingrained racial discomfort among the white majority, particularly to blacks in authority. A 1994 report by the House Armed Services Committee and a 1995 study by the General Accounting Office suggests that the discomfort level may be greater than the military acknowledges.[17] The House report, based on two thousand interviews with service members at nineteen bases in the United States and overseas, found no tolerance for overt racism anywhere but "subtle forms of racial discrimination or racial tension" almost everywhere. Both reports found that blacks were punished more often and more severely than whites, were disproportionately concentrated in support jobs, and were underrepresented in promotions. Blacks claim to be mentored less frequently than whites and feel they need to become "one of the good old boys" to rise through the ranks. Nor is the military free of the racial perception gap. In a 1992 air force survey, half the white cadets said that minorities have an unfair advantage in getting ahead, while 80 percent of the black cadets disagreed.[18] Other reports indicate that black and white service members separate when given the choice and the environment is less regulated. If a post has more than one enlisted club, for example, they often divide by race.

It is naïve to think that any American institution, even one as controlled as the military, is immune to the pulls and pressures of our racially separated society. But all the evidence on integration suggests that the greater the control and the more effective the social engineering, the more integrated the environment will be and the more likely the people involved will overcome prejudice in the rest of their lives. Even the critical House Armed Services Committee report acknowledges that strong leadership makes a difference and counters the centrifugal forces that otherwise would prevail: "Where leadership viewed the effort of providing and maintaining equal opportunity for all as requiring a daily, constant, multifaceted effort, the overall climate of the installation appeared positive (particularly where that leadership had significant tenure)."[19] Moskos and Butler reach almost the same conclusion: "As a rule of thumb, the more military the environment, the more complete the integration. Interracial comity is stronger in the field than in garrison, stronger on duty than off, stronger on post than in the world beyond the base."[20] Indeed not a single racial incident was reported during the Persian Gulf War.

Like the Shaker Heights and Corning examples, integration in the military has taken time, patience, and commitment. The military also started fairly early, motivated by the racial divisions, fights and near mutinies that hamstrung the fighting forces during Vietnam. Also, like our other examples, race in the military is brought out into the open, not avoided, and color-conscious means are used to achieve color-blind results. Moskos and Butler explain: "The Army is not race-blind; it is race-savvy. Cognizance of race is used to further nonracist goals."[21] Finally, once you join the military there is nowhere to flee unless you choose to drop out. There are no all-white schools, suburbs, or social clubs in which to hide. It is as close to a total institution as we get, which makes the social engineering that is necessary for integration easier to implement. The Corning example is somewhat similar because the company's isolation makes taking a new job especially burdensome. The more people make the choice to give up some choice, the greater the opportunity to create and enforce an integrated culture.

It is poignant to read in *All That We Can Be* that retired black generals who have had responsibility for thousands of soldiers and complex military systems rarely find jobs in the outside world commensurate with their rank and abilities. "It is difficult not to conclude that the discrimination these people overcame in the military overtakes them again when they return to civilian life."[22] Despite this, Moskos and Butler still believe the army can serve as a model for racial integration in America. They are like Don DeMarco, Shaker Heights' former housing director, who wholeheartedly believes that the right mix of "public policy and investment" can lead to an integrated America. We wish we could believe too. But we can't. That's because America's integration success stories have occurred in special circumstances unlikely to be replicated in the rest of the country, and on terms that most Americans are unwilling to accept. In a 1990 interview with the *Washington Post*, the head of DEOMI described the military's experiment with integration much like containing a disease. "If we don't keep the emphasis going," he said, "it's like reverting to pre-Pasteur biology: The epidemics will come back."[23] In the rest of America, the epidemic, though less visible, has never left. Sadly, we see little evidence that the majority of Americans— particularly white Americans—will ever swallow the medicine and submit to the procedures that ultimately might rid us of this disease.

CHAPTER ELEVEN

Toward a More Racially Honest America

Psychologists describe a person in denial as someone who refuses to accept reality and believes in illusory choices about the future. For many in denial the illusions overwhelm their identity and govern their lives. Successful therapy helps a person own up to the truth and find realistic ways to deal with it. Continuing to deny the truth only accelerates self-destructive behavior. It is a lesson we apply to race relations in America. If for most of this book we say the race relations glass is half empty, it is only because America continues to cling to an illusory integration ideal that tantalizes us with promise but disappoints us in fact. But if we admit the truth, if we accept that real integration will likely never happen in America, then the glass begins to look half full, if not more than that. It is really a matter of changing expectations, of making them more realistic. If we can never reach the racial promised land, we should at least strive for the racially honest land. Let us rid ourselves of the polemics, agendas, illusions, and accusations and begin to mold the clay we have been given.

We have little patience with those who deny the racial progress of the past fifty years. America is far better off racially than at any other time in our history, and it is fantasy to dispute it. But we also have little patience with those who mistake this progress for real integration and suggest we are on the way to a color-blind America. Anyone who makes this claim has not looked beyond the surface of American life, or is saying it for political gain. Our families, lives, and communities may intersect more than ever before, but that still does not mean they are integrated. For after the workday is done, or after the integrated television show signs off, our lives remain starkly separated. As much as we'd like to think of ourselves as one people indivisible, we must begin to see ourselves as two peoples bound together in one country. We may strive for equality, seek a common purpose, fight for the same flag, and influence our respective cultures, but ultimately we are separated by history, choice, psychology, and circumstance. To say this is not to admit failure but to admit the truth—and to throw down a challenge about how to make it better. Race in America may never be as good as our dreamers dreamed, but it can be better than what our pessimists fear.

To those who say that the only alternative to the integration ideal is separate but equal, we vehemently disagree. That is bumper stick analysis. Rather, we must think with more nuance, with greater respect for the subtlety of our racial dynamics, with greater attention to the give and take of our racial separation. The old categories simply don't fit.

Since our purpose in writing this book is to examine rather than prescribe, we are hesitant to recommend any comprehensive models for the future. One idea worth exploring, however, is what we call racial coexistence, which acknowledges the reality of black-white separation but keeps the boundary line porous and easy to cross. It's very similar to the way different nationalities coexist in some other countries—for example, the French and Flemish in Belgium, or the French, Italians, and Germans in Switzerland. These countries are not without problems; the centrifugal pull of ethnicity threatens their very nationhood at times. But when the coexistence works well, it creates a constructive and beneficial relationship between the different groups, one marked by a grudging respect, a balance of power, a mutual dependence, and a shared commitment to country. In these countries, harmony between the different groups is less important than honesty. In Brussels, the French and the Flemish work together by day but go their separate ways at night, all with a minimum of hostility because they expect no more from each other. In this coexistence the majority understands it must guarantee the minority a strong and permanent stake in society, economically and politically. Deny that stake, ignore the social contract, and the trouble really begins.

Of course, we do not want to take the comparison with other countries too far. Unlike the situation in these other countries, black and white Americans do not speak different languages and do not live in separate regions of the country. Our boundary lines are more subtle, even if they are just as resilient. We live in the same regions but in different neighborhoods; we speak the same language but choose different media; we share the same history but perceive it differently. Racial coexistence in America must take our own special circumstances into consideration.

Racial coexistence is certainly not ideal. But it may be the best our nation can accomplish. We must be realistic about our possibilities. To an America that normally accepts no limits on human potential and believes in our unique ability to tackle every problem and fulfill every ideal, the idea of coexistence certainly seems pinched, almost un-American. It's as if we are giving up, admitting doubt and defeat. But let's not be too hard on ourselves, for it is wrong to say we have failed when our goal was never realistic in the first place. Whatever shortcomings we have on race, they predate the current generation by centuries—indeed, they were first encoded in our culture nearly four hundred years ago when the first Africans were brought here against their will. We should actually commend ourselves for trying so earnestly during the last half century to make the best of our faults. So rather than focus only on what we have not done, let us also consider what we still can do. Let us consider the possibility that accepting our racial reality may ultimately turn out to be very liberating—as in the biblical expression that the truth shall make us free. If we stop tearing ourselves apart over an ideal we cannot achieve, it might free us to think creatively about the society we realistically might become. No longer would our leaders be able to find refuge in integration symbolism and color-blind rhetoric. No longer would they be able to score points by paying lip service to the integration ideal. Instead, they would have to come up with real solutions and guarantees to make our coexistence work.

For black Americans, eliminating the integration expectation may lift a heavy burden from their shoulders. The integration ideal puts blacks under enormous and constant pressure. Every day blacks ask themselves questions that go to the heart of what Du Bois meant by "twoness" in America. When do I assimilate? When do I stand back? Am I a black American? Or am I just an American? What will I gain? What will I have to give up? Once freed from the integration illusion, from the protestations of their fellow citizens that they truly want integration, blacks may find themselves emancipated from this corrosive and deep ambivalence.

This is not meant to discourage those in America who want to pursue the integration ideal. If communities want to follow the Shaker Heights model, they should be encouraged and funds should be made available to help make it work. If people want to pursue interracial dialogue as small groups are doing in more than two hundred communities across the country—let the conversations begin. Integration is still the most compelling racial ideal we have, even if only a handful of us are willing to do the hard work necessary to achieve it. But let us have no illusions. Despite the efforts of the few integrationists, white America is not about to make integration a national cause—and black America is increasingly unwilling to put up with the continuing frustration of trying. If one hundred fifty people from different parts of town talk every week in each of these two hundred communities, that still makes only 30,000 of us—about the population of Shaker Heights. They are far from a critical mass. Ever since the civil rights days of the 1960s, whites have spent very little time seeking interracial dialogue but instead have expended a great deal of energy fighting busing, affirmative action, and other programs designed to create integration. Now these programs are in retreat, enervated if not yet defeated. There is no evidence that whites have any further interest in integration other than the perfunctory celebration of the integration ideal and the disavowal of blatant discrimination. So we must make the best of what we have. If we cannot achieve integration, we must at least achieve greater racial honesty.

Racial honesty, however, will not come without controversy and pain. Confronting a state of denial is never easy. That said, we make three proposals to promote racial honesty in America. Our first proposal is this: We should reconsider the concept of the "minority" in American life, for this concept represents a serious problem in the way black America is understood and seen. The word minority has become so ingrained in our political culture that we rarely pause to consider its ramifications for blacks. Yet blacks are ill served by the dilution of the black American experience into the minority American experience. When blacks are treated as just another minority, the black experience is drained of its special moral claim on our society and history.

In many ways the minority concept is a political idea that arose at a peculiar moment in history, at a time when the modern American welfare state was born. Legislators seeking to justify social programs sought as broad a net as possible—so programs spurred by the black condition were broadened to include others in need. At about the same time, the political left began to romanticize Third World revolution, making solidarity with people of color a shibboleth of the liberal social justice movement. Because blacks and other disadvantaged groups faced similar economic obstacles and similar discrimination, it was assumed they all shared a common interest and belonged together as protected groups under the law. This impulse to embrace is certainly commendable. It seems appealing and fair. The problem is that it is grounded not in history but in politics and ideology. It is based on a snapshot of the present, not an understanding of how we got there. So blacks, instead of standing out as a unique nationality that helped to build this country through unrequited sweat and involuntary sacrifice, become just another aggrieved minority group whose history carries no more weight than the plight of other aggrieved minorities. They become just one among many people of color whose common experience is how they were wronged by the white majority. Their unique American story is subsumed by interest-group liberalism, making them just another political group with outstretched palms, a special interest vying for the same affirmative action programs as Aleuts and Samoans.

To deal honestly with race in America, blacks must recapture their special moral claim, and the rest of the nation must honor it. An apt analogy is the Jewish concern when the word "Holocaust" is used to describe other acts of genocide or mass murder. Jews by no means want to diminish the tragedy and genocide of others. They are often the first to speak out when a crime against humanity takes place. But they claim ownership of the word holocaust as a way to define the unique and singular circumstances of their own unspeakable horror. Blacks must also defend their special status and moral claims. The black experience is qualitatively different from the experience of every other American. Unlike every other ethnic group but one, Native Americans, blacks are not and never have been immigrants, and the black journey in America must not be mistaken for the immigrant journey in America. Whatever hardship immigrants have incurred has been in pursuit of the immigrant's American dream. Whatever hardship blacks have incurred has been a direct or indirect result of their involuntary enslavement. The typical immigrant ancestor is thankful his forebears came to America; the typical black American looks backward only in pain. These are two different histories, two different states of mind, two different claims on society. Moreover, as we described earlier in the book, current trends are beginning to bear out this historical distinction between blacks and recent immigrants. Despite certain similarities in their economic circumstances today, there is strong evidence that Asians and Hispanics are following a classic assimilation script not too different from that of immigrants a century ago. That is not the case with blacks. Society seems to be assimilating today's immigrants in a way it has never integrated blacks. These trends make it all the more imperative that we restore both the historical and moral dimensions to our understanding of America's blacks.

Reconsidering the minority concept also might finally put to rest that specious comparison between the accomplishments of blacks and the accomplishments of immigrants. If blacks are just another minority, it is fully justified to compare their progress with that of recent immigrants. It is common for whites to ask why blacks can't succeed like Koreans, for example—and the answer only further confirms white prejudices about blacks. To uncouple blacks from this comparison requires that we affirm the full texture and uniqueness of black history in America. Rather than compare blacks with other groups, we should compare them with where they themselves started. Rather than ask why black small business development lags behind that of Hispanics, we could dwell on the remarkable progress of a people only four or five generations removed from auction blocks and chains. It might enable us to see the problems blacks have today not as failure but as part of their unfinished American business. That the majority of blacks today live in or around the middle class must be seen as nothing less than an extraordinary triumph over a legacy that includes enslavement, the forced separation of families, the denial of educational opportunities, and an emancipation that meant Jim Crow, legal segregation, and slavery without shackles. Black history must be viewed as both tragic and heroic. It is and should be the parable that governs society's image of blacks. But it deserves to stand alone and must not be diluted by any kinship with the suffering of others, no matter how understandable that kinship may be.

Our second proposal to promote racial honesty moves us into the turbulent waters of the affirmative-action dispute. Our focus is not on which side to take in the policy debate, but rather on what the policy debate says about our national inability to be honest about race. We submit that in large part the affirmative-action controversy stems from dissembling and dishonesty on both sides as they press their cases. While our sympathies lie with affirmative-action proponents, neither they nor the opponents are leveling with the American people. The result is an ideological circling of wagons that makes the American people even more unwilling to be candid about race.

The affirmative-action debate should start with a simple, straightforward, and incontestable proposition: in a truly integrated America there would be no need even to raise the idea of affirmative action. In a truly integrated America whites would have black neighbors and recommend them for jobs as effortlessly as they now do with their white friends and neighbors— and vice versa. In a truly integrated America the distribution of income, wealth, and hiring power among blacks would mirror that among whites, which would then be reflected in comparable test scores and career achievements. In a truly integrated America, black and white children would attend the same schools and have the same contacts to help with their college admissions, jobs, and careers. In a truly integrated America, no white employer would assume a black person to be incompetent or less intelligent because of the color of his skin. In a truly integrated America, even subtle racial discrimination would not be an issue. In such a world there would be no need even to think about affirmative action. An individual's ability to perform to potential would not be influenced by race.

The problem is, we are far from being a truly integrated nation. The simple fact that progress has to be forced and maintained—that it doesn't happen by itself—is evidence enough. So the question becomes: Should affirmative action exist because integration doesn't? And this is where affirmative-action opponents don't come clean with the American people. They use the integration illusion to rationalize their political agenda, denying even the conditions that give rise to the affirmative action debate. For when asked if America has truly integrated, they respond evasively that we've made great progress. Often they hide behind the alluring rhetoric of Martin Luther King's dream, pretending that discrimination and prejudice are mere flecks of irritating dandruff, and claiming that Americans, for the most part, are fair-minded people who judge each other not by the color of their skin but by the content of their character. They even suggest that affirmative action actually hurts integration because it makes whites resent blacks and blacks question their own achievements. What these affirmative-action opponents do, in effect, is dissemble. They know that the most effective way to undermine affirmative action is to say we are already color-blind or can act that way. They avoid speaking the truth about integration because they disagree with the one remaining policy to address it.

If affirmative-action opponents were truly honest, they would say no, America is not integrated, and we aren't even close. They would say that subtle discrimination is rampant and that the racial imbalances in society continue to skew everything from test scores to equal opportunity. They would maintain that the obstacles blacks face in America today far outweigh any hardship affirmative action imposes on whites. They would acknowledge that white discomfort with blacks shows up in areas that have nothing to do with affirmative action, such as when a few black families move onto the block, and that most whites would probably question a black colleague's competence whether or not he got the job through affirmative action. They would also admit that the nation already is divided, affirmative action or not. And they would sound no different from affirmative-action supporters in spotlighting the nation's lack of racial integration. But then they would say that while they don't really have an alternative policy to right the imbalance and promote integration, they just don't like the fact that hard-working whites are being asked to foot the bill. They would concede that affirmative action is a well-intended policy designed to generate opportunity for blacks, but that opportunity shouldn't come at the expense of qualified whites. What a breath of fresh air it would be for affirmative-action opponents to speak honestly about integration in America but simply to say they just don't like this particular policy. Rather than harping on the problems with affirmative action, they could be leading the charge to educate the nation about our racial reality and defying us to come up with alternative proposals. Of course, to do so might weaken their position and anger their constituents, who have no interest in questioning the integration illusion. But such would be the price of racial honesty.

Affirmative-action proponents don't come fully clean with the public either. They emphasize the need for affirmative action to ensure fairness to blacks, but they waffle on the issue of possible unfairness to whites.

The pro-affirmative action case is built on a straightforward and logical premise: because integration doesn't exist, some sort of affirmative action should. At least in theory, the rationale goes, affirmative action serves as a counterbalance in a world consciously or unconsciously ordered by color. It is supposed to influence employment and education decisions that aren't covered by antidiscrimination laws. For example, anyone in the work world knows that the best way to find a job is not through the classifieds but through personal contacts and informal networks. Such networks also help with admission to college and graduate school, though to a lesser extent. The network usually builds on family, friends, neighborhood, church, social club, alma mater or professional association—what used to be called the old-boy network. But rarely are these networks integrated. That is where affirmative action is supposed to step in. Whites who use a network are not consciously discriminating. They are not purposely excluding blacks. They are merely following the age-old tendency of bosses and institutions to recreate themselves. But in a nonintegrated society, white institutions that recreate themselves end up predominantly white. Unless impelled to do otherwise, it is very hard for outsiders to break in and grow. You often hear an employer explain a hiring decision by saying that someone does or does not "fit in." But too often that reflects a subtle or unconscious bias that works against blacks. Affirmative action is designed to offset that bias. It is the equivalent of a new network to counterbalance the old.

Affirmative-action proponents also operate under another premise: a black person's qualifications in a nonintegrated society do not always reflect that person's potential, and this is too often manifested in a poorer education or preparation but not in lower ability. Practically speaking, it means that we should de-emphasize the role of test scores and paper qualifications and focus more on an individual's demonstrated potential. The military does precisely that when it sets a basic standard and assumes that anyone above it has the potential to perform as capably as anyone else. If blacks fall at the lower end of the qualifications scale, that matters little to a military convinced that anyone who meets the standard and passes basic training has the ability to operate sophisticated technology and serve the country well. That's why the military provides ongoing training and education. Done this way, affirmative action does not just bring someone in the door—it helps that person fulfill his or her potential.

Years ago one of us had the black star of the university basketball team in class. He did very poorly on his first assignment, which was nothing new to him, but it wasn't acceptable to his professor. With rewrite after rewrite the student began to blossom and grow, and by the end of the term he was performing at the class average. He later said his teachers used to pass him because he was the star, but they didn't expect much from him. They assumed he didn't have much to offer academically. But as his performance in this class showed, that student belonged at the university, though not only because he could dunk. He had the academic potential, even if his academic records didn't always show it. This is how the military does it, and it is the linchpin of any successful affirmative-action program.

Whether you agree or disagree with these premises, they are at least credible and fully defensible. Affirmative-action proponents make a vigorous case. But the problem is not what these affirmative-action supporters say, but what they leave out: they are very quiet about the incontestable fact that some affirmative action involves preferential treatment for blacks that in one way or another discriminates against whites. It is a case of two wrongs trying to make a right. Instead of admitting it, affirmative-action supporters run from it. They talk about diversity, saying there are no losers in a racially diverse society. They say that whites have a built-in privilege just for being white. They argue that affirmative action levels the playing field only by pulling blacks up, not by dragging whites down. There are degrees of truth in all of this, but Houdini would be proud. That's because they contort the reality of the eighteen-year-old daughter of a Ukrainian immigrant plumber who didn't get into her college of choice even though her test scores and grades were higher than those of some successful minority applicants—or of the white male journalist with more clips, more experience, and more awards than the black female who got the editing job. What else can we call this if not discrimination? That discrimination like this doesn't happen all the time under affirmative action doesn't mean it doesn't happen or couldn't happen. That blacks face similar discrimination much more frequently doesn't mean it's not discrimination when it happens to whites. That whites in general have privileges in this society doesn't mean every individual white benefited from that privilege. That the discrimination was designed to provide someone an opportunity does not make it easier on the person whose opportunity was denied. Let's face it honestly: whatever the compelling justification for it, some affirmative action involves actual or potential discrimination against whites.

We certainly understand why affirmative-action proponents bob and weave around this issue. They see opponents scoring points by fanning white fears about losing jobs and unfair treatment. They know that polls and focus groups show how white resistance to affirmative action jumps when it's labeled preferential treatment and reverse discrimination. Given that the thinking behind affirmative action is much more difficult to communicate than the "content of our character" sound bite the other side uses to make its case, affirmative-action proponents are understandably tired of getting bloodied. But avoiding the issue just makes it worse. It leaves the impression that supporters have something to hide and are afraid to admit the truth.

The true irony here is that if any side should be using the ideas and language of Martin Luther King, Jr., it should be the affirmative-action proponents. Let us remember that King himself called for "discrimination in reverse . . . a sort of national atonement for the sins of the past"; he also supported "a policy of preferential treatment to rehabilitate the traditionally disadvantaged Negro." King knew such ideas would chill even some of his closest allies, all of whom were dedicated to a color-blind America. But he also believed that the only way to get to a color-blind America was to pursue color-conscious remedies. What distinguished King was his willingness not only to acknowledge reverse discrimination but to argue openly and honestly that it was morally justified and in the best interest of both whites and blacks. He did not run from the ramifications of his ideas—he embraced them.

For affirmative-action supporters to retrieve the high moral ground, they must follow King's lead and turn preferential treatment into a positive good that all Americans should be proud to support. They must show how continued inattention to the built-in bias of a predominantly white society sows future discord and social division. They must make the case that the sacrifice involved may not serve the individual good of affected whites but does serve the common good of all Americans. It is the same sacrifice we ask of taxpayers whose sweat and hard-earned dollars go to supporting a Chrysler bailout or AIDS research or a military hospital or a high-tech research and development grant to a corporation. Each of these involves preferential treatment for some and financial sacrifice from many, all done for the common good. Certainly affirmative-action proponents should be able to argue that of all the institutions, interests, and individuals in America, few have a stronger claim on our sacrifice than the people whose ancestors sacrificed their own freedom to build this nation and who continue to live with the daily legacy of a society that has never fully thanked or embraced them. The moral case for reverse discrimination must be told and retold if affirmative action is ever to survive.

Now imagine a public discourse in which affirmative-action opponents could acknowledge our racial failings and commit themselves to real and substantial efforts to root out discrimination and achieve equal opportunity; and imagine if affirmative-action supporters could acknowledge the vulnerabilities and fears of whites but plead for acceptance in the name of a higher social good. Though it may not lead to complete agreement on these issues, at least we would be making honest choices on honest information with an honest dialogue based on honest emotions. That's still far from the racial promised land, but it brings us much closer to the honesty and respect we need to coexist together in peace.

Our third and final proposal aims to bring racial honesty literally to the living rooms and kitchen tables of every American home. For it is in the home where Americans express their baldest sentiments about race, it is in the home where the beliefs and behaviors that pull us apart receive either tacit or outright approval, and it is in the home where our racial images and assumptions reproduce themselves. So it must be in the home that we begin the long process of mending the breach. The problem is, blacks and whites rarely visit each other's homes. They rarely talk with each other about race, and when they do talk they generally talk past each other. And even if every black family in America paired with a white family for racial dialogue, more than 80 percent of all the white families would be left out. So one-on-one racial dialogue is a pipe dream at best. That leaves only one realistic way to bring racial honesty into the home: through the mass media and especially through the power of television advertising. Even if we never integrate in America, at least we can keep ourselves racially honest through a virtual dialogue in the media.

No medium today has greater influence over our attitudes, choices, and behaviors than advertising, particularly television advertising. Corporations currently spend more than $150 billion a year promoting their products, and there's a good reason why: it works. In 1996 Coca-Cola, Pepsi, and Dr Pepper/Seven Up spent nearly $500 million on advertising for soft drinks alone. That same year the top ten computer hardware companies spent more than $1 billion on advertising and the top ten fast-food companies spent nearly $2 billion. Nike and Reebok combined for nearly $300 million; Crest, Colgate, Aquafresh and Mentadent combined for nearly $150 million; three disposable-diaper companies spent $100 million; and the top ten cereal brands bought nearly a quarter of a billion dollars in ads. In 1997 alone Pizza Hut committed $200 million to promote the "chunkier toppings and fresher ingredients" of its new pizza pies. Advertising also sells us more than products. Every election year political campaigns and advocacy groups spend hundreds of millions of dollars to persuade us their candidates inspire trust or their issues will improve our lives.

Just imagine the impact if even a fraction of these resources could be dedicated to an issue that cuts to the very core of our national identity. Just imagine if the amount spent familiarizing us with "chunkier toppings and fresher ingredients" could be spent educating us on subtle discrimination or alerting us to the racial hurt we cause each other. Imagine if that money could be used for ads that challenge white middle-class homeowners to rethink why they consider selling when a black middle-class family moves in next door, or for ads that lay bare majority-white assumptions about black intelligence or competence, or for ads that challenge blacks to consider that some white reactions might be motivated not by race but by the pressures of just living a hard and stressful life. Imagine an ad that shows two women, one black and slightly overweight, the other white and well-tailored, and then asks us to choose which one is the welfare mom and which one is the business executive—to be followed by another ad that shows two men, one black in sweats and one white in a polo shirt, which asks us to choose the ex-convict and the business executive. In short, such a campaign must take chances with the message. It cannot be limited to nice and safe themes about racial harmony—like an updated Coca-Cola commercial featuring harmony on a hillside, or a spot saying that we may be different on the outside but we're no different on the inside. The messages must penetrate the veil of the integration illusion and address the real and daily issues that keep us apart.

In the hands of the creative and resourceful advertising industry, there is no limit to the assumptions and stereotypes such a campaign can challenge. Like a product ad campaign, this race campaign must be ongoing. It must saturate the airwaves and keep reinforcing the ideas behind it. The story must be told over and over. Advertisers know that constant exposure is the only way to keep sales up. A one-month campaign or one that runs spots intermittently ultimately will prove futile and meaningless. For the campaign to work, significant amounts of money must be dedicated to it over a sustained period of time. Recently, President Clinton initiated a $400 million prime-time ad campaign against drug abuse that would be funded by public and private money. Why couldn't we dedicate as much if not more to remedying our nation's original sin, to the issue that has divided us since the beginning and will continue to divide us for generations to come, to the problem that is the progenitor of so many others. If our elected leaders are too timid to finance such a campaign, we must find other creative ways to do it. Perhaps the plaintiffs in big class-action lawsuits against racial discrimination—such as the one that resulted in the $176 million settlement with Texaco—could stipulate that the offending companies reserve some of their advertising budget each year for this type of frank and candid race relations campaign.

Nothing quite so ambitious and far-reaching has ever been tried, so we have no way to anticipate the response or predict the result of a campaign like this. But we do know that race cuts so deep into our national tissue that repeated exposure to racial images sends a shudder throughout the body politic—as when the civil rights movement shifted white attitudes toward racial bigotry or when the race riots shifted them back or when the O. J. Simpson trial briefly unmasked the integration illusion. We also know that extensive advertising has been able to influence and change our social behaviors—witness the public health campaigns on smoking, seatbelts, and drunk driving. The smoking example is especially relevant, because it challenged not only a habit but a way of life and status symbol as well. When the Federal Communications Commission forced television stations in the late 1960s to give antismoking groups free airtime to counteract cigarette advertising, the antismoking ads were so successful that within two years the cigarette companies voluntarily pulled their ads from television just to keep their opponents off the air. Once these antismoking ads no longer aired regularly, tobacco sales that had been fairly flat began to rise again. One can only imagine how a similar campaign could work to educate Americans about race.

We have no illusions that racial honesty will ever integrate our families, lives, schools, or communities. We have no illusions that any idea short of a miracle will ever make us truly color-blind. But we do hope that a more racially honest America can build bridges and challenge the stereotypes and images that too often guide our decisions and actions. If racial honesty leads us to even a small amount of the mutual understanding and respect that integration promised, then the anger, alienation, and fear that riddle our lives today will give way to a coexistence marked by reciprocity, trust, and a genuine commitment to common cause. It may not be the promised land, but it may be as close as our nation ever will get.

Postscript

This book has brought us on an intellectual journey to a destination quite different from where we wanted to go. Integration is an ideal both of us would prefer to see realized in our lifetimes. A truly color-blind, integrated America is a vision we share. We believe it is in the best interest of all Americans, black and white. Part of us wants to buy in to the integration illusion, to praise the emperor's clothes, to embrace the hope of the dreamers that yes, it can work. We want a happy ending. But try as we might, the facts simply fail to accommodate our desires, and the racial reality stubbornly refuses to change. We must conclude, regrettably, that integration is an illusion borne of hope and desire, that our very devotion to the ideal ironically helps us avoid a real reckoning on race, and that for our nation to move beyond today's racial endgame we must relinquish the hope of ever reaching the racial Promised Land. In writing this book we faced the choice of telling a truth we did not want to tell or of perpetuating a fiction that we wanted to believe. There wasn't much of a choice.

It is wrenching to reach this conclusion. We may be scholars, but we have dreams, too. As troubling as our findings may be, deep down we have always hoped that this book would serve as a challenge to America, a spur to wake us from our deep denial and move us toward a truly color-blind nation. Our research tells us such an awakening is at best remote and unlikely, at worst impossible and beyond hope. Yet hope we will. "Yes, I am personally the victim of deferred dreams, of blasted hopes," said Martin Luther King in his 1967 Christmas Eve sermon, "but in spite of that I close today by saying I still have a dream, because, you know, you can't give up in life. If you lose hope, somehow you lose that vitality that keeps life moving, you lose that courage to be, that quality that helps you go on in spite of all." May our hearts somehow, in some way, prove our heads wrong.

Notes

Chapter 1

1. Selwyn Raab, "Ex-Workers Charge Bias at the Statue of Liberty," *New York Times*, December 1, 1996, p. 49.

2. John Lewis, "Why We Marched in '63," *Newsweek*, October 23, 1995, p. 33.

3. Nathan Glazer writes about this wishful thinking in his book *We Are All Multiculturalists Now* (Cambridge: Harvard University Press, 1997), p. 148.

4. Tom Teepen, "Tracings of Racism in America," *Atlanta Journal-Constitution*, July 13, 1993, p. A19.

5. Audrey Edwards, "Coming Together," *Essence*, October 1995, p. 100.

6. For example, coverage of a public meeting about District of Columbia school closings lingered on the image of black and white parents holding hands (WUSA-TV, April 28, 1997). The interracial-embrace image is also a staple of still photography, as in the poignant photos after a murder in Spotsylvania, Virginia (*Washington Post*, May 8, 1997, p. A19), and during the Oklahoma City bombing trial of Timothy McVeigh (*Washington Post*, May 22, 1997, p. A4).

7. Mark Shields, "What We Have Overcome," *Washington Post*, August 12, 1983, p. A17.

8. *The Gallup Poll Monthly*, November 1995.

9. Richard Cohen, "Thankful to Be Here," *Washington Post*, November 28, 1996, p. A31.

10. Charles Krauthammer, "A Question of American Identity," *Washington Post*, October 13, 1995, p. A25; James K. Glassman, "Is America Finally Going Color-blind?" *Washington Post*, June 3, 1997, p. A19; Jim

Sleeper, *Liberal Racism* (New York: Viking, 1997), p. 3; John Updike, "A Letter to My Grandsons," *Self-Consciousness* (New York: Knopf, 1989), p. 195; Justice Scalia's opinion is from *Adarand Constructors, Inc., v. Pena, Secretary of Transportation et al.*, 1995.

11. President Clinton is quoted in Martin Kasindorf, "A Great Divide: Clinton 'Surprised' by Black-White Split After O.J. Verdict," *Newsday*, October 11, 1995, p. A3. For other examples of whites being shocked by black anger, see Mike Clary, "Race Relations—St. Petersburg Violence Seen as a Continuation of a Trend," *Los Angeles Times*, November 26, 1996, p. A5, and Jason DeParle, "The Races in Teaneck: A Special Report—Killing Reveals Racial Divide Beneath Model Community," *New York Times*, April 30, 1990, p. A1.

12. Numerous are the polls that show goodwill among whites. Almost every daily newspaper and weekly newsmagazine has conducted a race relations survey in the past decade, and while many highlight various racial flashpoints, they also point out the good news of changing, and more tolerant, attitudes among whites. Surveys in *USA Today*, the *New York Times*, the *Washington Post*, the *Wall Street Journal*, *Newsweek*, and *Time* generally sample the national population, while other newspapers focus more on local attitudes. Also common are surveys by advocacy organizations such as People For the American Way, education groups such as Phi Delta Kappa, and civic organizations such as the Metro Chicago Information Center. The survey information cited here comes from these sources.

13. This quip has been attributed to the late Saul Alinsky, a prominent Chicago neighborhood activist.

14. Stern is quoted in David Remnick, "The Accidental Anarchist," *New Yorker*, March 10, 1997, p. 64.

15. See Rob Hotakainen, "A Rough Road to School Desegregation," *Minneapolis Star-Tribune*, April 23, 1993, p. 1B.

16. The Cambridge school story is told in Robin D. Barnes, "Black America and School Choice: Charting a New Course," *Yale Law Journal*, June 1997, pp. 2375–2409. The New York school questionnaire story is told in Jane Lazarre, *Beyond the Whiteness of Whiteness* (Durham: Duke University Press, 1996), p. 34.

17. For information on Long Island, see Ford Fessenden, "Pattern of Bias," *Newsday*, May 18, 1992, p. 5.

18. Philip Bennett and Victoria Benning, "Racial Lines Recast by New Generation, Greater Interaction Has Failed to Span the Divide," *Boston Globe*, September 13, 1992, p. 30.

19. See Richard Morin, "Polling in Black and White," *Washington Post*, November 5, 1989, p. C5.

20. For the University of Illinois study and for other information on

race relations in Chicago, see the excellent article by Gretchen Reynolds, "The Real Silent Majority: African American Middle Class of Chicago," *Chicago*, November 1995, pp. 84–93.

21. "The Negro in America," *Newsweek*, July 29, 1963, p. 34.

22. The Elks Club leader is quoted in "Rogue Elk," *Newsweek*, December 13, 1971, p. 70.

23. Harlon Dalton, *Racial Healing* (New York: Doubleday, 1995), p. 62. Dalton is the Yale law professor.

24. The Rand Corporation study is cited in Michael A. Fletcher, "Race Board's Focus Turns to Economic Gap," *Washington Post*, January 15, 1998, p. A8.

25. Todd Gitlin, *The Twilight of Common Dreams* (New York: Metropolitan Books, 1995), p. 115.

26. For information on West Indian immigrants, see Malcolm Gladwell, "Black Like Them," *New Yorker*, April 29–May 6, 1996, pp. 74–81, and Sam Fulwood III, "U.S. Blacks: A Divided Experience," *Los Angeles Times*, November 25, 1995, p. A1.

27. Justice Marshall is quoted in Tony Mauro, "*Brown* Ruling 'Broke Back of American Apartheid,' " *USA Today*, May 12, 1994, p. 2A.

28. Sources for this paragraph include Richard Lacayo, "Between Two Worlds," *Time*, March 13, 1989, p. 60; Douglas S. Massey and Nancy A. Denton, *American Apartheid* (Cambridge: Harvard University Press, 1993), p. 87; Margaret Usdansky, "Segregation: Walls Between Us," *USA Today*, November 11, 1991, p. 1A; Margery Austin Turner and Chris Hayes, *Poor People in Poor Neighborhoods in the Washington Metropolitan Region* (Washington, D.C.: The Urban Institute, 1997), p. 2; Margery Austin Turner, "Segregation by the Numbers," *Washington Post*, May 18, 1997, p. C3; Glazer, *We Are All Multiculturalists Now*, p. 145; "Segregation and Cities," *Society*, September 19, 1996, p. 2; Rochelle L. Stanfield, "The Split Society," *National Journal*, April 2, 1994, p. 764; Roderick Harrison and Daniel Weinberg, *How Important Were Changes in Racial and Ethnic Residential Segregation Between 1980 and 1990?* (Washington, D.C.: U.S. Bureau of Census, 1992).

29. We are grateful to the University of Michigan demographer Reynolds Farley for sending a preliminary draft of his paper, "Increasing Interracial Marriage: Trends Revealed by the Census and Census Bureau Surveys," October 1996. Other intermarriage statistics are from Peter D. Salins, *Assimilation American Style* (New York: Basic Books, 1997), pp. 158–160. There is some dispute over the percentage for Jews—some say it is less than 40 percent—but the 52 percent estimate is most commonly cited. The Spickard quote comes from the testimony of the Harvard sociologist Mary C. Waters before the House Committee

on Government Reform and Oversight's Subcommittee on Government Management, Information, and Technology, May 22, 1997.

30. Colin Powell, *My American Journey* (New York: Random House, 1995), p. 381.

31. For the racial identity of children, see the Mary C. Waters congressional testimony cited in note 29.

32. For intermarriage numbers in Britain, see "Race Relations—Integrated but Unequal," *The Economist*, February 8, 1997, p. 58; see also W. F. Deedes and Victoria Combe, "Life Is No Longer a Matter of Black and White," *Daily Telegraph*, December 28, 1994, p. 13.

33. Edmund S. Morgan, *American Slavery, American Freedom* (New York: W. W. Norton, 1975), p. 333.

34. Kenneth Clark, quoted in David Maraniss, "An Icon of Integration and the Durability of Racism," *Washington Post*, March 4, 1990, p. A22.

35. Bradley is quoted in E. J. Dionne, Jr., "What *Is* His Vision?" *Washington Post*, August 25, 1996, p. C7.

36. Leonard Steinhorn developed this theme in "Living in a Different World—A Minority Experience," *Atlanta Constitution*, July 6, 1992, p. A11.

37. For a social and political portrait of America broken down by ethnic group, see *The State of Disunion*, an extensive survey by the Postmodernity Project of the University of Virginia published in 1996. See also *The Gallup Poll Monthly*, October 1995, which asked blacks who is to blame for the present condition of blacks. Forty-one percent of blacks blamed themselves, 15 percent blamed whites, and 30 percent blamed both.

Chapter 2

1. Personal interview with Assistant Attorney General Deval Patrick, December 13, 1996; the appraisal experience is described in Joseph Boyce, "L.A. Riots and the 'Black Tax,' " *Wall Street Journal*, May 12, 1992, p. A24. See also Jean Bryant, "For Blacks and Whites in the Region, It's Still a House Divided," *Pittsburgh Post-Gazette*, April 14, 1996, p. A1, and NBC's *Dateline*, "Why Can't We Live Together," June 27, 1997, and Kevin Helliker, "To Sell to Whites, Blacks Hide Telltale Ethnic Touches," *Wall Street Journal*, March 26, 1998, pp. B1–2.

2. Douglas S. Massey and Nancy A. Denton, *American Apartheid* (Cambridge: Harvard University Press, 1993), p. 114.

3. The best and most comprehensive study of racial housing preferences is the University of Michigan's Detroit Area Study. See also the *Detroit Free Press*, October 10, 1992.

4. The material in this paragraph is drawn from the following sources: Gretchen Reynolds, "The Real Silent Majority: African American Middle Class of Chicago," *Chicago* Magazine, November 1995, pp. 84–93;

"Michigan Woman Stays in Face of White Flight," *ABC World News Tonight*, May 20, 1996; William P. O'Hare and William H. Frey, "Booming, Suburban, and Black," *American Demographics*, September 1992, pp. 30–38; Carla J. Robinson, "Racial Disparity in the Atlanta Housing Market," *The Review of Black Political Economy*, Winter–Spring 1991; Melissa Campanelli, "The African-American Market: Community, Growth, and Change," *Sales and Marketing Management*, May 1991, p. 76; Ford Fessenden, "Pattern of Bias," *Newsday*, May 18, 1992, p. 5; William B. Falk and Robert Fresco, "We the People—Island Becomes a New Frontier for Migrating Minority Settlers," *Newsday*, March 17, 1991, p. 5; statistics on the New Jersey communities come from a graphic in the *New York Times*, February 7, 1997, p. B4; David Michelmore and Carmen J. Lee, "Busting Busing," *Pittsburgh Post-Gazette*, June 11, 1995, p. A1; Bryant, "For Blacks and Whites in the Region, It's Still a House Divided"; Edward Martin, "Housing Options Increase for Minorities," *The Business Journal of Charlotte*, February 27, 1995, p. 19; Adam Nossiter, "Duke Country Has Few Blacks," *Atlanta Journal-Constitution*, June 30, 1991, p. A10.

5. "Race and Public Housing," *Washington Post*, December 20, 1985; Bill Steigerwald, "A Model for Racial Harmony," *Pittsburgh Post-Gazette*, April 14, 1996, p. A14.

6. David J. Kennedy, "Residential Associations as State Actors: Regulating the Impact of Gated Communities on Nonmenbers," *Yale Law Journal*, December 1995, p. 761–793. See also Dale Maharidge, "Walled Off," *Mother Jones*, November–December 1994, pp. 26–33.

7. On the exurbs, see Joel Kotkin, "White Flight to the Fringes," *Washington Post*, March 10, 1996, pp. C1–2. The Utah executive is quoted in Kotkin's article.

8. For the Chicago information, see an analysis by Ron Grossman and Byron P. White, "Poverty Surrounds Black Middle Class," *Chicago Tribune*, February 2, 1997, p. 1.

9. Sam Fulwood III, *Waking from the Dream* (New York: Anchor, 1996), p. 189.

10. Susan McHenry, executive editor of *Emerge* magazine, interviewed in *Fortune*, November 2, 1992, p. 128.

11. For the real estate appraisers' book, see David R. Sands, "Borrowing Bias," *Washington Times*, June 21, 1992, p. A13.

12. For bias testing in housing, see Caroline E. Mayer, "Minorities Said to Face Bias in House Hunting," *Washington Post*, April 9, 1997, p. C9.

13. For the broker who was threatened, see Michael Alexander, "Housing Split: No End to Trend," *Newsday*, September 24, 1990, p. 7; the "by any means necessary" quote is in J. Linn Allen, "Civil Wrongs," *Chicago Tribune*, November 10, 1993, p. 1; the self-steering quote is in Sharon

Lotliar, "Realtors Targeted as Suburb Fights White Flight," *Chicago Sun-Times,* May 31, 1995, p. 1.

14. On rental discrimination, see Peter Feuerhard, "The Canary Report: Racial Poison in New York," *Commonweal,* November 3, 1995, p. 7; "Letters to the Editor," *Cincinnati Enquirer,* March 5, 1995; Jean Bryant, "For Blacks and Whites in the Region, It's Still a House Divided," *Pittsburgh Post-Gazette,* April 14, 1996; Benjamin Weiser, "Co-op Must Pay $640,000 for Denying Sublet to a Black," *New York Times,* May 14, 1997, p. A20; Caroline E. Mayer, "Study Finds Rental Housing Bias Falling but Still Frequent in Area," *Washington Post,* February 18, 1997; Jeannye Thornton, David Whitman, and Dorian Friedman, "Whites' Myths About Blacks," *U.S. News & World Report,* November 9, 1992, pp. 41, 43; oral statement by Deval L. Patrick, assistant attorney general, Office of Civil Rights, Department of Justice, to the Subcommittee on the Constitution, House Judiciary Committee, December 7, 1995.

15. "Racism Charges Return to Dearborn," *New York Times,* January 5, 1997, p. A13; "Under Suspicion," *People* magazine, January 15, 1996, pp. 40–47; "Earl Graves Jr. Receives Apologies from NY Metro–North Police," *Jet,* June 5, 1995, p. 35; the young journalist is Chad G. Glover, "Still Second-Class Citizens," *Essence,* September 1994, p. 48; the Long Island lawyer is quoted in Katti Gray, "Long Island Blacks: System Targets Us," *Newsday,* October 5, 1995, p. A7; Henry Louis Gates told this story to Tom Wicker, *Tragic Failure* (New York: William Morrow, 1996), p. 87.

16. The "black-a-block" question for the Oak Park community relations director is quoted in "Soul-Searching in a Pioneering Town," *Newsweek,* March 7, 1988, p. 37. For other sources on mixed neighborhoods, see Andrew Wiese, "Neighborhood Diversity: Social Change, Ambiguity, and Fair Housing Since 1968," *Journal of Urban Affairs,* volume 17, number 2, 1995, pp. 107–129; J. Linn Allen, "Divergent Courses: Some Urban Areas Defy Pressures and Remain Ethnically Balanced," *Chicago Tribune,* July 28, 1996, p. 1; Carol Jouzaitis and Jerry Thornton, "Blacks, Whites Chip Away at Racial Barriers," *Chicago Tribune,* April 30, 1991, p. 1; Roper Center for Public Opinion Research, *The Public Perspective,* "Race Relations in the Eighties: A Polling Review," January–February 1990.

17. The scholar quoted is Richard A. Smith, "Creating Stable Racially Integrated Communities: A Review," *Journal of Urban Affairs,* volume 15, number 2, 1993, pp. 115–140. For sources on Matteson, see Juanita Poe, "Rapidly Changing Matteson Sets a Course to Woo Whites," *Chicago Tribune,* April 17, 1995, p. 1; Lee Bey, "Color Matteson Campaign Misguided," *Chicago Sun-Times,* March 9, 1996, p. 15; NBC *Dateline,* "Why We Can't Live Together," June 27, 1997. We are grateful to

Claritas, Inc., the marketing research firm, for the 1997 estimates and 2002 projections of Matteson's population.

18. "Voices in Black and White," *Cleveland Plain Dealer,* November 22, 1992, p. 1A.

19. See Peter Applebome, "Schools See Re-emergence of 'Separate But Equal,' " *New York Times,* April 8, 1997, p. A10; the cash-poor district is in Darlington, South Carolina.

20. For recent trends in school desegregation, see Gary Orfield, Mark D. Bachmeier, David R. James, and Tamela Eitle, "Deepening Segregation in American Public Schools: A Special Report from the Harvard Project on School Desegregation," *Equity & Excellence in Education,* September 1997, pp. 5–24. The Harvard Project on School Desegregation is considered the leading authority on school desegregation issues.

21. See Arlynn Leiber Presser, "Broken Dreams," *ABA Journal,* May 1991, pp. 60–64; Bill Schackner, "For Blacks and Whites in Our Region, School Desegregation Gets a Failing Grade," *Pittsburgh Post-Gazette,* April 21, 1996, p. A1; Ovetta Wiggins, "Symbols of Segregation Endure," *Bergen Record,* April 11, 1995, p. B1; Focus Group Transcripts and Focus Group Report to the Montgomery County Hate/Violence Committee, Montgomery County, Maryland, November 1993; Walt Harrington, "Black and White and the Future," *Washington Post Magazine,* November 24, 1991, pp. 25–39.

22. E. Jean Carroll, "The Return of the White Negro," *Esquire,* June 1994, pp. 100–107; see also Marjorie Rosen and Leah Eskin, "Wardrobe Wars," *People* magazine, January 31, 1994, p. 60.

23. For the information on Cleveland, see Julian E. Barnes, "Segregation, Now," *U.S. News & World Report,* September 22, 1997, p. 28. The College Board study is detailed in *Redeeming the American Promise,* a 1995 report by the Atlanta-based Southern Education Foundation, pp. xx, 28. The Georgia superintendent is quoted in "Georgia Superintendent Battles a Subtle Racism," *New York Times,* February 2, 1995, p. A10; Harvard Law professor Christopher Edley, Jr., related his son's story in a private correspondence with Leonard Steinhorn; see also "Racial Harm Is Found in Schools' 'Tracking,' " *New York Times,* September 20, 1990; Neal Thompson, "Tale of Two Schools," *Bergen Record,* April 10, 1995, p. A1; Debra Lynn Vial, "School Integration's Failed Promise: How North Jersey Parents and Towns See the Issue," *Bergen Record,* April 16, 1995, p. A1; Ovetta Wiggins, "Symbols of Segregation Endure," *Bergen Record,* April 11, 1995, p. B1; William Celis, III, "School System Found to Be Biased Against Bright Minority Students," *New York Times,* November 5, 1993, p. A22.

24. For an example of a teacher choosing the white student over the black, see Vial, "School Integration's Failed Promise"; for the packets

handed to white and black parents, see Ellis Cose, "The Realities of Black and White," *Newsweek,* April 29, 1996, p. 36, in which he describes a New York City experiment by the activist group ACORN to test how black and white parents would be received in the schools. For white surprise when black students get good grades, see Montgomery County, Maryland, Focus Group Transcripts and Focus Group Report.

25. See the 1995 report by the Southern Education Foundation, *Redeeming the American Promise*. The report powerfully demonstrates the persistence of a dual system of segregated higher education in the South and shows how blacks "have limited access" to predominantly white four-year institutions.

26. John T. McQuiston, "Black Students Lose Suit over a Police List," *New York Times,* February 10, 1997, p. 46; see Southern Education Foundation, *Redeeming the American Promise*, p. 4, for a survey finding that 51 percent of black students at majority white institutions say they have heard faculty make inappropriate remarks about minority students; the classic case of a white professor's rejection by black students happened at Harvard Law School in the early 1980s when black students said it was "insulting" that the white former director of the NAACP Legal Defense Fund, Jack Greenberg, was asked to teach a course on civil rights law; in the early 1990s a black professor at San Francisco State University, Robert C. Smith, was boycotted when he offered a course on black politics that did not meet the approval of the Ethnic Studies program—see Larry Gordon and David Treadwell, "On Race Relations, Colleges Are Learning Hard Lessons," *Los Angeles Times,* January 4, 1992, p. A1; for the phrase "ideologically black" we are indebted to Michael Meyers, executive director of the New York Civil Rights Coalition; the Cornell University controversy, which occurred in the spring of 1996, unfolds in the winter and spring editions of the 1996 *Cornell Daily Sun.*

27. "Battleground Chicago," *Newsweek,* April 3, 1995, p. 31. The various incidents are culled from news reports.

28. The administrator who tracked dining hall seating is David C. Smith, dean of admissions and financial aid at Syracuse University, who wrote "Bring the '60s Racial Agenda to the '90s," *Newsday,* October 22, 1990, p. 47; for information on black fraternities and sororities, see Isabel Wilkerson, "Black Fraternities Thrive, Often on Adversity," *New York Times,* October 2, 1989, p. A1; the University of Iowa unity rally is described in Mel Elfin, "Race on Campus," *U.S. News & World Report,* April 19, 1993, pp. 52–56; examples of separate graduations include 1993 at Cornell, where black students separated themselves and marched together, and 1991 at Northern Illinois University, where

blacks held their own ceremony; Natasha Tarpley, "Voices From the College Front," *Essence,* October 1993, p. 66.

29. Isabel Wilkerson, "Racial Harassment Altering Blacks' Choices on College," *New York Times,* May 9, 1990, p. A1; Robert A. Bennett, "Having Your Say," *Black Enterprise,* August 1995, pp. 65–75.

30. For workplace surveys, see Stuart Silverstein, "Workplace Diversity Thrives Despite Backlash," *Los Angeles Times,* May 2, 1995, p. A1; "Diversity in Corporate America," *Washington Post,* January 26, 1997, p. H4; National Association of Black Journalists, *Muted Voices: Frustration and Fear in the Newsroom,* 1993.

31. U.S. Department of Labor, *A Report on the Glass Ceiling Initiative,* September 1991, p. 16; Richard E. Lapchick, "1996 Racial Report Card," published by Northeastern University's Center for the Study of Sport in Society; the Grand Metropolitan executive is quoted in Sheryl Hilliard Tucker, "Black Women in Corporate America—The Inside Story," *Black Enterprise,* August 1994, p. 60.

32. The Texaco information can be found in Kurt Eichenwald, "The Two Faces of Texaco," *New York Times,* Money and Business Section, November 10, 1997, p. 1; the Federal Glass Ceiling Commission found that minorities leave jobs at more than twice the rate of white males; the *Business Week* quote is from "Race in the Workplace," July 8, 1991, p. 50.

33. The Texaco reference is in Eichenwald, "Two Faces of Texaco"; the Circuit City information comes from Sharon Walsh, "Jury Finds Circuit City Stores Allowed Pattern of Racial Bias," *Washington Post,* December 3, 1996, p. A1.

34. Ellis Cose, *The Rage of a Privileged Class* (New York: HarperCollins, 1993), pp. 47–48.

35. The black lawyer is quoted in Donald Woutat, "A Firm Focus on Diversity," *Los Angeles Times,* April 14, 1994, p. A1; the *Business Week* quote is from "White, Male, and Worried," January 31, 1994, pp. 50–55; the study is summarized in Barbara R. Bergmann, *In Defense of Affirmative Action* (New York: HarperCollins, 1996), pp. 42–44.

36. The statistics on advertising can be found in Joseph M. Winski, "The Ad Industry's 'Dirty Little Secret,' " *Advertising Age,* June 15, 1992, p. 16; the statistics on lawyers can be found in Rita Henley Jensen, "Minorities Didn't Share in Firm Growth," *National Law Journal,* February 19, 1990, p. 1; the number of blacks in the various fields is from 1994 Department of Labor statistics.

37. See Katha Pollitt, "Subject to Debate—Affirmative Action," *The Nation,* March 13, 1995, p. 336; James Ledbetter, "The Unbearable Whiteness of Publishing," *Village Voice,* July 25, 1995, pp. 25–28 (Part 1), and August 1, 1995, pp. 29–31 (Part 2); Colbert I. King, "Diversity, the GOP and the Press," *Washington Post,* August 21, 1996, p. A25.

38. For information on Hollywood, see the excellent article in *People* magazine, "What's Wrong with This Picture," March 18, 1996, pp. 44–52; see also Jenny Houtz, "Black Humor," *Electronic Media,* April 8, 1996, p. 31; The source on the publishing industry is Ledbetter, "The Unbearable Whiteness of Publishing."

39. Sources include King, "Diversity, the GOP and the Press"; Walterene Swanston, "Angry White Men," *American Journalism Review,* September 1995, p. 42; the number of black reporters is provided by the organization Fairness and Accuracy in Reporting; Michel McQueen, now with ABC News, is one of the black journalists who has been asked by a white editor whether she can cover the black community objectively; the Sam Fulwood III quote is from our interview with him, November 18, 1996; information on sports journalism was found in Gregory Clay, "Panel on Race in Sports Practices Diversity," *Austin American-Statesman,* January 18, 1997, p. C9.

40. Discriminatory practices at employment agencies are well known. See, for example, Anne Kornhauser, "Tracking Down Employment Discrimination," *The Recorder,* May 8, 1991, p. 1, and "Deciphering a Racist Business Code," *Time,* October 19, 1992, pp. 21–22; the ABC *Prime Time Live* show aired September 26, 1991. For studies documenting discrimination in hiring, see Margery Austin Turner, Michael Fix and Raymond J. Struyk, "Opportunities Denied, Opportunities Diminished: Racial Discrimination in Hiring," *Urban Institute Report 91–9,* 1991; Arthur Brief *et al.,* "Beyond Good Intentions: The Next Steps Toward Racial Equality in the American Workplace," *Academy of Management Executive,* 1997, vol. 11, no. 4, pp. 55–68. For references to hiring and personnel studies, see Sam Fulwood III, "Support for Integration Has Grown, Many Still Hold Negative Stereotypes of Others," *Los Angeles Times,* January 9, 1991, p. A13; David S. Broder, "Blunt Talk About Race," *Washington Post,* April 21, 1991, p. B7; Richard Morin and Lynne Duke, "Prejudice Is in the Eye of the Beholder, Poll Indicates," *Washington Post,* March 8, 1992, p. A24; "Discrimination Follows an Internal Script," *Wall Street Journal,* October 19, 1994; Michele Galen, "Diversity: Beyond the Numbers Game," *Business Week,* August 14, 1995, p. 60; Michael A. Fletcher, "Race Board's Focus Turns to Economic Gap," *Washington Post,* January 15, 1998, p. A8. The Circuit City executive is quoted in Walsh, "Jury Finds Circuit City Stores Allowed Pattern of Racial Bias."

41. The Dallas case is described in Todd Bensman, "Mixing it Up," *Dallas Morning News,* May 24, 1995, p. A1; the New York courts are described in "Courts of Shame," editorial, *New York Times,* June 14, 1991, p. A26; the Chicago police supervisor told his story in Studs Terkel,

Race: How Blacks and Whites Think and Feel About the American Obsession (New York: The New Press, 1992), pp. 261–263.

42. Long Island police numbers are in Bill Mason and Richard C. Firstman, "Police Relations with Black Communities Still Strained," *Newsday*, September 17, 1990, p. 28; for the Pittsburgh information, see Jim McKinnon, "Police Battle Public Distrust," *Pittsburgh Post-Gazette*, May 5, 1996, p. A16; the Palm Beach Gardens situation is described in Bob Herbert, "Workaday Racism," *New York Times*, November 11, 1996, p. A15; the firefighter numbers come from Romeo O. Spaulding of the International Association of Black Professional Fire Fighters; the Long Island fire department information comes from Letta Taylor, "In the Ranks: After Years of Efforts, Minority Firefighters Remain Few," *Newsday*, December 19, 1994, p. A7; Los Angeles' unwritten policy is described in James Rainey, "Fire Department's Shining Image Clouded by Audit," *Los Angeles Times*, January 3, 1995, p. A1.

43. See Morin and Duke, "Prejudice Is in the Eye of the Beholder."

44. For an article describing how comments from blacks and women are received at meetings, see Alison Bass, "Studies Find Workplace Still a Man's World," *Boston Globe*, March 12, 1990, p. 39; for white attitudes toward black-owned businesses, see Fulwood, "Support for Integration Has Grown," in which he describes research by the Georgia Tech economics professor Thomas Boston.

45. Lawrence Otis Graham is quoted in Kevin McKenzie, "Visiting King Site Guided Author Now Helping Minorities," *Memphis Commercial Appeal*, December 26, 1993, p. C1; on the way blacks advise other blacks at work, see Rhonda Reynolds, "Avoiding the Looks That Kill Careers," *Black Enterprise*, June 1995, p. 281–288, and Jacquelyn Powell, "Protective Coloration," *Washington Post*, April 3, 1997, p. A1.

46. The study describing "burn out" and more frequent job changing is the 1993 National Study of the Changing Workforce, conducted by the Families and Work Institute. See also "Conflict in the Workplace," *Society*, May 1994, p. 2.

Chapter 3

1. The source on Lima, Ohio, is David Ogul, "Facing Racism," *Press-Enterprise* (Riverside, California), October 6, 1996, p. A1.

2. Sources for this paragraph include Gayle White, "Blacks, Whites Rarely Share Church Pews," *Atlanta Journal-Constitution*, July 11, 1991, p. A4; David Maraniss, "Facing Racial Issues in a Liberal Religion," *Washington Post*, March 5, 1990, p. A1; "Power and Higher Power: Carter's Spiritual Journey," *New York Times*, December 15, 1996, p. A30; Robert

Shogan, *Promises to Keep: Carter's First Hundred Days* (New York: Thomas Y. Crowell, 1977), pp. 58–73.

3. See Larry B. Stammer, "After 'Memphis Miracle,' Work Goes On," *Los Angeles Times,* October 26, 1996, p. B5; the minister is quoted in Tom Topousis and Ruth Padawer, "A Message of Racial Equality," *Bergen Record,* January 21, 1992, p. B1.

4. The Plaza Methodist Church story was told in a report by *CBS News* correspondent Bill Whitaker, "CBS News Extra: O.J. in Black and White," October 23, 1996; the Beaumont, Texas, information comes from "Black and White United Methodist Church Congregations Merge into One Church in Beaumont, Texas," *Jet,* March 11, 1996, p. 55; the Philadelphia church is described in David Maraniss, "Facing Racial Issues in a Liberal Religion," *Washington Post,* March 5, 1990, p. A1.

5. For a description of black lives in predominantly white suburbia, see Jere Downs, "Blacks in Suburbs: A Balance," *Philadelphia Inquirer,* March 16, 1997, p. B1.

6. For racial separation in arts and culture, see Gretchen Reynolds, "The Real Silent Majority: African American Middle Class of Chicago," *Chicago,* November 1995, pp. 84–93; Paul Bonner, "Area Arts Groups Turn Spotlight on Audience," *Durham (N.C.) Herald-Sun,* April 25, 1996, p. C3; and Peggy Cooper Cafritz, "Culture in Black and White," *Washington Post,* January 20, 1991, p. B5. The college-town club is described in Cornelius F. Foote, Jr., "Subtle Racial Tension Continues at Mostly White Institutions," *Washington Post,* March 22, 1990, p. D3.

7. The black woman at the black club is quoted in Laura Blumenfeld, "Another Friday Night on Division Street: Two Downtown Bars, One Barrier," *Washington Post,* August 12, 1994, p. F1.

8. The Denny's material comes from *United States of America* v. *Flagstar Corporation and Denny's Inc.,* Amended Consent Decree; sources for the fitness club information include Jay Mathews, "Undercover Bias Busters," *Newsweek,* November 23, 1992, p. 88, and Ronald D. White, "All-Too-Believable Stories of Bigotry," *Washington Post,* December 19, 1990, p. A3; the Buffalo mall case is described in "Johnnie L. Cochran Jr. Takes Case of Black Teen Killed by Dump Truck on Her Way to Work," *Jet,* August 19, 1996, p. 37.

9. See Anna Borgman, "When It Comes to Their Hair, Blacks, Whites Often Part Ways," *Washington Post,* December 25, 1996, p. B1.

10. Sources for the health-care information include David Barton Smith, "The Racial Integration of Medical and Nursing Associations," *Hospital and Health Services Administration,* September 22, 1992, p. 387; Ellis Cose, "The Color Bind," *Newsweek,* May 12, 1997, p. 58; Ellis Cose, *Color-Blind* (New York: HarperCollins, 1997), pp. 114–117; David Maraniss, "Prescription Written in Black and White," *Washington*

Post, April 3, 1991, p. A1; Dr. Garvey is quoted in "A World Apart—Segregation on Long Island," *Newsday,* reprint of special series, September 16, 1990, p. 23; the Nicholas Lemann quote is from "Taking Affirmative Action Apart," *New York Times Magazine,* June 11, 1995, p. 36.

11. See Dari Giles, "Summer Resorts—Black Resort Towns are Enjoying a Renaissance Thanks to Buppies and Their Families," *Black Enterprise,* August 1994, pp. 90–91; Ron Stodghill II, "A Return to the 'Black Eden,' " *Business Week,* October 30, 1995, p. 18; Vanessa E. Jones, "Freaknik Beckons the Young," *Memphis Commercial Appeal,* April 19, 1996, p. 1C; Jill Jordan Sieder, "Mardi Gras Blues," *U.S. News and World Report,* February 3, 1992, p. 16.

12. Eugene Morris, "The Difference in Black and White," *American Demographics,* January 1993, p. 49; Richard Shenkman, "Myth America Pageant," *Eastsideweek,* July 3, 1996, p. 18–19; Fern Shen, "Ocean City's Shores Chilly for Some Blacks," *Washington Post,* July 19, 1992, p. B1.

13. Bureau of National Affairs, "Paid King Holiday Still Unusual in Most Sectors," *Bulletin to Management,* January 9, 1997, p. 1; "On King Day, Teach Kids," editorial, *Atlanta Journal-Constitution,* January 17, 1992, p. A10; Ruby L. Bailey, "Remembering the Dream," *Detroit News,* January 15, 1996, p. B1; Jo Ann Zuniga, "Blowing His Own Horn—15,000 Cheer MLK Day Parade," *Houston Chronicle,* January 16, 1996, p. A13.

14. The Ted Koppel quote is from the April 1, 1997, *Nightline;* Bill Bradley gave his speech on race relations to the National Press Club in Washington, D.C., July 16, 1991.

15. Sources for the baseball information include Richard E. Lapchick, *1996 Racial Report Card* (Boston: Northeastern University, Center for the Study of Sport in Society, 1997); *ABC World News Tonight,* April 15, 1997; Claire Smith, "Fewer Blacks Follow Robinson's Baseball Lead," *New York Times,* March 30, 1997, p. A1; Claire Smith, "The Race Issue Extends Beyond the Playing Field," *New York Times,* April 10, 1997, p. D33; Brent Staples, "A White Man's Place to Be," *New York Times,* April 8, 1997, p. A14; Marc Fisher, "Segregation Lives Where Jackie Once Did," *Washington Post,* April 15, 1997, p. A1; Mark Maske and Tyler Kepner, "Baseball Tries to Reclaim Minority Interest," *Washington Post,* July 25, 1997, p. C1; Michael Hiestand, "Sport Seeks Fan Growth," *USA Today,* May 15, 1997, p. 3C.

16. The baseball player was then Atlanta Brave David Justice; for the *USA Today* reporter, see Dick Patrick, "A Different Track—Whites Take Flight from Speed Sports," December 19, 1991, p. 1C.

17. See Richard E. Lapchick, *1996 Racial Report Card,* published by Northeastern University's Center for the Study of Sport in Society, pp. 26–27; "All-USA Picks Fit Pattern," *USA Today,* December 17,

1991, p. 6C; the University of Iowa wide receiver is quoted in Jim Ecker, "Agents Lining Up for Chance to Market Hawk," *Cedar Rapids Gazette,* article posted on the newspaper's Website, December 19, 1997.

18. See Lapchick, *1996 Racial Report Card,* pp. 26–27.

19. For the fan study, see Lawrence M. Kahn, "Racial Differences in Professional Basketball Players' Compensation," *Journal of Labor Economics,* January 1988, pp. 40–61. See also Jim Meyers, "Fan Preference Causes Pay Disparity," *USA Today,* December 18, 1991, p. 4C; the Associated Press report on Zoeller is cited in Michael Wilbon, "Fuzzy's Words Obscure Larger Picture," *Washington Post,* April 30, 1997, p. C7; John Hoberman, *Darwin's Athletes* (New York: Houghton Mifflin, 1997), pp. xv–xvi.

20. The women's basketball coach is quoted in Jan Crawford Greenberg, "In College Sports, at Least, Racial Playing Field Is Level," *Chicago Tribune,* September 6, 1996, p. 1; for information on the college scene, see Ed Sherman, "Degrees Elude Black Athletes," *Chicago Tribune,* March 31, 1993, p. 1 of the sports section; William C. Rhoden, "Athletes on Campus: A New Reality," *New York Times,* January 8, 1990, p. A1; Joe Bower, "Can a Coach Enforce Racial Harmony?" *USA Weekend,* October 20, 1996, p. 14; *College Sports* magazine, October 1994; Bradley's NBA contemporary is Chet Walker, *Long Time Coming* (New York: Grove Press, 1995), p. 214; see also "Black Football Players Tell Why Integration Doesn't Always Work off the Field," *Jet,* October 7, 1996, p. 52.

21. Walker, *Long Time Coming,* p. 46.

22. Joshua Solomon, "Reliving 'Black Like Me': My Own Journey into the Heart of Race-Conscious America," *Washington Post,* October 30, 1994, p. C1; see also "White Man Who Altered Himself to Look Black Reveals Chilling Account of Racism, Oppression," *Jet,* December 26, 1994/January 2, 1995, p. 26.

23. Personal interview with Assistant Attorney General Deval Patrick, December 13, 1996.

24. Patrick interview, December 13, 1996.

25. See Joseph N. Boyce, "L.A. Riots and the 'Black Tax,' " *Wall Street Journal,* May 12, 1992, p. A24; "Prejudice Is Still a Fact of Life for Blacks," letter to the editor, *New York Times,* May 17, 1991; Jerelyn Eddings et al., "The Covert Color War," *U.S. News & World Report,* October 23, 1995, pp. 40 ff.; C. Fisher, "Black, Hip and Primed (to Shop)," *American Demographics,* September 1996, pp. 52–58; Marjorie Whigham-Desir, "The Real Black Power," *Black Enterprise,* July 1996, pp. 60 ff.; Gregory Freeman, "It's Up to Whites to Find Sensitivity in Color Reaction," *St. Louis Post-Dispatch,* December 3, 1993, p. 5C; Avis Thomas-Lester and Valerie Strauss, "Girls Accuse Mall Guards of Racism," *Washington Post,* October 6, 1996, p. B1.

26. Stores that refuse to stock black products were the subject of a report on WTTG-TV *10 O'clock News*, Washington, D.C., November 6, 1997. For other articles on the black consumer experience, see Richard Lacayo, "Between Two Worlds," *Time*, March 13, 1989, pp. 58–68; Lena Williams, "When Blacks Shop, Bias Often Accompanies Sale," *New York Times*, April 30, 1991, p. A1. For the black police detective's story, see Whigham-Desir, "The Real Black Power." What black parents tell their kids is described in Focus Group Report to the Montgomery County Hate/Violence Committee, Montgomery County, Maryland, November 1993. Store preferences are described in Fisher, "Black, Hip and Primed (to shop)."

27. "Maryland State Police Settle Lawsuit over Racial Profiles," *Jet*, January 23, 1995; Paul W. Valentine, "Md. State Police Still Target Black Motorists, ACLU Says," *Washington Post*, November 15, 1996, p. A1; ABC's *Nightline*, April 15, 1997; Harris Poll commissioned by the Teens, Crime and Community Project of the National Institute for Citizen Education in the Law and the National Crime Prevention Council, conducted in Fall 1995 and released the following January by these two organizations in a publication entitled *Between Hope and Fear*; Montgomery County, Maryland, Focus Group Report.

28. Ellis Cose, *The Rage of a Privileged Class* (New York: HarperCollins, 1993), p. 28. For examples of indignities, see Robin Givhan, "A Beauty's Mark," *Washington Post*, May 2, 1997, p. C1; Karen Grigsby Bates, "Excuse Me, Your Race Is Showing," *Washington Post*, January 26, 1997, p. C5; Williams, "When Blacks Shop"; "Interview with Hank Aaron," *Sport*, February 1993, pp. 71–75; Sam Fulwood III, "Blacks Find Bias Amid Affluence," *Los Angeles Times*, November 20, 1991; Jerelyn Eddings et al., "The Covert Color War," *U.S. News & World Report*, October 23, 1995, pp. 40 ff.; Freeman, "It's Up to Whites to Find Sensitivity in Color Reaction"; Marshall O. Lee, "Mugged by Bill Cosby," *Essence*, April 1993, p. 46.

29. The information on television is based on material provided by BBDO Advertising, particularly the special report the firm publishes annually on black television viewers. We are grateful for the assistance of BBDO's senior vice president for special markets, Doug Alligood.

30. The 20th Century-Fox executive is quoted in Kim Masters and Jacqueline Trescott, "Why Hollywood Keeps Blacks Waiting," *Washington Post*, March 24, 1996, p. G1; the Miramax president is quoted in Nina J. Easton, "Good News/Bad News of the New Black Cinema," *Los Angeles Times*, June 16, 1991, p. 5; for the status of black films in the industry, see Maximillian Potter, "Black by Popular Demand," *Premiere*, January 1996, pp. 39–41, and Betsy Streisand, "True Story, Big Studio, Black Film," *U.S. News & World Report*, March 10, 1997, p. 66.

31. The material on country music comes from the Country Music Association Website and Bruce Feiler, "Has Country Music Become a Soundtrack for White Flight?" *New York Times*, October 20, 1996, p. 38. The *Billboard* editor was quoted in Feiler's article. Feiler is writing a book about country music.

32. See, for example, "Urban Radio: The Invitation Medium," *R&R*, September 15, 1995.

33. Marc Fisher, "Colors of the Radio Spectrum," *Washington Post*, December 3, 1996, p. E1.

34. These readership statistics are from the Simmons Market Research Bureau.

35. The *Vogue* editor, Anna Wintour, is quoted in Amy M. Spindler, "Taking Stereotyping to a New Level in Fashion," *New York Times*, June 3, 1997, p. A23; the 1991 study was conducted by the New York City Department of Consumer Affairs.

36. The *Washingtonian* statistics were compiled by our graduate student Theresa Spinner for her master's thesis, "A Survey of Feature Stories on African Americans Published in *Washingtonian* magazine, 1986–1996," submitted to the American University School of Communication, August 1997, p. 28.

37. The *New York Times* editor is Joseph Lelyveld, who is quoted in David Shaw, "Negative News and Little Else," *Los Angeles Times*, December 11, 1990, p. A1.

38. See David Shaw, "The Simpson Legacy," *Los Angeles Times*, October 9, 1995, pp. 1–12.

39. The black columnists we tracked are Clarence Page of the *Chicago Tribune*, William Raspberry of the *Washington Post*, Bob Herbert of the *New York Times*, and Brent Staples of the *New York Times*; the white columnists are David Broder of the *Washington Post*, Anthony Lewis of the *New York Times*, and William Safire of the *New York Times*.

40. Kirk A. Johnson, "Black and White in Boston," *Columbia Journalism Review*, May–June 1987, pp. 50–52.

41. For the appeal of special marketing to blacks, see Joel Herche and Siva Balasubramanian, "Ethnicity and Shopping Behavior," *Journal of Shopping Center Research*, Fall 1994, pp. 66–79; Janice C. Simpson, "Buying Black," *Time*, August 31, 1992, p. 52; "Marketers Pay Attention! Ethnics Comprise 25% of the U.S.," *Brandweek*, July 13, 1994, p. 26; Marcia Mallory, "Waking Up to a Major Market," *Business Week*, March 23, 1992, pp. 70–71; and, Jerome D. Williams, William J. Quails and Sonya A. Grier, "Racially Exclusive Real Estate Advertising: Public Policy Implications for Fair Housing Practices," *Journal of Public Policy and Marketing*, Fall 1995, pp. 225 ff.

42. New York City Department of Consumer Affairs, *Invisible People:*

The Depiction of Minorities in Magazine Ads and Catalogues (New York: Department of Consumer Affairs, 1991).

Chapter 4

1. A 1982 undergraduate paper by Steve Greenberg, a former American University student of Leonard Steinhorn's, provided valuable information for the Motown discussion. We are also grateful to *Billboard* magazine for sending information on its Rhythm & Blues charts. See also Michael Haralambos, *Right On: From Blues to Soul in Black America* (New York: Drake Publishers, 1975), pp. 93–134.

2. John Lewis, "Why We Marched in '63," *Newsweek*, October 23, 1995, p. 33.

3. "Crisis of Color, '66," *Newsweek*, August 22, 1966, p. 22. A year later, in its August 21, 1967, edition, *Newsweek* made the same point: "The closer he gets, the more threatening he looks."

4. Bower Hawthorne was interviewed by *U.S. News & World Report*, November 11, 1963, p. 84.

5. For the 1995 quote, see Dan Balz, "Racial Issues Weigh Heavily on Minds of Nation's Voters," *Washington Post*, November 6, 1995, p. A10; the 1966 quote is from "They're Trying to Go Too Fast," *Newsweek*, August 22, 1966, p. 25.

6. The white New Yorker is quoted in "Says a White Mother: 'We Have Rights, Too,' " *U.S. News & World Report*, October 26, 1964, p. 77; the southern congressman, Rep. John Bell Williams of Mississippi, is quoted in "The Other Washington," *Newsweek*, July 1, 1963, p. 22; the "advocate of racial equality" is quoted in "Middle Class Negroes Should Assume More Responsibility," *U.S. News & World Report*, July 15, 1963, p. 61.

7. Louis Harris, "The 'Backlash' Issue," *Newsweek*, July 13, 1964, p. 24.

8. The 1963 Harris Poll and *Newsweek* quote can be found in "How Whites Feel About Negroes: A Painful American Dilemma," *Newsweek*, October 21, 1963, pp. 44–57.

9. The Wilkins quote is from a *U.S. News & World Report* interview with him, September 25, 1967, p. 83; the "popular to be a Negro" quote is from "A Look at the Rise of the Negro Middle Class," *U.S. News & World Report*, July 15, 1963, p. 60; Julian Bond is quoted in "Black America Now," *Newsweek*, February 19, 1973, p. 29.

10. The Tennessee and Indiana quotes are from "How Whites Feel About Negroes: A Painful American Dilemma," *Newsweek*, October 21, 1963, p. 45; the Queens, New York, woman is quoted in "Says a White Mother: 'We Have Rights, Too,' " p. 72.

11. "How Whites Feel About Negroes: A Painful American Dilemma," p. 44.

12. See "The Negro Problem at a Glance," *U.S. News & World Report,* June 10, 1968, pp. 62–63.

13. For job statistics, see Joe T. Darden, "Black Residential Segregation Since the 1948 *Shelley* v. *Kraemer* Decision," *Journal of Black Studies,* July 1995, pp. 680–691.

14. Information on Washington, D.C., can be found in "A Look at the Rise of the Negro Middle Class," *U.S. News & World Report,* July 15, 1963, p. 57; the Baltimore example is described in great and illuminating detail by W. Edward Orser, *Blockbusting in Baltimore* (Lexington, Ky.: University Press of Kentucky, 1994); residential tipping in Chicago is mentioned in "What Must Be Done," *Newsweek,* November 20, 1967, p. 37; the *U.S. News & World Report* quote can be found in "Racial Crisis Ahead for Neighborhood Schools," July 8, 1963, p. 47.

15. See "The Negro Problem at a Glance." Had blacks emigrated to the suburbs in numbers equal to their 12 percent population share, about 200,000 would have moved to the suburbs each year from 1960 to 1966.

16. For information on Levittown, see John C. Gebhardt, "The Real Birth of Affirmative Action," *Commonweal,* February 9, 1996; Paula Span, "Mr. Levitt's Neighborhood," *Washington Post,* May 27, 1997, pp. 1–2; Bruce Lambert, "At 50, Levittown Contends with Legacy of Racial Bias," *New York Times,* December 28, 1997, pp. 23, 24; Levitt is quoted in David Halberstam, *The Fifties* (New York: Villard Books, 1993), p. 141.

17. For information on Wyandanch, see D. J. Hill, "Proud but Often Powerless, Wyandanch Residents Try to Stabilize Their Community," *Newsday,* September 23, 1990, p. 8 ff.; King made this statement about black housing preferences in a January 1965 *Playboy* interview, which was cited in Ellis Cose, *Color-Blind* (New York: HarperCollins, 1997), p. 104.

18. The realtors' code is cited in David R. Sands, "Borrowing Bias," *Washington Times,* June 21, 1992, p. A13.

19. On the government's role in housing, see John M. Stahura, "Rapid Black Suburbanization of the 1970s: Some Policy Considerations," *Policy Studies Journal,* Winter 1989–90, pp. 280–281; Irby Park, "Realtors Back Fair Housing," *Chattanooga Free Press,* April 20, 1997, p. M1; Rochelle L. Stanfield, "The Split Society," *National Journal,* April 2, 1994, p. 762; Douglas S. Massey and Nancy A Denton, *American Apartheid* (Cambridge: Harvard University Press, 1993), chapter 2; Douglas S. Massey, "Public Housing: Roots of Urban Underclass Linked to High-Density Projects," *Dallas Morning News,* September 15, 1996, p. 1J; Bob Fitch, "The Case of the Disappearing Work," *In These Times,*

December 9, 1996, pp. 34–35. The report of the 1968 Kerner Commission (officially titled the National Advisory Commission on Civil Disorders), which was appointed by President Johnson to investigate the causes of racial unrest, also cites "urban renewal" as a major cause of racial discontent.

20. *Time* cites a study of nearly 1,900 neighborhoods in forty-seven cities that found that housing values rose significantly in all-black and mixed neighborhoods throughout the 1950s: "Civil Rights: A Modest Milestone," August 19, 1966, p. 20.

21. On the Michigan governor, see Theodore White, "Backlash: Anti-Negro Feeling and the Coming Election," *Life*, October 16, 1964, pp. 100–110; the Harris Poll is discussed in Louis Harris, "The 'Backlash' Issue," *Newsweek*, July 13, 1964, p. 25.

22. The Michigan Civil Rights Commission statistic comes from "What the Negro Has—and Has Not—Gained," *Time*, October 28, 1966, p. 33; according to an August 23, 1965, article in *U.S. News & World Report*, civil rights leaders were turning their sights on an integration "that whites cannot escape by fleeing to white neighborhoods or to the suburbs."

23. "What Negroes in the North Are Really After," *U.S. News & World Report*, June 10, 1963, p. 40.

24. The statistics on individual cities come from "Government's Plan to Desegregate the Suburbs," *U.S. News & World Report*, October 10, 1966, p. 77; for Chicago, see "What New Turn in Negro Drive Means," *U.S. News & World Report*, June 17, 1963, p. 41, "Racial Crisis Ahead for Neighborhood Schools," *U.S. News & World Report*, July 8, 1963, p. 48, and "Why a Big Northern City Faces a Crisis in Schools," *U.S. News & World Report*, August 9, 1965, p. 62; for Englewood, N.J., see "What New Turn in Negro Drive Means," *U.S. News & World Report*, June 17, 1963, p. 41 and "March on Gwynn Oak Park," *Time*, July 12, 1963, p. 18.

25. For Baltimore, see Orser, *Blockbusting in Baltimore*, p. 113; for Roosevelt High School in Washington, D.C., see "Integration—Then Resegregation," *U.S. News & World Report*, November 25, 1963, p. 80.

26. The quote and examples are from Forrest R. White, "*Brown* Revisited," *Phi Delta Kappan*, September 1994, pp. 12–20.

27. The urban educator and the Pittsburgh school board report are both quoted in "Big-City Schools in Trouble?" *U.S. News & World Report*, September 27, 1965, pp. 44–47.

28. The Great Neck NAACP leader was quoted in "Busing at Great Neck," *Newsweek*, February 17, 1969, p. 70.

29. The material on unions is from a variety of sources, including Louis

Uchitelle, "Affirmative Action: Labor's Faltering Experiment," *New York Times,* July 9, 1995, p. 1, 18; "What New Turn in Negro Drive Means," *U.S. News & World Report,* June 17, 1963, p. 42; "The Right to a Job," *Newsweek,* August 5, 1963, p. 52; "The Negro's Search for a Better Job," *Newsweek,* June 8, 1964, p. 83; "Jobs for Negroes: How Much Progress in Sight?" *Newsweek,* July 15, 1963, p. 70.

30. The foremost expert in this area, the Harvard sociologist William Julius Wilson, focuses primarily on the worsening of conditions in the early 1970s and doesn't trace the problem back much earlier than that. See Wilson, *When Work Disappears: The World of the New Urban Poor* (New York: Alfred A. Knopf, 1996).

31. On the total number of blacks in the workforce between 1957 and 1966, see "What the Negro Has—and Has Not—Gained," *Time,* October 28, 1966, p. 32; for the figures on Detroit and St. Louis, see Joe T. Darden, "Black Residential Segregation Since the 1948 *Shelley* v. *Kraemer* Decision," *Journal of Black Studies,* July 1995, pp. 680–691.

32. The *Newsweek* quote is in "The Hard-Core Ghetto Mood," *Newsweek,* August 21, 1967, p. 21.

33. Herbert Hill quoted in "The Negro's Search for a Better Job," *Newsweek,* June 8, 1964, p. 79.

34. Representative Pucinski is quoted in " 'A Major Turning Point' Against Negro Movement," *U.S. News & World Report,* October 3, 1966, p. 46; the quotes from the September 9, 1963 edition of *U.S. News & World Report* are on p. 35; the *Newsweek* poll finding is in "How Whites Feel About Negroes: A Painful American Dilemma," *Newsweek,* October 21, 1963, p. 56; the *New York Times* poll was reported in the September 21, 1964, edition of the paper; Cleveland Mayor Ralph Locher is quoted in "The Negro Vote," *U.S. News & World Report,* April 27, 1964, p. 36.

35. Louis Harris, "The 'Backlash' Issue," *Newsweek,* July 13, 1964, pp. 24–27.

36. Whitney Young is quoted in "Integration: 'Reverse Reaction'?" *Newsweek,* August 12, 1963, p. 19; the Chicago Urban League director is quoted in "The Turning Point," *Time,* October 7, 1966, p. 30.

37. The prominent Democrat is quoted in "Now A New Worry for Kennedy: The White Vote in '64," *U.S. News & World Report,* September 9, 1963, p. 37; the Chicago Republican quote and "the silent issue" comment are from "Politics: JFK's Lost Votes," *Newsweek,* October 21, 1963, pp. 55–56.

38. Reagan is quoted in Michael Lind, "The Southern Coup," *The New Republic,* June 19, 1995, p. 26.

39. The Wallace quotes are from "Democrats: Shaking Eyeteeth," *Newsweek,* May 4, 1964, p. 22; the Wisconsin Wallace voter is quoted in

"After Wisconsin—New Turn in Politics," *U.S. News & World Report,* April 20, 1964, p. 32.

40. White, "Backlash: Anti-Negro Feeling and the Coming Election," pp. 104–110.

41. "Outlook: the Hope for Peace," *Newsweek,* October 21, 1963, p. 57.

42. White, "Backlash: Anti-Negro Feeling and the Coming Election," p. 109.

43. Kenneth Clark is quoted in "What Negroes in the North Are Really After," *U.S. News & World Report,* June 10, 1963, p. 39; Harold R. Isaacs, "Integration and the Negro Mood," *Commentary,* December 1962, pp. 487–497; King is quoted in "Races: The Revolution," *Time,* June 7, 1963, pp. 17–18.

44. A summary of the UCLA study can be found in "An American Tragedy, 1967," *Newsweek,* August 7, 1967, p. 33.

45. Baldwin is quoted in the May 17, 1963, edition of *Time,* pp. 26–27.

46. Norman Podhoretz, "My Negro Problem—and Ours," *Commentary,* February 1963, pp. 93–101.

47. Ross Barnett is interviewed in "The Negro's Future in the South," *U.S. News & World Report,* June 3, 1963, pp. 60–64.

48. See Stokely Carmichael, "What We Want," *New York Review of Books,* September 22, 1966, pp. 5–8; Justice Thomas wrote this opinion in the 1995 case *Missouri* v. *Jenkins.*

Chapter 5

1. The Federal Bureau of Investigation defines violent crime as murder and nonnegligent manslaughter, forcible rape, robbery, and aggravated assault, all of which involve force or threat of force. The Department of Justice estimate can be found in Herbert Koppel, "Lifetime Likelihood of Victimization," *Bureau of Justice Statistics Technical Report,* March 1987, p. 3.

2. For the university survey, see Alvin Sanoff, "Students Talk About Race," *U.S. News & World Report,* April 19, 1993, p. 61.

3. Anthony Walton, "Patriots," in *Lure and Loathing: Essays on Race, Identity, and the Ambivalence of Assimilation,* ed. Gerald Early (New York: Penguin, 1993), p. 255.

4. For white impressions of black odor, see "Prejudice: Widespread and Deep," *Newsweek,* October 21, 1963, p. 50, and " 'They're Trying to Go Too Fast,' " *Newsweek,* August 22, 1966, p. 25.

5. See Gordon W. Allport, *The Nature of Prejudice* (Garden City, N.Y.: Doubleday Anchor Books, 1958), pp. 134–136; for the relationship be-

tween prejudice and beauty, see H. Hoetink, *Slavery and Race Relations in the Americas* (New York: Harper Torchbooks, 1973), pp. 192–210.

6. Thomas Jefferson, *Notes on the State of Virginia* (Chapel Hill, N.C.: University of North Carolina Press, 1955), pp. 138–139.

7. Stanley Crouch, "Another Drink of the Blues: The Race Card in the Simpson Case," *Los Angeles Times*, July 31, 1994, p. M1.

8. According to the 1990 NORC survey, 62 percent of whites saw blacks as lazier than whites, 56 percent as more prone to violence, and 57 percent as less intelligent. The 1994 NORC survey found that 61 percent of whites saw blacks as lazier and less hard-working. The questions about intelligence and violence were not asked in 1994.

9. "Southern Exposure," *Washington Post*, July 15, 1995, pp. A10–11.

10. Kevin Helliker, "To Sell to Whites, Blacks Hide Telltale Ethnic Touches," *Wall Street Journal*, March 26, 1998, pp. B1, 2; for the focus group quote, see Lynne Duke, "Racial 'Perception Gap' Emerges as Young Whites Discuss Blacks," *Washington Post*, December 24, 1991, p. A4.

11. See Keith Harriston, "Student Faked Racially Tinged GW Rape Story," *Washington Post*, December 11, 1990, p. A1.

12. Samuel L. Gaertner, "Nonreactive Measures in Racial Attitude Research: A Focus on 'Liberals,' " in P. A. Katz, ed. *Towards the Elimination of Racism* (New York: Pergamon Press, 1976), pp. 183–211; Samuel L. Gaertner and John F. Dovidio, "The Aversive Form of Racism," *Prejudice, Discrimination and Racism*, ed. Dovidio and Gaertner (Orlando, Fla.: Academic Press, 1986), p. 65; Patricia Devine, "Stereotypes and Prejudice: Their Automatic and Controlled Components," *Journal of Personality and Social Psychology*, vol. 56, no. 1, 1989, pp. 5–18 (see p. 12). Devine is more hopeful than other researchers that the impact of these stereotypes can be minimized through a prolonged and systematic effort to reduce prejudice. For an analysis that concludes that whites who offer seemingly nonprejudiced responses are merely covering up their real but socially undesirable attitudes, see F. Crosby, S. Bromley, and L. Saxe, "Recent Unobtrusive Studies of Black and White Discrimination and Prejudice: A Literature Review," *Psychological Bulletin*, 87, pp. 546–563.

13. Interview with Dr. Alvin Poussaint, March 12, 1997.

14. The survey numbers on outlawing intermarriage can be found in the National Opinion Research Center's 1993 General Social Survey. See also a 1996 *Washington Post* survey, which found that 16 percent favor outlawing intermarriage—cited in "Southern Exposure," *Washington Post*, July 15, 1996, pp. A10–11. In a 1995 *Washington Post* survey, cited in *Jet*, October 2, 1995, p. 22, 60 percent of white women said they wouldn't marry a black man. For white concern about a sister dating a black man, see Tom Squitieri, "Black/White in the USA," *USA Today*,

September 22, 1989, p. 1A; for white concern about a close relative marrying a black, see Carl McClendon, "Black and White," *St. Petersburg Times,* October 9, 1994, p. 1A.

15. Edmund S. Morgan, *American Slavery, American Freedom* (New York: W. W. Norton, 1975), p. 328.

16. Toni Morrison is quoted in Bonnie Angelo, "The Pain of Being Black," *Time,* May 22, 1989, p. 120.

17. This voting phenomenon is described in Chandler Davidson and Bernard Grofman, eds., *Quiet Revolution in the South* (Princeton, N.J.: Princeton University Press, 1994).

18. W. E. Burghardt Du Bois, *The Souls of Black Folk* (Cutchogue, N.Y.: Buccaneer Books, 1976), pp. 16–17.

19. William Raspberry, "Harmful Little Nothings," *Washington Post,* June 3, 1996, p. A15.

20. The black executive is quoted in Clay F. Richards, "Poll: Prejudice a Fact of Life," *Newsday,* September 17, 1990, p. 26; Charlayne Hunter-Gault, "The Burden of Being Black in America," *Fortune,* November 2, 1992, p. 118; Earl Graves is quoted in John Diconsiglio, "The Color of Money," *Scholastic Update,* December 8, 1995, p. 7.

21. The survey is cited in William Raspberry, "No, We Are Not Obsessed By Wealth," *Washington Post,* February 6, 1987, p. A23.

22. Judy Scales-Trent, *Notes of a White Black Woman* (University Park, Pa.: Pennsylvania State University Press, 1995), p. 31.

23. Anthony Walton, "Willie Horton and Me," *New York Times Magazine,* August 20, 1989, p. 77.

24. Personal interview with Sam Fulwood III, November 18, 1996.

25. Focus Group Transcript from the Montgomery County Hate/Violence Committee, Montgomery County, Maryland, November 1993.

26. For the black suicide rates, see Fern Shen, "Suicide Rates Increase for Young Black Males," *Washington Post,* July 21, 1996, p. B1.

27. See Warren Leary, "Discrimination May Affect Risk of High Blood Pressure in Blacks," *New York Times,* October 24, 1996, p. A20; Brent Staples, "Death by Discrimination," *New York Times,* November 24, 1996, p. 14; and Felicia R. Lee, "Doctors See Gap in Blacks' Health Having a Link to Low Self-esteem," *New York Times,* July 17, 1989, p. A11.

28. For reasons of privacy, we prefer not to disclose who made these comments to us.

29. John Higham, *Send These to Me: Jews and Other Immigrants in Urban America* (New York: Atheneum, 1975), p. 236.

Chapter 6

1. The "synthetic experience" of television is described in G. Funkhouser and F. Shaw, "How Synthetic Experience Shapes Reality," *Journal of Communication* vol. 40; no. 2 (1990), pp. 75–87.

2. Benjamin DeMott, *The Trouble with Friendship: Why Americans Can't Think Straight About Race* (New York: Atlantic Monthly Press, 1995).

3. We developed the phrase "virtual integration" in 1995 when discussing ideas for this book and did not know that another author, John Hoberman, was planning to use the same phrase in his 1997 book, *Darwin's Athletes*.

4. Clarence Page, *Showing My Color: Impolite Essays on Race and Identity* (New York: HarperCollins, 1996), p. 252.

5. The singer's quote is from Henry Louis Gates, Jr., "Thirteen Ways of Looking at a Black Man," *The New Yorker,* October 23, 1995, p. 63.

6. The Michael Jordan reference is found in Lynn Hirschberg, "The Big Man Can Deal," *New York Times Magazine,* November 17, 1996, p. 49.

7. These and other facts can be found in Greg Braxton, "Roots Plus 20," *Los Angeles Times,* January 26, 1997, p. 8. See also Jacqueline Trescott, " 'Roots,' Wrapped Around the American Psyche," *Washington Post,* February 16, 1997, p. G5.

8. We also tracked ABC on Tuesday, September 30, 1997, and channel-surfed through all three networks on Monday, October 6, 1997.

9. The 11 percent figure comes from Christopher P. Campbell, *Race, Myth and the News* (Thousand Oaks, Calif.: Sage Publications, 1995), p. 38; Geoffrey Garin is quoted in Ronald Brownstein, "4 Decades Later, Legacy of *Brown vs. Topeka* Is Cloudy," *Los Angeles Times,* May 15, 1994, p. A1.

10. The comedian Patton Oswalt was quoted in the *New York Times,* March 4, 1997, p. C11.

11. The Center for Media and Public Affairs statistic is cited in Rick Du Brow, "Portrayals of Latinos on Television Regressing," *Los Angeles Times,* September 7, 1994, p. A5.

12. We are grateful to the Screen Actors Guild for supplying these figures on advertising. For the 1989 study, see Robert E. Wilkes and Humberto Valencia, "Hispanics and Blacks in Television Commercials," *Journal of Advertising,* vol. 18, no. 1 (1989), pp. 19–25.

13. P. W. Matabane, "Television and the Black Audience: Cultivating Moderate Perspectives on Racial Integration," *Journal of Communication,* vol. 38, no. 4 (1988), p. 26.

14. For the survey showing that a majority of whites get their information about blacks from the media, see Matthew P. Smith, "Bridging

the Gulf Between Blacks and Whites," *Pittsburgh Post-Gazette*, April 7, 1996, p. 1.

15. Personal interview with Paula Walker, March 10, 1997.

16. Ben H. Bagdikian, "Editorial Responsibility in Times of Urban Disorder," in *The Media and the Cities*, ed. Charles U. Daily (Chicago: University of Chicago Center for Policy Study, 1968), p. 15.

17. We have drawn on the following research studies for our information: Robert M. Entman, "Modern Racism and the Images of Blacks in Local Television News," *Critical Studies in Mass Communication*, vol. 7 (1990), pp. 332–345; Robert M. Entman, "Blacks in the News: Television, Modern Racism, and Cultural Change," *Journalism Quarterly*, Summer 1992, pp. 341–361; Robert M. Entman, "Representation and Reality in the Portrayal of Blacks on Network Television News," *Journalism Quarterly*, Autumn 1994, pp. 509–520; Robert M. Entman, *Violence on Television: News and "Reality" Programming in Chicago* (Chicago: Chicago Council on Urban Affairs, 1994); George Gerbner, "Women and Minorities on Television: A Study of Casting and Fate," *Report to the Screen Actors Guild and the American Federation of Radio and Television Artists*, June 1993; Daniel Romer, Kathleen H. Jamieson, and Nicole DeCoteau, "Differential Standards of Newsworthiness and Ethnic Blame Discourse on Television News: A Study of Crime Reporting in Philadelphia," unpublished paper sent to us by its authors. Research on the Los Angeles station is described in Howard Kurtz, "A Guilty Verdict on Crime, Race Bias," *Washington Post*, April 28, 1997, pp. 1, 4, who cites the findings of University of California–Los Angeles professors Shanto Iyengar and Franklin Gilliam, Jr. See also Du Brow, "Portrayals of Latinos on Television Regressing"; and Mark Lorando, "TV's 'Average' Reveals Double Standard," *New Orleans Times-Picayune*, September 13, 1993, p. A9.

18. Research by the University of California–Los Angeles professors Shanto Iyengar and Franklin Gilliam, Jr., is reported in Kurtz, "A Guilty Verdict on Crime, Race Bias."

19. The murder coverage statistics are from the Center for Media and Public Affairs press release, "In 1990s TV News Turns to Violence and Show Biz," August 12, 1997; for the drop in the nationwide homicide rate, see Vincent Schiraldi, "The Latest Trend in Juvenile Crime," *Washington Post*, January 11, 1998, p. C5.

20. Mark Lorando, "Mass Media Wields Power That Reinforces Prejudice," *New Orleans Times-Picayune*, September 13, 1993, p. A7.

21. The public's reliance on TV news for information on crime is described in Stephen Braun and Judy Pasternak, "With Terror on Its Mind," *Los Angeles Times*, February 13, 1994, p. A16.

Chapter 7

1. Mark Whitaker, "And Now What?" *Newsweek*, October 30, 1995, p. 28.

2. For examples, the noted political scientist Seymour Martin Lipset uses the phrase "invisible man" when describing the black middle class in *American Exceptionalism* (New York: W. W. Norton, 1996), pp. 134–135.

3. Stanley B. Greenberg, *Middle Class Dreams: The Politics and Power of the New American Majority* (New York: Times Books, 1995), p. 39.

4. R. W. Apple, Jr., "It's Hard Running up the Middle," *New York Times*, August 11, 1996, section 4, page 1.

5. Jason DeParle, "Class Is No Longer a Four-Letter Word," *New York Times Magazine*, March 17, 1996, pp. 40–43.

6. For the quote on the Baltimore Orioles player, see Mark Maske, "Surhoff's Position is Clear," *Washington Post*, March 24, 1997, p. C3. The quote about John Stockton is found in John Hoberman, *Darwin's Athletes: How Sport Has Damaged Black America and Preserved the Myth of Race* (New York: Houghton Mifflin, 1997), p. 49. Hoberman offers a more elaborate analysis of this phenomenon in sports; see pp. 47–51.

7. Ulrich B. Phillips, *American Negro Slavery* (Baton Rouge: Louisiana State University Press, 1969), pp. 298, 328, 341–342. The book was originally published in 1918 and was widely viewed as the authority on slavery until the mid-1950s.

8. "Freedom—Now," *Time*, May 17, 1963, p. 23.

9. Jesse Jackson quoted in John Leland and Allison Samuels, "The New Generation Gap," *Newsweek*, March 17, 1997, p. 59.

10. Baldwin quoted in "Freedom—Now," p. 27.

11. *Mississippi Burning*'s director, Alan Parker, is quoted in Richard Corliss, "Fire This Time," *Time*, January 9, 1989, p. 58. The films listed are but a few of the films in this genre.

12. Dr. Thomas W. Matthew, president of National Economic Growth and Reconstruction Organization (NEGRO), is quoted in "New Meaning for Black Power," *U.S. News & World Report*, July 22, 1968, p. 32.

13. Bradley is quoted in Timur Kuran, "Race and Social Mistrust: Seeds of Racial Explosion," *Current*, December 1993, p. 4.

14. Whitney Young is quoted in "Negro Leaders—More Militant Now?" *U.S. News & World Report*, April 22, 1968, p. 19.

15. The unnamed Johnson administration official is quoted in "Civil Rights: A Turning Point," *New York Times*, September 19, 1966, p. A1.

16. "Race in the Workplace," *Business Week*, July 8, 1991, p. 50.

17. The Chicago teenager is quoted in Christopher John Farley, "Kids and Race," *Time*, November 24, 1997, p. 91.

18. A 1995 U.S. Department of Labor study concluded that there is "no widespread abuse" of affirmative action programs in employment

and that a "high proportion" of reverse discrimination claims are "without merit." Critics of this study, however, suggest that many whites never bring discrimination claims. See Kevin Merida, "Study Finds Little Evidence of Reverse Discrimination," *Washington Post*, March 31, 1995, p. A2.

19. For images of the entitled black during Reconstruction, see Eric Foner, *Reconstruction: America's Unfinished Revolution 1863–1877* (New York: Harper & Row, 1988), especially the photo insert between pages 194 and 195. We were led to these particular images in the Foner book by the American University Law Professor Jamie B. Raskin in "Affirmative Action and Racial Reaction," *Howard Law Journal*, Summer 1995, pp. 541–543.

20. Richard Harwood, "America's Unchecked Epidemic," *Washington Post*, December 1, 1997, p. A25.

21. Franklin E. Zimring and Gordon Hawkins, *Crime Is Not the Problem: Lethal Violence in America* (New York: Oxford University Press, 1997), p. 81.

22. The *Nightline* broadcast was aired April 27, 1989.

23. Sharon Cotliar, "Oak Park Struggling to Get Along," *Chicago Sun-Times*, July 24, 1994, p. A8.

24. On the advertising executives, see Marilyn Kern-Foxworth, *Aunt Jemima, Uncle Ben, and Rastus* (Westport, Conn.: Greenwood Press, 1994), p. 159.

25. Howard Bryant, "The Search for Role Models," in *Thinking Black*, ed. by DeWayne Wickham (New York: Crown, 1997), pp. 81–85.

26. "Tenn. Man Admits Fabricating Tale of Traffic Dispute in Son's Death," *Washington Post*, October 24, 1996, p. A7.

27. For the private-school story, see Patricia Elam Ruff, "Private School, Private Pain," *Washington Post*, February 23, 1997, pp. C1–2.

28. Interview with Henry Louis Gates, Jr., "A 'Race Man' Argues for a Broader Curriculum," *Time*, April 22, 1991, p. 16.

29. Michel McQueen, "People with the Least to Fear from Crime Drive the Crime Issue," *Wall Street Journal*, August 12, 1992, p. A1.

30. Donald L. Chatman, "Willie Horton and Me," letter to the editor, *New York Times*, September 24, 1989, section 6, p. 12.

31. Jerome G. Miller, *Search and Destroy: African-American Males in the Criminal Justice System* (Cambridge, U.K.: Cambridge University Press, 1996), p. 8.

32. The Amnesty International Report, issued in June 1996, is entitled *Police Brutality and Excessive Force in the Now York City Police Department*. The black police executive is quoted in "Black Officers Protest Shooting of Colleague," *New York Times*, November 27, 1997, p. A41.

33. The Los Angeles Times survey is cited in Jeannye Thornton and

David Whitman, "Whites' Myths About Blacks," *U.S. News & World Report*, November 9, 1992, p. 44.

34. *Between Hope and Fear: Teens Speak Out on Crime and the Community*, a 1996 study of teen attitudes conducted by Louis Harris and Associates for the National Crime Prevention Council and the National Institute for Citizen Education in the Law. See especially pp. 63–77.

35. Michiko Kakutani, "Common Threads," *New York Times Magazine*, February 16, 1997, p. 18.

36. The black high school girl is quoted in Laura Blumenfeld, "Black Like Who?" *Washington Post*, July 20, 1992, p. C5.

37. John Hoberman, *Darwin's Athletes*, pp. 34–35.

38. The black teen is quoted in Blumenfeld, "Black Like Who?"

Chapter 8

1. The eight-hundred-pound gorilla incident occurred in March 1997 and was covered by the *Washington Post*, the source of this material. See the following articles by the *Post* reporter Lisa Frazier, " 'Gorilla' Quip Prompts Calls for Resignation," March 5, 1997; " '800-Pound Gorilla' Quip Tears Open Old Wound," March 8, 1997; "Desegregation Appointee to Keep Post," March 11, 1997.

2. Leonard Steinhorn first developed the perception gap concept in his 1991 article, "Building a New American Consensus on Race Relations," *Journal of Intergroup Relations*, Spring 1991, pp. 33–53.

3. The writer is Marc Elrich, "The Stereotype Within," *Washington Post*, February 13, 1994, pp. C1, C4.

4. The "politeness conspiracy" phrase has been attributed to Thomas Kochman, currently a diversity consultant in Chicago and the author of *Black and White Styles in Conflict* (Chicago: University of Chicago Press, 1981).

5. The school calendar incident is described in Peter Maas, "Howard School's Scrapped Calendar Becomes a Lesson in Sensitivity," *Washington Post*, August 21, 1996, pp. C1, C6.

6. The defense forensic expert is Henry Lee, and the juror is cited in "The Verdict's Aftermath," *U.S. News & World Report*, October 16, 1995, p. 34.

7. Some whites went further than calling the jury unreasonable. Radio talk-show host Rush Limbaugh said the verdict was "about low I.Q.s on the jury," as if jurors were unable to comprehend the scientific evidence.

8. For information on investigations into black elected officials, see James Neff, "Is Justice Blind?" *George*, October 1996, pp. 126–129, 153–155.

9. Farrakhan gave his speech to the National Press Club on July 30, 1984.
10. Many of the ideas in this section are drawn from Steinhorn, "Building a New American Consensus on Race Relations."
11. Diane Colasanto, "Public Wants Civil Rights Widened for Some Groups, Not for Others," Gallup Poll News Service, December 20, 1989.
12. William Raspberry, "Needed: A Conversation About Race," *Washington Post*, March 24, 1995, p. A23.
13. See C. Gray Wheeler, "30 Years Beyond 'I Have a Dream,' " *The Gallup Poll Monthly*, October 1993, p. 4.
14. Lee Sigelman and Susan Welch, *Black Americans' Views of Racial Inequality: the Dream Deferred* (Cambridge, U.K.: Cambridge University Press, 1991), p. 165.

Chapter 9

1. For the *New York Times* article, see Robert Pear, "Civil Rights Moves Are Faintly Praised," July 17, 1983, Section 4, p. 2; for the *Time* magazine article, see Maureen Dowd, "Suddenly It Was All Action—To Counter Criticism, a Volley of Civil Rights Initiatives," July 25, 1983, p. 24.
2. David Gergen quoted in Herbert H. Denton, "Reagan Proclaims Concern for Blacks," *Washington Post*, September 16, 1992, p. A1; the other, unnamed, administration official is quoted in Juan Williams, "Civil Rights Week Meant to Improve Reagan's Image," *Washington Post*, July 17, 1983, p. A2.
3. Reagan's comment on segregated schools is quoted in Kenneth O'Reilly, *Nixon's Piano: Presidents and Racial Politics from Washington to Clinton* (New York: Free Press, 1995), p. 370.
4. The Harris Poll, commissioned by the NAACP Legal Defense and Educational Fund, was reported in Lee May, "See Heavy Losses and Few Gains—Blacks Look Back with Anger at Reagan Years," *Los Angeles Times*, January 20, 1989, p. A1.
5. The 20 percent number is cited in Molly Ivins, "GOP: What You See Isn't What You Get," *Austin American–Statesman*, August 21, 1996, P. A15.
6. The Republican convention secretary was quoted in Diane Stafford, "GOP Still a Hard Sell for Minorities," *Kansas City Star*, August 15, 1996, p. A14.
7. Bennett is quoted in Kathy Sawyer, "King Scholars Steal Bennett's Best Lines," *Washington Post*, January 15, 1986, p. A8.
8. King's "discrimination in reverse" quote is found in "The Right to a Job," *Newsweek*, August 5, 1963, p. 52; he called for "radical changes in the structure of society" in his book *Where Do We Go From Here: Commu-*

nity or Chaos (New York: Harper & Row, 1967), p. 133; his plea for a "Bill of Rights for the Disadvantaged" is found in his 1964 book *Why We Can't Wait* (New York: New American Library, 1964), pp. 137–141; his quote on "preferential treatment" is found in Coretta Scott King, "Man of His Word," *New York Times*, November 3, 1996, p. A15.

9. See King, *Why We Can't Wait*, pp. 134–141.

10. The Wilkins quote is from "What the American Negro Wants—Interview with Roy Wilkins, Head of the NAACP," *U.S. News & World Report*, April 29, 1963, p. 51.

11. Taylor Branch, *Parting the Waters: America in the King Years 1954–63* (New York: Simon & Schuster, 1988), pp. 918–919. For another analysis of Kennedy's civil rights record, see O'Reilly, *Nixon's Piano*, pp. 189–237.

12. In an interview with the journalist Anthony Lewis after President Kennedy's death, Robert Kennedy so much as acknowledged that he and his brother rarely thought about the black situation in the South during the 1960 campaign and had little more than a political interest in the plight of blacks. See O'Reilly, *Nixon's Piano: Presidents and Racial Politics from Washington to Clinton*, p. 237.

13. The Kennedy staffer is quoted in "On the March," *Newsweek*, September 2, 1963, pp. 17–21.

14. The quotes and ads are drawn from Joe McGinniss, *The Selling of the President 1968* (New York: Trident Press, 1969).

15. "The Supreme Court: Integration Now," *Time*, November 7, 1969, p. 19.

16. Nixon is quoted in Thomas Byrne Edsall and Mary D. Edsall, "Race," *The Atlantic*, May 1991, p. 66.

17. "A Dream—Still Unfulfilled," *Newsweek*, April 14, 1969, p. 25.

18. Clinton is quoted in Martin Kasindorf, "A Great Divide—Clinton 'Surprised' by Black-White Split After O.J. verdict," *Newsday*, October 11, 1995, p. A3.

19. See Stanley B. Greenberg, *Middle Class Dreams: The Politics and Power of the New American Majority* (New York: Times Books, 1995).

20. Bill Clinton and Al Gore, *Putting People First* (New York: Times Books, 1992), pp. 63–66.

21. Speech to the Democratic Leadership Council, May 2, 1992.

22. Speech to the University of Texas at Austin, October 16, 1995.

Chapter 10

1. We conducted a telephone interview with Shaker Heights' mayor, Patricia S. Mearns, on December 15, 1997. Also participating in that interview was Sheryl King–Benford, the Shaker Heights law director and

interim director of the Center for Housing and Community Life. The Shaker Heights section of this chapter also draws on phone interviews with community leader and integration pioneer Dr. Winston Richie (December 29, 1997) and former housing director Donald DeMarco, now president and executive director of the Fund for an Open Society (January 13, 1998). Also worth consulting are the following articles and books on integrated housing in general and Shaker Heights: W. Dennis Keating, *The Suburban Racial Dilemma: Housing and Neighborhoods* (Philadelphia: Temple University Press, 1994), chapter on Shaker Heights, pp. 96–113; Andrew Wiese, "Neighborhood Diversity: Social Change, Ambiguity, and Fair Housing Since 1968," *Journal of Urban Affairs*, vol. 17, no. 2, 1995, pp. 107–129; Richard A. Smith, "Creating Stable Racially Integrated Communities: A Review," *Journal of Urban Affairs*, vol. 15, no. 2, 1993, pp. 115–140; Jonathan Tilove, "Integration Maintenance Criticized: Desegregation Feels like Discrimination to Some," *New Orleans Times-Picayune*, February 21, 1993, p. A3; Isabel Wilkerson, "One City's 30-Year Crusade for Integration," *New York Times*, December 30, 1991; Andrew Cassel, "Why a Town Pays to Integrate," *Orlando Sentinel Tribune*, June 30, 1991, p. G1; Richard C. Firstman, "Trying Hard to Keep That Racial Mix; Shaker Heights, Oak Park: Tale of Two Midwest Suburbs," *Newsday*, December 9, 1990, p. 7.

2. See Ann Scott Tyson, "How One Illinois Community Is Fighting 'White Flight,' " *Christian Science Monitor*, July 21, 1995, p. A1.

3. Telephone interview with Dr. Winston Richie, December 29, 1997.

4. Telephone interview with Mayor Patricia S. Mearns, December 15, 1997.

5. Telephone interview with Donald DeMarco, January 13, 1998.

6. The Corning section is drawn from a number of sources, including a telephone interview with Gail Owens Baity, manager of human resources for Corning's Advanced Materials Division, on January 14, 1998, and a conversation in Washington, D.C., between Leonard Steinhorn and Corning's former chairman Jamie Houghton on May 29, 1997. See also the following articles: "Affirmative Action; Why bosses like it," *The Economist*, March 11, 1995, p. 29; "25 Best Places for Blacks to Work," *Black Enterprise*, February 1992, p. 71; Claudia H. Deutsch, "Managing: Listening to Women and Blacks," *New York Times*, December 1, 1991, Section 3, p. 25; Peter T. Kilborn, "Affirmative Action: How to Make It Work," *New York Times*, October 4, 1990, p. A1; Cindy Skrzycki, "Bringing a Bit of City to the Company Town: Corning Inc. Upgrades to Attract, Keep Good Workers," *Washington Post*, August 12, 1990.

7. The "revolving door" concept is described in "Race in the Workplace," *Business Week*, July 8, 1991, p. 50.

8. Telephone interview with Gail Owens Baity, January 14, 1998.

9. Telephone interview with Gail Owens Baity, January 14, 1998.

10. Charles C. Moskos and John Sibley Butler, *All That We Can Be: Black Leadership and Racial Integration the Army Way* (New York: Basic Books, 1996), p. 2.

11. The intermarriage information comes from Reynolds Farley, "Increasing Interracial Marriage: Trends Revealed by the Census and Census Bureau Surveys," preliminary draft, October 1996. We are grateful to Farley for sharing this draft with us.

12. The housing integration information comes from Reynolds Farley and William H. Frey, "Changes in the Segregation of Whites from Blacks During the 1980s: Small Steps Toward a More Integrated Society," *American Sociological Review,* vol. 59. February 1994, pp. 23–45.

13. The former air force captain is Debra Dickerson, "The Martial Melting Pot," *U.S. News & World Report,* December 23, 1996, pp. 32–34.

14. The 1994 bias complaint information for the army comes from Moskos and Butler, *All That We Can Be,* pp. 62–63.

15. For the navy numbers and other information on bias complaints, see Richard A. Serrano, "Military Affirmative Action Efforts Held Up as a Model," *Los Angeles Times,* December 30, 1995, p. A1.

16. Moskos and Butler, *All That We Can Be,* p. 1.

17. "An Assessment of Racial Discrimination in the Military: A Global Perspective," report of the Committee on Armed Services, U.S. House of Representatives, December 30, 1994; untitled report by the General Accounting Office to The Honorable Ronald V. Dellums, April 7, 1995.

18. See 1995 General Accounting Office report to Rep. Dellums for the 1992 air force study.

19. "An Assessment of Racial Discrimination in the Military," p. 4.

20. Moskos and Butler, *All That We Can Be,* p. 2.

21. Ibid., p. 71.

22. Ibid., p. 50.

23. Col. Patrick Connor is quoted in David Maraniss, "U.S. Military Struggles to Make Equality Work," *Washington Post,* March 6, 1990, p. A1.

Authors' Interviews

In researching this book, the authors conducted interviews with the following people:

Douglas Alligood, senior vice president for special markets, BBDO Advertising

Gail O. Baity, human resources manager, Advanced Materials Division, Corning Incorporated

Angela Glover Blackwell, senior vice president, Rockefeller Foundation

David S. Broder, columnist, *Washington Post*

Julian Bond, chairman of the board, NAACP

Hodding Carter III, president, Knight Foundation

Donald DeMarco, former housing director, Shaker Heights, Ohio, and president of Fund for an Open Society

Sam Fulwood III, author and reporter, *Los Angeles Times*

Andrew Hacker, author of *Two Nations: Separate, Hostile, and Unequal,* and professor of political science, Queens College

Sheryl King-Benford, law director and interim director, Center for Housing and Community Life, Shaker Heights, Ohio

Patricia Mearns, mayor, Shaker Heights, Ohio

Michael Meyers, executive director, New York Civil Rights Coalition

Jack Nelson, reporter and former Washington bureau chief, *Los Angeles Times*

Clarence Page, columnist, *Chicago Tribune*

Deval Patrick, former U.S. Assistant Attorney General for Civil Rights

Alvin Poussaint, psychiatrist and professor, Harvard Medical School

Winston Richie, realtor, Shaker Heights, Ohio, resident since 1955

Jim Sleeper, author of *The Closest of Strangers* and *Liberal Racism*
Alvin Thornton, professor of political science, Howard University
Paula Walker, vice president and news director, WNBC-TV, New York City
Roger Wilkins, professor of history, George Mason University
Charles V. Willie, professor of education, Harvard University
Robert Woodson, president, National Center for Neighborhood Enterprise

Index

· A NOTE ON THE TYPE ·

The typeface used in this book is a version of Baskerville, originally designed by John Baskerville (1706–1775) and considered to be one of the first "transitional" typefaces between the "old style" of the continental humanist printers and the "modern" style of the nineteenth century. With a determination bordering on the eccentric to produce the finest possible printing, Baskerville set out at age forty-five and with no previous experience to become a typefounder and printer (his first fourteen letters took him two years). Besides the letter forms, his innovations included an improved printing press, smoother paper, and better inks, all of which made Baskerville decidedly uncompetitive as a businessman. Franklin, Beaumarchais, and Bodoni were among his admirers, but his typeface had to wait for the twentieth century to achieve its due.